"We have clearly shown that a child has a need to observe, to reflect, to learn, to concentrate, to isolate himself, and also from time to time to suspend his activities in silence. And we have done this so clearly that we can say with all confidence that the idea that a small child is in a state of rest when he is outside a place suited for his education is erroneous. Rather, it is our duty to direct a child's activities, sparing him useless efforts which would dissipate his energies, divert his instinctive search for knowledge, and be a frequent cause of nervous disorders and hindrance to his growth. The education of even a very small child, therefore, does not aim at preparing him for school but for life."

—Maria Montessori

Also by Maria Montessori

THE SECRET OF CHILDHOOD

Available from Ballantine Books

THE DISCOVERY
OF THE CHILD

Maria Montessori

Translated by
M. Joseph Costelloe, S.J.
The Creighton University

BALLANTINE BOOKS • NEW YORK

This American edition of *La scoperta del bambino*, in a new translation by M. Joseph Costelloe, S. J., is based on the 6th edition of the work, published by Garzanti, Milan, Italy, 1962. It has been licensed for publication in the United States by Maria M. Montessori, Director General of the Association Montessori Internationale, Amsterdam.

Library of Congress Catalog Card Number: 67-24813

ISBN 0-345-29390-8

This edition published by arrangement with Fides Publishers, Inc.

Manufactured in the United States of America

First Ballantine Books Edition: March 1972
Seventh Printing: June 1980

Contents

iL

Introduction

If at the time of the publication of the Third Italian Edition of this work I felt obliged to justify the reprinting of something that had been written at the beginning of my work, I now feel an all the greater need of such an apology at the publication of the present edition forty-two years later. My motives have always been the same, but the development of my work and the conclusions reached from the revelations given by the children in our schools have far surpassed our fondest expectations. It would have been impossible to bring this book up to date without completely rewriting it both for form and contents. Circumstances do not permit this, and it would require a whole series of specialized publications referring to various psychological and educational aspects of our extensive experiences throughout the world. Some of these have already been published, for example, *The Secret of Childhood, The Absorbent Mind, Education for a New World, Educating the Human Potential, Psycho-Arithmetic, Psycho-Geometry*, and so forth, but others are still in preparation.

In the present edition I have simply sought to clarify certain problems and especially to point out the fact that our work has resulted in something more than the creation of a new method of education. The conclusions which we have reached are expressed in the new title: *The Discovery of the Child*. After the first few chapters I have given a rapid review of the most recent developments. But the reader is asked to keep in mind the fact that the greater parts of this book was written at the beginning of our endeavors and that it often refers to scientific theories and experiments that were then popular or to situations that were familiar in those days. Times have changed, and science has made great progress, and so has our work; but our principles have only been confirmed, and along with them our conviction that mankind can hope for a solution to its problems, among which the most urgent are those of peace and unity, only by turning its attention and energies to the discovery of the child and to the development of the great potentialities of the human personality in the course of its formation.

MARIA MONTESSORI

Poona, November 1948

1. On the Application of Science to the School

I do not intend to elaborate a treatise on the science of education: these preliminary notes have the modest end of setting forth the rather interesting results of a teaching experience which would seem to open up a way for the practical application of new methods tending to make greater use of scientific experiments in education without removing its natural foundations in speculative principles. For many years it has been maintained, with some exaggeration, that education should tend to forsake the purely speculative fields, as already had been done by medicine, in order to establish itself on foundations that are the result of experimentation. Physiological, or experimental, psychology, which from Weber and Fechner to Wundt and Binet, has come to be organized into a new science, seems almost destined to furnish it with a substratum like that which the old psychology furnished to the philosophy of education. The application of morphological anthropology to the study of children seems also to be another cardinal factor in the new education.

But as a matter of fact, a system of "scientific pedagogy" has never been worked out or defined. It is something vague and frequently discussed, but also something which in reality does not exist.

Some years ago there arose in Italy the so-called "schools of scientific education." The object of these schools, which were sponsored by experienced physicians, was to train teachers in the new methods of education. They were a great success and won the approval of all the teachers of Italy. Even before these new theories had been introduced into Italy from Germany and France, Italian anthropologists had interested Italian teachers in making careful observations of

children during their various stages of growth and in the
advantages of using precise instruments for measurements.
Sergi, for example, had gone about for almost fifty years
assiduously spreading the idea of seeking through scientific
observations a means of renovating the educational system.
"Today," Sergi used to say, "there is an urgent need of
reform in the methods of education and instruction, and
anyone who fights under this standard fights for the regeneration of man."

Sergi's writings have been collected in a single volume,
Educazione ed Istruzione. In this he published the lectures
and conferences which he had given to further this movement, and he stated that it was his conviction that the way to
renewal was to be found in *a methodical study of the one to
be educated, carried out with the help of educational anthropology and experimental psychology*:

> For several years I have fought for an idea which, the
> more I reflect on it, the more convinced I am of its
> usefulness for the instruction and education of man: If we
> are to obatin our objectives by natural means, we must
> have at our disposal numerous precise observations on
> human conduct and especially that of children, upon whom
> we must base the foundations of education and culture.
>
> Education, it is true, does not exist in measuring one's
> head, height, and so forth; but such means point the way
> to it, for we cannot educate anyone until we have firsthand
> knowledge of him.

Sergi's authority gave rise to the conviction that once an
individual came to be known through experimentation, the
art of educating him would naturally develop. But this, as so
often happens, confused his followers, who failed to distinguish between the experimental study of a child and his
education. Since the former was made to appear as the
natural means to attain the latter, educational anthropology
was called *scientific education.* Converts to the new system
carried as their standard the "Biographical Chart," convinced
that once this flag was finally raised in a school the victory
would be won.

The so-called "schools of scientific education" therefore
instructed teachers in taking bodily measurements, in the use

of instruments for the measurement of sense perceptions, and in drawing up case histories. In this way a body of scientific teachers was formed.

Actually, in other countries nothing more or better was being done.

In France, in England, and especially in America, studies were made in anthropology and educational psychology in the elementary schools under the illusion that a reform of the schools could be effected through the taking of physical and psychic measurements. The same tendency was followed in the later studies of the individual, beginning with the psychology of Wundt and continuing on to the tests of Binet, but the same ambiguity remained. Further, these investigations were almost never carried out by teachers but by physicians. As a rule, these men were more interested in their own particular field of study than in education. They sought to contribute to the advancement of experimental psychology and physical measurements rather than to organize their work and achievements in a way that would form the long awaited foundation for a scientific system of education. In brief, anthropology and psychology were never used as a means of education, and, on the other hand, the teachers did not rise to the level of the physical scientists.

Nevertheless, progress in education demands a true cooperation of these two in thought and practice, a cooperation that would bring scientists directly into the noble field of teaching and which would raise the teachers from the lower cultural level which they occupy today. In order to implement this eminently practical ideal, a University School of Teaching was founded at Rome with the hope of raising education from its position as a secondary branch in the faculty of philosophy to an independent faculty which, like that of medicine, would include a wide area of teaching fields, among which would be educational anthropology, and experimental psychology.

Nevertheless these sciences continued to develop on their own, and education as such remained in the old philosophical rut where it had originated and where it remained untouched, let alone transformed.

But today education is not so much interested in science as in humanity and civilization, which has only one fatherland, the world. And all those who have made some contribution to so great a cause, even if this was more of an attempt than a complete success, deserve to be respected by society.

And so it is that we, who work for a single goal, are as it were the members, or the different ages, of the same person; and those who come after us will attain the goal, because there were those who believed and worked before them.

Similarly, we believed that by carrying the hard and arid rocks of laboratory experimentation into old and crumbling schools we might be able to rebuild them. Many have looked upon materialistic and mechanistic science with excessive hopes. It is precisely because of this that we have entered upon a false and narrow way which must be surmounted if we are to revitalize the art of educating future generations.

It is not easy to train teachers in the methodology of the experimental sciences. After we have taught men and women how to make physical and psychic measurements as exactly as possible, we have only machines of doubtful value. By showing them how to make experiments we have certainly not formed *new teachers*. But what is even more significant, we have left the teachers on the threshold of the experimental sciences but have not admitted them into the more profound and nobler areas where scientists are actually formed.

But what is a scientist?

A scientist is not simply one who can manipulate all the physical apparatus in a laboratory, or produce various chemical reactions, or prepare slides of organic tissues for examination under a microscope. Much more frequently it is the assistants or members of the laboratory's staff who are most skilled in the techniques of experimentation.

We may define a scientist as one who during the course of an experiment has perceived something that leads to a further investigation of the profound truths of life and has lifted the veil which hid its fascinating secrets, and who, in the pursuit of this knowledge, has felt so passionate a love for the mysteries of nature that he forgets himself. A scientist is not one who can make use of different instruments, but one who knows nature. This sublime lover displays the external signs of his calling like a monk. We may describe a scientist as one who lives in his laboratory forgetful of the outside world and who at times may act eccentrically, as when he is careless about his dress, because he no longer thinks about himself. He is one who looks so continuously through a microscope that he becomes blind, who deliberately contracts tuberculosis, or who infects himself with cholera in his eagerness to know the ways in which these diseases are spread. He is one who knows that a chemical mixture may be explosive but prepares it anyway, and is blown up.

This is the type of man to whom nature reveals her secrets and crowns with the glory of discovery.

A scientist thus possesses a "spirit" that surpasses any mechanical skill. And a scientist has reached the summit of his discipline when his mental attitude has triumphed over his mechanical abilities. Science itself will be enriched by him not only with new natural discoveries but with new philosophical syntheses.

I personally believe that we should give more attention to imparting a *spirit* to teachers than scientific techniques, that is, our aim should be towards what is intellectual rather than material.

Thus, for example, when the scientific training of teachers was thought to consist in a communication of certain mechanical skills, there was no intention of making an elementary teacher a perfect anthropologist, an expert experimental psychologist, or a master of child hygiene. He was only being guided towards the field of experimental science and being taught how to manipulate various instruments. In the same way, we must now inspire a teacher with a "scientific outlook," though one that is limited to a particular field, the school.

We must create in the soul of the teacher a general *interest in the manifestation of natural phenomena* until he comes to the point where he loves nature and experiences the anxiety of one who has prepared an experiment and is waiting for new data to appear.

Scientific instruments are like the alphabet, and one must know how to use them to be able to read the secrets of nature. Just as a book containing the highest thoughts of an author is dependent upon the alphabet for the composition of the individual words, so nature, through the techniques of experimentation, reveals her own countless secrets.

If the print is sufficiently clear, anyone who has learned how to spell from a simple reader can, in the same mechanical way, go through one of Shakespeare's plays.

One who has learned nothing more than how to make

experiments is like one who spells out the literal sense of the words from a child's reader. And we shall have teachers on this same elementary level if we limit their training to the acquiring of techniques.

We must, therefore, make them interpreters of the spirit of nature, just as one who, after he has learned how to spell, one day finds himself able to comprehend the thoughts of Shakespeare, or Goethe, or Dante by the means of written symbols.

As is obvious there is a great difference between these two types of reading and the way is long. And yet it was only natural that we should have made the first error. A child who has gone through a speller has the illusion that he knows how to read, and, as a matter of fact, he can read the signs over shops, the headings of newspapers, or any word or phrase that actually meets his eyes. It would be very simple for him to imagine that, when he enters into a library, he knew how to appreciate the *sense* of all the books he saw there. But if he would try to read them, he would soon realize that "to know how to read mechanically" is of little value and he would leave the library to return to school.

The same mistake is made when new teachers are simply taught how to take physical measurements and perform psychological experiments.

* * *

Let us set aside the difficulties of preparing teacher-scientists in the accepted sense of the word. Let us not even attempt to outline a program for such a preparation since this would take us too far afield. Let us suppose, instead, that through long and patient exercises we have already trained our teachers *in the observation of nature*, and that we have raised them, for example, to the level of those zoologists who go out into the woods and fields to witness the early activities of some family of insects in which they are interested. He may be weary from his walk, but he is still watchful. He is only intent in not revealing his presence in the least degree so that the insects may carry out peacefully hour after hour those natural operations which he is anxious to observe.

Let us imagine that these teachers have reached the stage of that scientist who patiently watches the spontaneous movements of protozoa under his microscope. It seems to him that these tiny creatures reveal a shadowy consciousness or instinct in the way they avoid each other or select their food. He then disturbs their tranquil life with an electric current and notices how some group themselves about the positive and others about the negative pole. He then exposes them to a strong light and sees how some hasten towards, while others flee from, it. In this way he studies their various reactions, trying to discover if the creature's attraction to, or rejection of, the stimuli is of the same character as that which makes it avoid others of its own kind or move towards food. In other words, the scientist wants to know if movements of this sort are prompted by a kind of consciousness or, better, by a natural instinct, rather than by some physical attraction or repulsion like that which exists between a magnet and iron. And we may also imagine that this scientist, finding that it is two o'clock in the afternoon, is delighted to realize that he has been working in his laboratory instead of at home, where he would have been called for dinner, thus interrupting both his interesting observation and his fast.

Let us imagine, I say, that a teacher, apart from his own special training, has reached the stage where he feels this same kind of interest, though to a lesser degree, in observing natural phenomena. But even then his preparation would not be adequate.

A teacher is destined by his own special work to observe not simply insects or protozoa but man. And the man he is destined to observe is not one busy about his daily occupations, like those of insects when they wake up in the morning, but man when his intellectual life is awakening.

One who desires to be a teacher must have an interest in humanity that connects the observer with the observed more closely than that which joins the zoologist or biologist to nature; and since this union is more intimate, it is necessarily more delightful. A man cannot love an insect or a chemical reaction without giving up something of himself, and such a surrender seems to anyone who watches it dispassionately to be a kind of suffering, a distortion of one's own life, a martyrdom.

But the love of one man for another can be so pleasant and simple that not only privileged souls but even the ordinary run of men can attain it without effort. Teachers, when they have acquired something of the "scientific spirit," should comfort themselves with the thought that they will soon experience this delight in their observations.

To gain some idea of this second kind of spiritual preparation, we must try to enter into the minds of Christ's first chosen followers as they heard him speak of a kingdom of God which was far greater than any they could see on earth. One of the disciples began to wonder who would ever be great in this kingdom, and he asked him with childish curiosity: "Master, who will be the greatest of all in the kingdom of heaven?" And Christ, caressing the head of a little child who was gazing rapturously up at him, replied: "Whoever can become like to this little child, he will be the greatest in the kingdom of heaven."

Now let us imagine an ardent mystic soul that observes all the revelations of a little child's mind, so that with mingled feelings of respect, love, holy curiosity, and longing for the very heights of heaven, he may learn the way of his own proper perfection and thus be able to bring it fairly into the midst of a classroom filled with little children.

And yet not even he would be the new educator whom we wish to form.

But let us strive to pour into a single soul the keen spirit of sacrifice of a scientist and the ineffable ecstasy of such a mystic, and we shall then have the perfect spirit of our "teacher."

Actually, he will learn from the child himself the ways and means to his own education, that is, he will learn from the child how to perfect himself as a teacher.

* * *

Let us imagine to ourselves one of our botanists or zoologists, skilled in the techniques of observation and experiment, who, for example, has made a field trip to study peronospera and has completed his observations in the field, and then, with the help of his microscope and laboratory equipment, carries out further research and experiments in growing the fungi and so forth. Let us imagine, then, that such a scholar has been chosen for his research to fill a scientific post in which he must carry out new studies on the hymenoptera. What would be his reactions if, when he arrived at his new post, he saw placed in front of him a box covered with a clear glass, at the bottom of which were fastened with pins beautifully preserved butterflies with their wings outspread? The young scientist would say that this was a child's game and not an object of scientific study, that the objects in the box represented an exercise which boys carry out in the parks, catching butterflies in a net fastened to a stick. An experimental scientist confronted with such objects could do nothing.

A similar situation would occur if we were to place a teacher who was also a scientist such as we have described in one of our present day schools, where the spontaneous expression of a child's personality is so suppressed that he is almost like a corpse, and where he is so fixed to his place at a desk that he resembles a butterfly mounted on a pin. There he spreads out his wings for the acquirement of arid knowledge symbolized by the vanity of a butterfly's wings.

It is therefore not enough to prepare a learned teacher; a school must also be prepared for him.

It is imperative that a school *allow a child's activities to freely develop*. For this is the essential change to be made if a scientific form of education is to come into being.

No one would dare to maintain that such a principle already exists in teaching and in the school. It is true that some teachers, led by Rousseau, have laid down fantastic principles with respect to a child's freedom and have expressed their confused desires for it, but the true concept of *liberty* is practically unknown to professional educators. Their concept of *liberty* is frequently that which people form for themselves when they rebel against slavery; or, at a higher level, it is that of a *liberty* always restricted because it is simply one more step up the ladder, the partial liberation of a whole, the liberation of a country, of a class, or of a mode of thought.

The concept of liberty which should inspire teaching is, on the other hand, universal: it is the liberation of a life repressed by an infinite number of obstacles which oppose its harmonious development, both physical and spiritual. This is a matter of the utmost importance, although up until now it has escaped the notice of most men!

It is not a problem to be neglected but rather one to be clearly stated. Anyone who would claim that the principle of liberty in education is active in schools today would make us smile as we would at a child who, gazing at a mounted butterfly, would insist that it was alive and ready to take wing.

A principle of repression that amounts at times almost to slavery has a firm grip on both schools and education.

A proof of this may be found in the use made of desks and seats to match. Here we may see a striking example of the mistakes made by earlier materialistic educators who stumbled badly in their efforts to use the scattered stones of science to rebuild the crumbling walls of the school. Children were formerly seated on long, dreary benches, then science came along and perfected the desk. All the discoveries of anthropology were drawn on for this task. The age of the child and the length of his legs were used to determine the right height for the seat. The distance between the seat and the desk itself was calculated with mathematical precision so that a child's back might not become curved. Then, finally, with a really profound insight, the desks were separated from each other and made so narrow that once a child sat down he could not stretch himself from side to side or move close to his neighbor; and the desk itself was so constructed that a child could be seen as far as possible in all his immobility. The hidden motive behind all this separation of the children was to prevent immoral actions in the classroom, even in kindergartens! What should one say of such excessive prudence in a society wherein it would be scandalous to teach principles of sexual morality for fear of corrupting the innocent? And yet we have science here lending its support to this hypocrisy by building machine-like desks. And this is not all. Complacency goes still further. Science has so perfected the desks that they guarantee a child's immobility, or, if one prefers, spare his every movement. Everything is so arranged that, when a child is firmly fixed at his desk, he is forced to assume a position thought to be conducive to his health. We find seat, footrest, and desk so arranged that a child cannot stand up. But then, when the seat is tilted, when the top of the desk is raised and the footrest turned up, he has just enough space to stand erect.

This is the way in which desks have gradually been perfected. All experts on the so-called "scientific system of education" have a model scientific desk. Not a few nations are proud of their own national desks, and their various refinements have won them patents and awards.

Many sciences have doubtlessly contributed to the construction of the desk. Anthropology has provided the measurements of a child's body and described the natural characteristics of his age. Physiology has explained the movements of a child's muscles. Psychology has described the precosity and perversion of instincts. And child hygiene, above all, has prevented curvature of the spine. The desk was, therefore, scientifically constructed according to the data furnished by anthropological studies made upon children and has thus furnished us with an example of a literal application of science to the school.

But it will not be long before there will be a change in this attitude in every country where there is a revival of interest in the welfare of children. In the face of so much progress made in the first decade of the twentieth century, it will seem to be incomprehensible that so many students of child hygiene, anthropology, and sociology did not bring to light the basic error of the desk.

It will not be long before people will run their hands in amazement over these model desks or look at pictures of them and read the reason given for their construction, hardly trusting their senses.

The desks were adopted to prevent pupils from getting curvature of the spine!

And yet these same children were subjected to such a regime that even if they had been born healthy their spinal columns could have become twisted and they themselves humpbacked! And this could have happened to the spinal column, which, biologically speaking, is the most primitive and essential part of the skeleton, the main support of the living organism! It was something that could stoutly endure the fierce struggles that engaged both primitive and civilized man when they fought lions in the desert or hunted mammoths or quarried stone and bent iron and extended their dominion over the earth. And yet this spinal column cannot stand up but bends under the yoke of school!

It is incomprehensible that "*science*" should have perfected an instrument of slavery in the school without being in the least enlightened by the thought and efforts given to the creation of a free society.

Everyone knows the direction that has been taken by this reform. The poorly-fed workingman does not ask for tonics but for an improvement in his economic condition that will help him to eat better. The miner, who must work for many hours a day stretched out on his stomach, can easily rupture himself, but he does not ask for a truss. Instead, he looks for shorter hours and better working conditions so that he can lead an ordinary healthy life like other men.

And if during this same period of social reform we find that children are working in such an unhealthy environment in the classroom, and one so opposed to their normal development that their very bones become bent, we find an answer to this sad condition in an orthopedic desk.

Sometime ago a woman with obvious satisfaction, imagining that I approved of all of these scientific innovations in the schools, asked my opinion about a brace which she had invented for school children to complement the protective features of the desk. Physicians, as a matter of fact, have various means of treating curvature of the spine: orthopedic instruments, braces, and traction, that is, the periodic suspension of a child by the head or shoulders so that the weight of his body stretches and straightens the spinal column. And now that someone has suggested employing the brace, it will not be long before someone advises traction for the pupils!

All of this is a logical consequence of the material application of scientific methods to a decadent system of education. The same could be said of the use of anthropology and experimental psychology in contemporary schools.

The rational way to prevent scoliosis in children would be to change the type of work they do so that they would no longer be obliged to remain for many hours a day in a harmful position.

What the schools need is more liberty, not such a contraption as a desk.

Even if a desk were useful for a child's physique, it would still be an obstacle to a healthy environment because of the difficulty of moving it when the room is cleaned. Today there is a new trend for furniture in homes. It is being made lighter and simpler so that it can be easily moved about and dusted, if not actually washed, every day. But schools have remained blind to the transformations going on about them.

We must reflect on what will happen to the spirit of a

child whose body is condemned to grow in such an artificial and vicious fashion that his bones become deformed. When we speak of rescuing workingmen, we understand that under the more apparent evils, such as anemia, hernia, and so forth, there lies an even more serious wound afflicting the human soul that has been reduced to slavery; and this is what we aim at alleviating when we say that the workingman must regain his liberty. We know only too well that when a man's blood becomes impoverished or his system disordered his mind is darkened and rendered insensible. Moral degradation, hanging like a weight about the neck, has been the chief obstacle to human progress, and men's souls cry out for redemption far more than their bodies. And if this is so, what should we say about the education of children?

We know only too well this sorry spectacle. In a classroom a bustling teacher is busy pouring knowledge into the heads of his charges. To succeed in his task he must keep his pupils immobile and attentive even by force, making generous use of rewards and punishments in order to keep his condemned listeners in the proper frame of mind.

But rewards and punishments, to speak frankly, are the desk of the soul, that is, a means of enslaving a child's spirit, and better suited to provoke than to prevent deformities.

Actually, rewards and punishments are employed to compel children to conform to the laws of the world rather than to those of God. And these laws are practically always laid down for them by an adult invested with unlimited authority.

Too often a teacher commands because he is strong and expects a child to obey because he is weak. Instead of acting in this way, an adult should show himself to a child as a loving and enlightened guide assisting him along the way leading to the kingdom of heaven. Anyone who uses his talents can be exalted, and everyone can receive a reward, whether he has many talents or only a poor single one.

But in school there is only one prize for all those "of good will" who enter the race, a fact which generates pride, envy, and rivalries instead of that thrill coming from effort, humility, and love which all can experience. In this way we create a conflict not simply between the school and social progress but also between the school and religion. One day a child will surely ask himself if the prizes won at school were not rather obstacles on the way to eternal life, or if the punishments with which he was humiliated when he was in no position to defend himself did not make him one of those "hungering and thirsting after justice" whom Christ defended in the Sermon on the Mount.

Social life, it is true, has rewards and punishments that differ from those of the spirit, and adults see to it that a child's mind soon enough adapts itself to, and keeps itself within, the conventions of this world. They make use of rewards and punishments to make a child submissive to their will.

But if we take a close look at society, we shall see that it is gradually improving, that a life ruled by thought and reason is emerging triumphant. The yoke of the slave yields to that of the servant, and this in turn yields to that of the working-man.

All forms of slavery have a tendency to disappear. The history of human progress represents a series of conquests and liberations, and any failures in this regard are looked upon as regressions.

In some ways schools resemble governmental bureaucracies. Employees in the various departments of government are busy securing some distant but great advantage, but their results are not immediately visible. It is through them that the state carries on its great undertakings and provides for the general welfare of the people. But they themselves are scarcely aware of the importance of their work. Their immediate interest is in a promotion, just as a student is anxious to pass on to a higher grade at the end of the school year. The employee who loses sight of his lofty goal is like a degraded child or a tricked slave. His intrinsic dignity as a man has been reduced to the level of a machine, which needs to be oiled if it is to function properly since it does not have within itself a vital principle. He is urged on along his dry and disagreeable journey by such things as a desire for recognition. And the fear of not getting a promotion prevents him from leaving his job and ties him to his painstaking and monotonous labor just as the same fear keeps a student at his books. Corrections of a supervisor are exactly like the shouts of a teacher, and changes in poorly written letters are like marks made on a student's badly written exercise.

If the policies of an administration do not match up to the greatness of the country, if it is easily corrupted, it is because the mentality of a clerk has engulfed the magnanimity of the man who should be carrying out these functions. His vision has been restricted to a concern for trivialities, for rewards or punishments. It is not surprising then that power and favoritism have such a great influence on these servants of the state.

A country survives, however, since the integrity of most of its employees is strong enough to resist the corrupting influence of rewards and punishments. Honesty prevails somewhat in the same fashion as society itself triumphs over every form of poverty and death and marches on to new victories; and, like the instinct for freedom, it overcomes every obstacle as it goes on from victory to victory.

And it is this great inner drive that often lies hidden in the mind that makes the world progress.

No one who has ever done anything really great or successful has ever done it simply because he was attracted by what we call a "reward" or by the fear of what we call a "punishment." If an army of giants were to wage a war for no other reason than to win promotions, stripes, or medals, or simply to avoid being shot against a band of pygmies inflamed with a love for their country, the latter would certainly obtain the victory. When an army has lost the spirit of heroism, rewards and punishments can do no more than complete the work of its destruction by leading to its corruption.[1]

Every victory and every advance in human progress comes from some inner compulsion. A young student can become a great teacher or doctor if he is driven on by an interest in his vocation; but if he is motivated solely by the hope of a legacy or a good marriage or some other external advantage, he will never become a real teacher or doctor, and he will not make any great contribution to the world through his work. If a

---

[1] In everything that we say about rewards and punishments we do not intend to discount their basic, educational import, which is founded on human nature itself, but only to check their abuse and perversion so that instead of being means they become as it were an end. As a matter of fact, common sense tells us that rewards and punishments are a means for knowing practically, especially when minds are darkened by passion, that a work is good or evil, praiseworthy or reprehensible. Thus in a certain sense they are inseparable from work as effect is from cause, as moral beauty or foulness is from a human act.

young man must be punished or rewarded by his school or family to make him study for his degree, it would be better for him not to receive it at all. Everyone has a special inclination or special secret, hidden vocation. It may be modest but it is certainly useful. An award can divert such a calling and turn one's head to the loss of his true vocation.

We keep repeating that the world is making progress and that men must constantly be urged to pursue it. But true progress consists in the discovery of something hidden. Frequently it may be something that simply needs to be improved or perfected. No reward is offered for the discovery of something not foreseen; and, in fact, one who tries to bring it to light is frequently persecuted. It would be a disaster if poems were written solely with the hope of winning a state award. It would be better for a poet's vision to remain concealed within him and for the poetic Muse to disappear. A poem should flow from a poet's mind when he is not thinking of a reward or of himself; and even if he wins a prize, it should never make him proud.

But there is also an external award worthy of a man. When an orator, for example, sees the faces of his listeners light up with emotion, he experiences a thrill that can only be compared with the intense joy of one who discovers that he is loved. It is in touching and conquering the minds of others that we enjoy the only reward worthy of our efforts.

This happens to us at certain joyous moments given to us so that we may continue to live in peace. It may happen when we fall in love, or when a child has been conceived, or a book published, or a great discovery has been made, and we deceive ourselves with the thought that we are the happiest person in the world. And yet, if at that moment someone who is in authority, or who is over us like a teacher, should come up and offer us a medal or some other prize, he would rob us of our true reward. Disillusioned we would cry out: "Who are you to remind me of the fact that I am not supreme, that there is another so far above me that he can give me a reward?" Man's true reward can come from God alone.

As far as punishment is concerned, we do not mean to deny its social function and individual efficacy but merely its moral value and general necessity. It is most usefully employed with criminals, but these are relatively few, and social progress is not dependent upon them. The penal code threatens us with punishment if we are dishonest within the limits fixed by the law. But we are not honest because we fear the law; we refrain from theft and murder because we recognize the intrinsic evil of such acts. The penalty of the law simply makes us realize this more keenly, but the tenor of our lives should be such that it keeps us far from the possibility of committing evil acts.

Without going into the psychological aspects of the problem, we may still say that a delinquent, before he transgresses a law, is aware of its existence and of a penalty. In other words, he has felt the penal code bearing down upon him but has defied it, or he has been enticed to commit a crime under the impression that he could avoid the punishment. Nevertheless he has experienced within his own mind a struggle between the crime and its punishment. Whether the penal code effectively reaches its goal of hindering crime or not, it has undoubtedly been drawn up for a very limited class of individuals. The vast majority of the citizens are honest even when they are unaware of the sanctions of the penal law.

The real punishment of a normal man is for him to lose consciousness of his own strength and greatness. Such a punishment often falls upon men enjoying an abundance of what are commonly known as "rewards." But men, unfortunately, often do not notice the real punishments which threaten to overwhelm them.

* * *

Here education can be of help.

But instead, we keep children in a school restricted by objects that are degrading to both body and soul, the desk and material rewards and punishments. And why? To keep them silent and immobile. But where does this lead them? Unfortunately, nowhere!

Their education consists in mechanically filling their minds with the contents of a syllabus which is frequently drawn up by departments of education and imposed by law.

Confronted by such a forgetfulness of the continuity of our own lives with that of our children and their descendants, we should hang our heads in shame and cover our faces with our hands!

Truly there is an urgent need today of reforming the methods of instruction and education, and he who aims at such a renewal is struggling for the regeneration of mankind.

2. The History of Methods

If we wish to develop a scientific system of education, we must therefore strike out on a different road from that which has been followed so far.

Teachers must be trained and schools transformed at the same time. If we are to have teachers trained in observation and experimentation, it is necessary that they should be able to carry out these activities in the school.

A basic requirement for a scientific educational program must therefore be a school that will permit a child to freely develop his own personal life. If a system of education is to rise from a study of the individual student, it will have to come about in this way, that is, from the observation of free children who are watched and studied but not repressed.

It would be foolish to expect that a new type of education could arise merely from an examination of school children with the help of anthropology and experimental psychology.

Every branch of experimental science has developed from the use of its own peculiar method. The science of bacteriology has risen from the isolation and culture of microbes. Criminology, medicine, and education have had their origin in the application of anthropometric methods to individuals of various classes, such as criminals, the insane, the sick in clinics, and students. Experimental psychology needs as its starting point an exact description of the technique of performing an experiment.

In general, it is important to define the method and technique of experimentation and then, after making specific use of them, to wait for the results of the experiment. Investigations of this kind must be carried out without any preconceptions as to their final outcome. For example, if we wish to make a scientific study of a child's intelligence with relation to the development of his skull, we must take no account of the greater or less intelligence of the different students who heads are measured. This precaution must be taken so that the results of our research are not unconsciously vitiated by the preconceived notion that more intelligent children have more perfectly developed heads.

When one is performing an experiment, he must for the time being rid himself of all his prejudices, even those that may be the product of his own particular culture and background.

Accordingly, if we wish to conduct educational experiments, we must not have recource to kindred sciences but must free our minds so that they can proceed without hindrance in their search for the truths that belong properly and exclusively to teaching.

We must not therefore start from any fixed ideas about child psychology but with a program that will give a child his freedom so that we can deduce a truly scientific child psychology by observing his spontaneous reactions. It may well be that such a program holds great surprises in store for us.

* * *

Our problem then is to establish the method peculiar to experimental education. It cannot be that employed in other experimental sciences. If scientific education is to a certain extent connected with hygiene, anthropology, and psychology, and if it also to a certain extent adopts the technical methods used by all three, their actual use is limited to details in the study of the individual being educated. The methods of these sciences are analogous to, but quite different from, those of education and can therefore play only a subordinate part in teaching itself.

This particular study is concerned with the method used in experimental teaching and is the fruit of my own personal experiences in schools for very young children.

Actually, what I am presenting is only an introduction to a new system of education. It is one I have used with children between the ages of three and six, but I believe that the surprising results that have been obtained with them will be an incentive for further work along this line.

Although our system of education, which has had so much success, is not yet entirely complete, it already constitutes a sufficiently organic whole for it to be profitably adopted in schools for small children or for those in the first grade.[1]

In saying that the present work is the result of two years of experience, I am perhaps not quite correct. I do not believe that I could have discovered everything that I am going to describe simply through my own recent efforts.

The educational system employed in the Children's Houses actually has more remote origins. If my experiences with normal children have been rather brief, they are based on previous teaching experiences with abnormal children and thus represent a considerably longer period of thought.

Some ten years ago when I was an assistant instructor in the Psychiatric Clinic of the University of Rome, I had the opportunity of visiting the insane asylum to study the sick that were to be chosen as subjects for clinical instruction. It was in this way that I became interested in the mentally retarded children who were housed in the same asylum. At this time doctors were greatly interested in the treatment of thyroid glands, and this had led to a greater interest in mentally deficient children. I had completed my own internship as a physician and now turned my attention to the study of children's diseases.

It was thus through my concern for mentally retarded children that I became acquainted with the special method for teaching such unfortunates devised by Edward Seguin and I became quite interested in an educational treatment of various abnormalities such as deafness, paralysis, idiocy, rickets, and so forth, which was becoming popular with physicians at this time. The practical outcome of reflection on these problems was a conviction that education must be united with medical treatment for a cure of these disorders, and special emphasis was placed upon the use of physical therapy.

I differed from my colleagues in that I instinctively felt that mental deficiency was more of an educational than medical problem. At various congresses much was said about

[1] The method has now been extended and has been widely tried in elementary classes. It is described in *Self-Education in Elementary Schools*. More recently it has been pushed back to the time of birth and advanced to the age of adulthood. There are some secondary schools that follow the Montessori method, and they have received public approbation.

the medico-pedagogical method for treating and educating feeble-minded children, but at the Educational Convention held at Turin in 1898 I raised the question of their moral education and I must have struck a sympathetic chord in my audience since the idea, passed on by the physicians to the teachers in elementary schools, spread like a flash and aroused a great deal of interest.

I was, in fact, given an appointment by my teacher Guido Paccelli, who was then Minister of Education, to conduct a series of lectures for the teachers of Rome on the education of feeble-minded children. These lectures gave rise to a state institution for training teachers of retarded children which I directed for more than two years.

Connected with this institution was a class for extern students who, because of their mental deficiencies, were thought to be uneducable in the elementary schools. Later on, through the help of a charitable organization, there was founded an educational institute where, in addition to extern students, there were brought together all the mentally deficient children who till then had been living in the insane asylum in Rome.

I thus spent two years with the help of my colleagues in preparing the teachers of Rome in a special method of observing and educating feeble-minded children. But this was not all. What was even more important was that after I had gone to London and to Paris to study at first hand the education of the mentally deficient, I undertook the task of personally teaching the children and directing the work of the other teachers in our institute.

I was more than an elementary teacher. I stayed with the children and taught them myself from eight in the morning to seven in the evening without interruption. These two years provided me with my first and indeed my only true title as a teacher.

From the very beginning of my work with mentally retarded children in the years 1898 to 1900 I felt that the methods I was employing were not only a help to the mentally deficient but that they contained educational principles more rational than those then in use, especially since they were able to help a weak mind to develop. After I had left the school for the deficient children, this idea became even more fixed in my mind. Gradually I became convinced that similar methods applied to normal children would lead to a surprising development of their personalities.

It was then that I made a thorough study of the so-called "remedial education" and decided to study the education of normal children and the principles upon which it is based. I therefore enrolled as a student of philosophy at the university. I was animated with a deep faith. Although I did not know if I would ever be able to test the truth of my conviction, I gave up every other occupation in order to deepen it. It was almost as if I was preparing myself for an unknown mission.

The methods used in the education of the feeble-minded had their origin at the time of the French Revolution in the work of a physician whose writings occupy a place in medical history, since he was the founder of that branch of medical science known today as "otology," which deals with diseases of the ear.

He was the first to attempt a methodical education of the sense of hearing. He carried on his work at the institute for the deaf-mutes founded by Pereire in Paris and succeeded in restoring hearing to those who were only partially deaf. Later on, having had in his charge for eight years an idiot boy known as the "Savage of Aveyron," he extended the educational methods which had already been employed with such success in treating deafness to all the senses. Itard, who had been a student of Pinel, was the first teacher to observe a pupil in the same way that the sick were observed in hospitals, epecially those suffering from nervous disorders.

Itard's educational works are most interesting because of the minute descriptions which he gives of his educational efforts and experiences. Anyone who reads them today must admit that they were the first attempts at experimental teaching.

As a matter of fact, he derived from his scientific studies a series of exercises capable of modifying the personality by remedying those deficiencies which kept an individual in his inferior state. Itard actually succeeded in making semi-deaf children hear and speak, who otherwise would have remained deaf and dumb and as a consequence forever abnormal. This is indeed something quite different from a simple study of an individual, conducted through tests of experimental psychology. These only provide information with respect to one's actual mentality; they do not modify it or have any influence on methods of education. Here, on the other hand, the scientific techniques employed became a means of instruction and the educational approach itself was changed.

Itard, therefore may be called the founder of scientific education. The title does not really belong to Wundt or Binet, who were instead the founders of physiological psychology, which finds a ready application in schools.

This is a fundamental point that deserves to be clarified. In Switzerland, Pestalozzi became the father of a new effective system of education. But it was in Germany some fifty years later that Fechner and Wundt founded experimental psychology. The two trends grew and developed into separate schools. The older system of academic instruction continued to evolve on its old foundations, though at the same time students were given mental tests. These, however, had no influence whatever on education. The experiments which Itard had carried out somewhat earlier, were, on the contrary, a true beginning of a scientific education capable of modifying both educational methods and the pupils themselves. But since it had its origins in the treatment of defective children, the educational world did not give it serious attention.

The credit of having perfected a real educational system for defective children belongs to Edward Seguin. He was at first a teacher but later became a physician. Taking the experiences of Itard as his starting point, he modified and perfected the method during a period of ten years when he was treating children who had been taken from the asylum and brought together in a little school on the Rue Pigalle in Paris. His method was set forth for the first time in a book of more than six hundred pages published in 1846 in Paris with the title: *Traitement moral hygiène et éducation des idiots.*

Later on, Seguin emigrated to the United States, where he founded many institutions for the feeble-minded, and where, after twenty more years of experience, he published a second edition of his work, but with a different title: *Idiocy and Its Treatment by the Physiological Method.* The work was published in New York in 1866. In it Seguin clearly defined what he called a "physiological method" of education. He dropped the reference to the "education of idiots" that he had used earlier, as if it were something special for them, but now spoke of idiocy being treated by a "physiological method." If we reflect on the fact that education has always had psychology as its foundation, and that Wundt postulated a "physiological psychology," we must be struck by the similarity of these concepts; and we must suspect that the physiological method has some connection with "physiological psychology."

While I was an assistant at the Psychiatric Clinic, I had read with great interest Edward Seguin's French work. But I was not able to find in any library the English book published twenty years later in New York, although it was cited by Bourneville as dealing with a special problem of education. To my great surprise, I was not even able to find a trace of it in Paris, where Bourneville told me that he knew of its existence, but that it had never reached Europe. Nevertheless, I hoped to find a copy of it in London. Eventually, however, I had to conclude that the volume was not even to be found there either in public or private libraries. I made a vain quest for it, going from house to house of many English doctors who were well known for their work with defective children or who were in charge of special schools for them. The fact that this book was unknown even in England, even though it had been published in English, led me to believe that Seguin's system had not been understood. As a matter of fact, Seguin was frequently quoted in publications dealing with institutions for the feeble-minded, but the educational principles described in these works were entirely different from those used by Seguin himself. Almost everywhere practically the same methods used for normal children were used in the instruction of those who were defective. This was particularly true in Germany. A German friend of mine who had gone there to help me in my research noted that there was special teaching material available but it was rarely used and was as a rule kept in the museums associated with the schools for the feeble-minded. The Germans defended the principle that it is well to adopt the method used with normal children for those who are retarded, but it must be admitted that this method is more objective in Germany than it is with us.

I continued my studies at Bicêtre for a considerable length of time. There I saw that more use was made of Sequin's apparatus than of his system, and yet the French text was available to the teachers. The teaching there was purely mechanical, and all the teachers followed the rules to the letter. However, I noticed everywhere, both in London and in Paris, a desire for fresh advice and new experiences since Seguin's claim that his method actually was effective in educating idiots was practically never fulfilled.

The reason for this failure can be easily understood. Everyone was thoroughly convinced that defective children, that is, inferior beings, should in the long run be educated in the same way as normal children. They had not realized that a new system of education had appeared upon the horizon, much less that it could raise defective children to a higher level. And they were even less aware of the fact that a method of education able to raise up defective children could also raise up those who were normal.

For two years after this I carried on my experiments in educating defective children in Rome. I followed the suggestions I found in Seguin's book and also discovered that Itard's admirable experiments were a veritable treasure. In addition to this, following the lead of these authors, I had a rich stock of teaching material made for my use. This material, which I did not see complete in any other institution, proved to be of excellent assistance in the hands of anyone who knew how to use it, though left to itself it was passed over unnoticed by the deficient children. I now understood why the teachers had become discouraged and abandoned his method. They were prejudiced by the conviction that they had to place themselves on the level of the one to be educated and this plunged them into a kind of general apathy. They knew that they were educating children of lesser talents and they therefore did not succeed. The same happens with teachers of very small children who think that one who tries to educate them must place himself at their level by engaging in games and frequently in silly talk.

Instead of acting in this way, it is necessary that we know how to awaken the man that lies asleep within the soul of a child. I felt this instinctively, and I believe that it was not the material but my voice which roused the children and encouraged them to use the material to teach themselves. I was guided in my work for them by the great concern which I had for their wretchedness and by the love which these unfortunate children can stir up in all who come near them. Seguin had earlier come to much the same conclusion. When

I read of his patient efforts, I realized that his primary means of instruction were spiritual. Indeed, at the end of his French work, he gives a résumé of what he had done and sorrowfully comes to the conclusion that all will be lost if *teachers* are not properly prepared. He has a very original idea about the preparation of teachers of defective children. His advice is almost like that which one would give to another on the arts of seduction. He would like to see them good-looking, pleasant-voiced, and very careful to do everything they can to make themselves attractive. Their bearing and their tone of voice should be studied with the same care as that taken by great actors preparing themselves for the stage since they must conquer minds which are weak and weary and fill them with the great emotions of life.

This action upon the child's spirit was a kind of secret key which opened up the way over a long series of teaching experiments wonderfully analyzed by Edward Seguin and which as a matter of fact are most efficacious for the teaching of idiots. I obtained surprising results from them, but I must confess that while my efforts showed results in the intellectual progress of my pupils, I was myself strangely exhausted. I felt as if I was giving up some of my own inner strength. What we call encouragement, comfort, love, and respect are actually a drain on one's soul, and the more lavish one is in this regard, the more one renews and reinvigorates the lives of those about him.

Without such an inner effort, the most perfect *external stimulus* passes unnoticed, as the sun did for Saul when he called out: "What is this? . . . It is a dense fog!"

This is not the place to describe the new experiments which I was then able to make on my own account. I will only note that at this time I attempted an original method of teaching the children how to read and write. These were elements in a child's education that were treated very imperfectly in the works of both Itard and Seguin.

I succeeded in teaching some of the defective children from the asylum how to read and write so well that I could present them for an examination that was conducted in the public schools for normal children. And they passed it successfully.

These results were so extraordinary that they seemed almost miraculous to those who saw them. My own opinion was, however, that the boys from the asylum had been able to compete with the normal children simply because they had been taught in a different way. Their psychic development had been encouraged whereas that of the normal children had been stifled and repressed. I kept thinking that if the special type of education which had been so marvelously effective with the retarded children could one day be applied to those who were normal, the miracle would disappear since the vast difference between the two mentalities would no longer be bridged. While everyone else was admiring the progress made by my defective charges, I was trying to discover the reasons which could have reduced the healthy, happy pupils of the ordinary schools to such a low state that in the intelligence tests they were on a level with my own unfortunate pupils.

One day one of the teachers assisting me with the retarded children at the institute gave me a passage to read from the prophet Ezechiel. It had made a profound impression upon her as a kind of prophecy about the education of these poor children:

> The hand of the Lord was upon me, and brought me forth in the spirit of the Lord: and set me down in the midst of a plain that was full of bones.
>
> And he led me about through them on every side: now they were very many upon the face of the plain, and they were exceeding dry.
>
> And he said to me: Son of man, dost thou think these bones shall live? And I answered: O Lord God, thou knowest.
>
> And he said to me: Prophesy concerning these bones; and say to them: Ye dry bones, hear the word of the Lord.
>
> Thus saith the Lord God to these bones: Behold I will send spirit into you, and you shall live.
>
> And I will lay sinews upon you, and will cause flesh to grow over you, and will cover you with skin: and I will give you spirit and you shall live, and you shall know that I am the Lord.
>
> And I prophesied as he had commanded me: and as I prophesied there was a noise, and behold a commotion: and the bones came together, each one to its joint.

And I saw, and behold the sinews, and the flesh came up upon them: and the skin was stretched out over them, but there was no spirit in them.

And he said to me: Prophesy to the spirit, prophesy, O son of man, and say to the spirit: Thus saith the Lord God: Come, spirit, from the four winds, and blow upon these slain, and let them live again.

And I prophesied as he had commanded me: and the spirit came into them, and they lived: and they stood up upon their feet, an exceeding great army.

And he said to me: Son of man: All these bones are the house of Israel: they say: Our bones are dried up, and our hope is lost, and we are cut off.

The words, "I will send the spirit into you and you shall live," seem indeed to refer to the immediate, individual work of the teacher, who encourages, incites, and assists his pupil, and lays the foundation for his education.

And the following words, "I will lay sinews upon you, and will cause flesh to grow over you, and will cover you with skin," recall the basic formula in which Seguin summarized his method. It is "to lead a child, as it were, by the hand from the education of the muscles to that of the nervous system and of the senses." It was in this way that Seguin taught idiots how to walk and how to keep their balance when performing difficult movements, such as in climbing stairs, jumping, and so forth, and finally how to refine their feelings, beginning with the education of the muscular, tactile, and heat sensations, and ending up with the education of the individual senses. All of this, however, was primarily concerned with a child's physical life. But the prophet had said: "Prophesy to the spirit ... and let them live again." Seguin had indeed led the mentally deficient from a physical to a spiritual life, "from an education of the senses to concepts, from concepts to ideas, and from ideas to a realization of right and wrong." But when such a wonderful work is finished, and when a retarded child, with the help of a detailed physiological analysis and a properly progressive method of education, has become a man, he is still inferior to others and will never be able to really adapt himself to his social environment: "Our bones are dried up, and our hope is lost, and we are cut off."

The chief contribution made by Pestalozzi to education was the principle that a teacher must have a special training that is not simply intellectual but which also touches the heart. According to him, education is basically "a contact of souls" and a teacher must feel "respect and sympathy" for the children he teaches. Still, this is only a first, if essential, step in the process of awakening the soul of the child. A child's own activities must then find the means that lead to its own development.

This second element in a child's education has been the contribution of scientific education. This is why we can say today, as the fruit of our own experience, that a teacher is "the catalyst" between a child, who may be disturbed, sleepy, or repressed, and the environment prepared for his education. Frequently this contact between a child and his environment cannot be established until he has first been freed from the burden of a previous repression and its harmful effects. In such a case, an attempt must be made to cure, or, as we say, "to normalize" the child before he is given the means for his development. Many of our teachers have suffered serious disappointment because of their lack of success. They began their work as if the child were well and overlooked his need for readjustment.

This was a further reason why Seguin's method was laid aside. The enormous expenditure of effort that it entailed did not seem to be justified by the meagerness of the results.

Moreover, everyone kept saying the same thing: "There is still so much to do for normal children."

* * *

My own experience with Seguin's method inspired me with confidence in it. After giving up my direct work with retarded children, I devoted myself to the study of his books and those of Itard. I felt the need of meditating upon them. I therefore did something which had not been done before and which perhaps few would care to repeat. I translated into Italian and copied out from beginning to end the writings of these two authors. I wrote them out by hand so that I would have time to weigh the meaning of each of the words and absorb the spirit of the authors. I had just about finished copying out the six hundred pages of Seguin's French book when I received from New York a copy of his second edition, published in English in 1866. An old copy of it has been found among the discarded books of a physician's private library in New York, and it had been readily given to the person who sent it to me. With the help of an English woman I translated it. The work did not contain any significant additions to Seguin's educational experiences but it did set forth more clearly the philosophy that lay behind the work he had described in his first volume. This teacher, who had studied retarded children for thirty years, set forth the idea that the same physiological method used with normal children would lead to a regeneration of all mankind. This method, as we have indicated, would have as its basis a study of the individual child and an analysis of the physiological and psychic phenomena appearing during the course of his education. Seguin's voice seemed to me to be like that of our Lord's precursor crying out in the wilderness. And my mind was deeply struck by the immense importance of a work which could potentially bring about a reform in the schools and in the whole concept of education.

At this time I was enrolled in the university as a student of philosophy. I was taking courses in experimental psychology, which had only recently been introduced into the universities, of Turin, Naples, and Rome. At the same time I was doing some research in educational anthropology in the primary schools. I used the opportunity to study the method used in the education of normal children. These studies later enabled me to teach educational anthropology at the University of Rome.

Such then was my preparation for my later work. I had become familiar with the scientific problems of the day and I was particularly interested in the new branches of medicine dealing with mental ills. I realized, as others did not, that a scientific education could not be based on the study and measurement of the individuals to be educated, but rather upon some kind of continuous treatment that could modify them. Itard had made use of a scientific method of education because he employed the measurements which he made of a child's hearing simply as a means to enable those who were partially deaf to hear better. In his treatment of the savage of Aveyron he had used scientific methods very much like those later devised by the founders of experimental psycholo-

32   The Discovery of the Child

gy, and in so doing he had succeeded in restoring an individual to society who had seemed so far removed from it that he was thought to be an idiot as well as deaf and dumb. In fact, Itard was so successful with this unfortunate child that he learned how to hear and understand what was spoken and also how to read.

In the same way Seguin, employing an analytical method much like that of Fechner, but more extensive, not only studied hundreds of retarded children gathered together in the asylum of Paris, but he transformed them into human beings capable of working together and receiving an intellectual and artistic formation.

I myself, by simply studying individuals and using scientific instruments and mental tests, had transformed retarded children who had been expelled from school as being uneducable into individuals who could enter into competition with normal children. They had been so transformed that they found a place in society as intelligent, educated persons. A scientific education is, therefore, one which, even though it is based upon science, modifies and perfects an individual.

A scientific education based upon objective research should also be able to transform normal children. But how? By raising them up above the normal level and making them better. The object of a science of education should be not only to "observe" but also to "transform" children.

This, then, was the conclusion to which I had come: we should not only observe but we should also transform the children in our care. Observation had given rise to the new science of psychology but it had not transformed the schools or the students. It had added something, but it had left the schools in their original condition since it had not brought about a change in the methods of instruction of education. If the new methods were to be employed along scientific lines, they should completely change the school and its methods and thus give rise to a new form of education.

The key to the scientific education of retarded children was that idiots and others of inferior intelligence did not respond to ordinary methods of teaching and could not carry out commands. It was therefore necessary to use other means to be adjusted to the varying capacities of different individuals.

Education of this type had been an object of research, of

experiments, of attempts to discover the potentialities of each of the students and of offering him means and motives which could awaken his latent energies so that he might continue to use, expand, and coordinate them through proper exercise.

A teacher when he is first confronted with one who is deaf or feebleminded is as helpless as if he were confronted with a newly born child. Only experimental science can point out the way to a new type of education suitable for such unfortunates.

I wanted to experiment with the various methods used successfully by Seguin with children when they first came to school at the age of six untrained and unlearned. But since we are constantly hampered by our habits and prejudices, I never thought of applying these same methods on preschool children. The opportunity of doing so came to me by pure chance. And yet it might have seemed logical to use the same methods on little children as those that had been employed for the retarded. It was generally thought that the former could not be educated or taught since their minds had not yet reached sufficient maturity.

It is impossible to compare retarded with normal children, if we consider children of different ages, that is, if we compare those who are abnormal and do not have a capacity for development with those who have not had time to develop, that is, very small children. Retarded children are judged to be intellectually much like normal children some years younger. Despite the fact that such a comparison fails to take into account the initial force innate in the different degrees of the two natures, it is not illogical.

Small children have not yet acquired a definite coordination of their muscular movements. Their walk is unsteady; they cannot carry out ordinary acts of daily life such as putting on their stockings, buttoning their clothes, tying their shoes, putting on gloves, and so forth. Their sense organs, for example, in the focusing of their eyes, are not as yet fully developed. Their language is rudimentary and shows the well-known defects of infant speech. Difficulty in concentrating, fickleness, and so forth are other traits of the same kind.

In his studies in infant psychology, Preyer has made an extensive comparison between pathological defects in speech and those that are normal in the course of a child's development. Methods proved effective in the mental training of retarded children could be of some assistance to all children, and should thus provide a sound method of instruction for all normal beings.

Many permanent defects, like those of speech, are acquired when one is a child because we neglect to take care of individuals at the most important period of their lives when their principal functions are formed and stabilized, that is, when they are between the ages of three and six.

This ambitious idea of being able to assist in man's development through scientific methods of education during that period of his life in which his intelligence and character are being molded had not struck me despite my keen interest in the question.

Herein lies the interest in this kind of "psychological discovery" and this scientific method of education.

As it had done so often in the past, for example, in the discovery of electricity, so here also chance played its part. As a matter of fact, chance, that is, a peculiar set of circumstances, must almost always provide the spark to an intuition. It is the peculiar set of circumstances which reveals what is new, and then, when intuition and interest have been awakened, these later can open up a new way for progress.

My own experience is interesting because, apart from previous studies and prejudices, it offered a complex environment that provided a perfect unity not only for the education of a child but for social life and sentiments as well.

The History of the Discovery of a Scientific Education for Normal Children

It was toward the end of the year 1906, and I had just returned from Milan, where I had been chosen to assist in judging the awards to be given at the International Exhibition in the section devoted to scientific education and experimental psychology. I was invited by the Director General of the Roman Association for Good Buildings to undertake the organization of infant schools in its tenement houses.

He had the magnificent idea of reforming a quarter filled with refugees and other unfortunate people like that of San Lorenzo in Rome. Here some thirty thousand people were living crowded together in conditions that were beyond civic control. Among them were unemployed laborers, beggars, prostitutes, and criminals recently released from prison, who had sought refuge within the walls of houses that were still unfinished because of the economic crisis which had interrupted all building activities in the area. An engineer by the name of Talamo conceived the idea of buying up these unfinished buildings and gradually completing them, thus making them habitable for the people. Along with this plan he had another that was truly admirable. He hoped to gather together all the children of preschool age (from three to six) in a kind of "home school."

Every tenement would have its own school, and since the association already had more than four hundred sites in Rome, the project had possibilities for development. But, in the meantime, the first school was to open in January, 1907, in a large tenement in the quarter of San Lorenzo. There the association already possessed fifty-eight buildings, and the directors of the association envisaged opening up sixteen schools in these dwellings.

This special type of school was christened with the charming name of *Casa dei Bambini* (Children's House). The first of these was opened on January 6, 1907, on the Via dei Marsi, 53, and I was entrusted with the responsibility of its direction. I perceived the social and educational importance of such an institution in all its immensity, and I insisted upon what at the time seemed to be an exaggerated vision of its triumphal future; but today many are beginning to understand that what I foresaw was true. In Italy, January 6th is a children's feast. It is the feast of the Epiphany and is celebrated like Christmas; there is a Christmas tree and children receive toys and other gifts. It was the 6th of January, then, that more than fifty children gathered together for the first time. It was interesting to note how different these little creatures were from those that usually attend preschools. They were timid and clumsy, and apparently stupid and irresponsible. They were unable to march in a row and the teacher had each one hold on to the smock of the one in front so that they walked in a kind of Indian file. They were in tears and seemed afraid of everything—of the beautiful ladies who were present, of the tree and the objects that hung from it. They would not accept the gifts or taste the sweets or answer when questioned. They were quite like a group of little savages. They certainly had not lived, like the little savage of Aveyron, in a woods with animals but in a forest belonging to a lost race beyond the pale of civil society. When the women saw this touching sight, many of them declared that only through a miracle could these children be educated, and they expressed the desire of seeing them after a year or two.

I was invited to speak, but since I was not able to enter into details about the structure and economics of the undertaking, I made a general reference to the work which I was starting and then read a part of the prophecy which is used in the Catholic Church for the solemnity of the feast of the Epiphany, the day chosen for the inauguration of the Children's House. The passage was taken from Isaiah 60:1-5:

Arise be enlightened, O Jerusalem: for thy light is come, and the glory of the Lord is risen upon thee.

For behold darkness shall cover the earth, and a mist the people: but the Lord shall arise upon thee, and his glory shall be seen upon thee.

And the Gentiles shall walk in thy light, and kings in the brightness of thy rising.

Lift up thy eyes round about, and see: all these are gathered together, they are come to thee: thy sons shall come from afar, and thy daughters shall rise up at thy side.

Then shalt thou see, and abound, and thy heart shall wonder and be enlarged, when the multitude of the sea shall be converted to thee, the strength of the Gentiles shall come to thee.

"Perhaps," I added as a kind of conclusion, "this Children's House can become a new Jerusalem which, if it is spread out among the abandoned people of the world, can bring a new light to education."

The daily papers criticized these words as being exaggerated.

This, then, was the meaning of the educational work that I carried on for two years in the Children's Houses. It represents the results of a series of experiments made by men in educating children according to new methods. It was not a mere application of techniques used by Seguin in infant schools, as anyone who consults his works can see. Still it is true that the foundations for the work of those two years could be traced back to the time of the French Revolution and the life-long labors of Seguin and Itard. As for myself, thirty years after the publication of Seguin's English work I took up his ideas and, if I may say it, his work with that same freshness and enthusiasm which he had inherited from his teacher, Itard, who had died in his devoted care. For ten years I experimented with the ideas and meditated upon the work of these remarkable men, whose heroic lives were passed in relative obscurity. My ten years of study can thus be added to the forty years of labor of Itard and Seguin. Fifty years of active preparation during a period of more than a century had, therefore, already transpired before this brief trial of only two years was attempted. I do not believe that I am wrong in saying that it represents the efforts of three physicians who, from Itard to myself, took the first steps on the way of psychiatry.

Description of the Conditions Surrounding the First Experiment: An Account of Its First Propagation

The environment in which the first Children's Houses had their origins must have been extremely favorable, since the surprising results obtained during those first years have never again been equaled.

This is one reason why it is worth analyzing the various elements that comprised this venture. In the first place, there must have been created among the people of the place and the families of the children a sense of peace and well-being, of cleanliness and intimacy that had hitherto been unknown. Moreover, the people themselves had undergone a kind of "moral selection." They were poor, honest, but without any particular profession. They lived from day to day on chance work, acting as porters, washer-women, or gathering violets and other flowers in the fields as they came to bloom. They lived surrounded by people who were coarse and immoral. And all of these unfortunates housed in the rebuilt apartments were without exception illiterate.

The children worked together in a kind of common paradise. Because of their parents' ignorance they received no education from their families. Neither were they influenced by the ordinary type of education that children receive in school. The mistress in the first Children's House was not a real teacher, but a woman with only a small amount of education who had worked as a domestic and had labored in the fields farmed by her family. She had no ideas about teaching, no principles of education. She was not responsible to anyone in authority, nor was she subject to the criticism of school inspectors.

During the day the children were abandoned by their fathers and mothers as they went out in search of work.

These circumstances, which might seem to preclude any favorable outcome for a school, proved to be a necessary condition. They created a neutral atmosphere as far as any educational influence was concerned.

The work of the school proceeded in a truly scientific fashion since it was not opposed by any obstacles. And this freedom from any hindrances contributed much to the happy outcome of the experiment. The Children's House was thus a kind of psychological laboratory, unharmed by any prejudices.

It was here that those surprising events took place which roused the curiosity and stirred up the admiration of the world such as "the unexpected manifestation of writing and of spontaneous reading," "spontaneous discipline," and "free social life."

It was precisely this group of raw and unkempt children that became a famous center of interest, drawing visitors from all parts of the world, and particularly from the United States, as if to an educational Mecca.

Because of this attraction, the quarter of San Lorenzo was visited by scientists, rulers, ministers of state, and members of the aristocracy, all of whom were eager to see close at hand these marvelous children. And from this center Children's Houses were later spread throughout the world.

After the establishment of the first Children's House on January 6th, others were opened a few months later on April 7th in apartments that had been reconditioned by the Association for Good Buildings. And on October 18, 1908, a Children's House was set up in the *Umanitaria* at Milan. This was the largest social institution in Italy, founded by Jewish socialists to assist the common people. It contained model homes for workmen, but it was also a center of propaganda.

An obscure and austere journalist was working there at the time, a fact that is perhaps worth recording since he later became notorious throughout the world. His name was Benito Mussolini.

The *Umanitaria* made a great contribution to our work by undertaking to build the same kind of scientific material that I had used in the first Children's House.

Later the Association for Good Buildings opened schools in apartments which it had in various sections of Rome, and it was at this time that people of the middle class obtained their wish of having a Children's House for their own sons and daughters. Later a Children's House was founded for the aristocracy by the English ambassador at Rome. It took in children from the highest social ranks.

After the disastrous earthquake which destroyed Messina in Sicily, some sixty children found in the ruins were brought together in a Children's House that was founded for them on the Via Giusti under the direction of the Franciscan Missionary Sisters of Mary. At the time these poor children were still in a state of shock from the terrible disaster which they had experienced. This house became famous for the transformation which it wrought on these children. It even became a source of inspiration for works such as the *Montessori Mother* by the American, Dorothy Canfield Fisher. Baron and Baroness Franchetti sponsored the first training program for teachers. Their original object was to prepare teachers for rural Italian schools, but teachers from nine different European countries registered for the first session. It naturally led to the opening of further Children's Houses in other regions. In 1913, on the very eve of the First World War there was organized under American initiative the first international course at Rome. This was attended by students from Europe, America, Africa, and India.

Such were the origins of the scientific education of children, and they gave great promise of having a profound influence on all education.

Children's Houses spread rapidly throughout the world despite prejudices against them and the difficulties created by the war. And today, during the Second World War, Children Houses are multiplying in India.

The history of the movement shows that the same kind of education, though with some adaptations, is applicable to all grades of society and to all nations of the world, and it may be used with children from happy homes as well as with those who have been terrified by an earthquake or some similar disaster. In our day the child has been revealed as a driving force that can bring new hope to people engulfed in darkness.

The Children's House has a twofold importance. It is socially important in that it is a "school within a house." It is educationally important, but its success here depends upon the application of the method which I learned through experience.

It deserves to be described for the contribution it can make to the progress of civilization.

Actually, it has solved many social and educational problems. Though it may once have seemed utopian, it has helped to transform the home. It touches directly the most important aspect of society, that is, man's own inner life.

3. The Teaching Methods Employed in Children's Houses

As soon as I realized that I had a school for small children at my disposal, I decided to make a scientific study of their education and strike out on a new path. Others had more or less confused child studies with education. They called the study of children "scientific education," even though the school itself remained unaffected by such studies. The new type of education, which I hoped to introduce, was, on the contrary, based on objective research which, it was hoped, would "transform the school" and act immediately upon the pupils, inspiring them with a new life.

As long as "science" limited itself to the attaining of further knowledge about children, without attempting to rescue them from the many evils which this same science had discovered in the schools and in the whole system of education, no real claim could be made for any such thing as a "scientific education." As long as those engaged in research limited themselves to posing "new problems," there was no reason to believe that a scientific education was in the process of evolving. A truly scientific education should give answers to problems and not merely point out the difficulties and dangers existing in the common schools, whether these were previously unknown or whether they were part and parcel of the whole system.

The discovery and demonstration of a hitherto unknown evil is the work of hygiene and educational experiments, but it is not a new system of teaching.

Child psychology could not of itself have discovered the natural characteristics and the consequent psychological laws that govern a child's development because of the abnormal conditions existing in the schools. These made the students adopt an attitude of weariness or of self-defense instead of enabling them to give expression to the creative energies that naturally belonged to them.

Even Wundt, the founder of psychological physiology, admitted that "the psychology of the child is unknown."

My intention was to keep in touch with the research of others, but to preserve my own independence. The only thing that I considered to be essential was Wundt's maxim that "all methods of experimental psychology can be reduced to one, namely, to carefully recorded observation."

When there is a question of dealing with children, however, another factor certainly enters in—a study of their growth. Here also I retained the same general rule but without subscribing to any specific claims about a child's activities according to his age.

Physical Growth

From the very beginning I took care to follow the growth of a child's body, studying and measuring it according to the principles of anthropology. But I simplified the measurements considerably and adopted an easier way to record the data. I also tried to arouse the children's interest in this procedure. Families periodically received the measurements of their children and at the same time the average normal measurements according to a child's age. The result of this was that parents could follow intelligently their children's physical development.

I had a machine constructed to take the measurements of the children. It had a metric scale ranging from fifty to one hundred and fifty centimeters. On the platform of this measuring device was placed a small movable stool thirty centimeters in height so that a child's measurements could be taken when seated. Today I advise that the machine be made with a double platform. On one side of it the height of a child can be measured when standing and on the other when seated. The scale for measuring the child when seated starts at the level of the stool. The horizontal rods that rest on a child's head run in grooves independently of each other. Two children can thus be measured at a time. A further advantage is that no time is lost in removing and putting back the stool or in calculating the differences on the metric scale.

With the help of this instrument I decided to take the

measurements of the children both standing and sitting every month. In order to take the most accurate measurements possible of a child's growth and to facilitate my research, I made it a rule that a child's height should be taken on the same date each month.

A child's weight should be taken every week on a pair of scales placed in the dressing room next to the bath. He is undressed and then weighed before his bath on the day of the week on which he was born. In this way the children's baths, about fifty in number, are distributed on the various days of the week. Five to seven children are bathed each day. Practically, a weekly bath presents a considerable number of difficulties, and it is often necessary to be somewhat theoretical about it. However, I planned the weekly bath as I have indicated with the intention also of regulating and guaranteeing it.

I believe that these are the only physical measurements which need to occupy the teacher and the only ones which are directly concerned with the school.

Other measurements should be taken by a pediatrician or at least by one who intends to specialize in this field, but in the meantime I took these measurements myself.

An examination made by a physician is necessarily complex, and to assist him in this work I have had printed forms for biographical information, an example of which is reproduced on page 44.

The form was simple, and I kept it so, because I want the physician and the teacher to be guided by the conditions of the environment in which they are making their observations. The data sought was carefully determined so that it would be respected and the research carried out in a proper fashion. I further advise the taking of the following measurements of each child once a year: the circumference and two diameters of his head, the circumference of his chest, his height, weight, and cephalic index, and other details that might be indicated by circumstances or advances made in anthropological studies. A physician should carry out these examinations within a week, or at least within a month, of the child's birthday, and if possible, on the day itself. By keeping to such a rule the physician also lightens his task. This permits a doctor to make his observations from time to time without being in the least overburdened with work. It is up to the teacher to keep the doctor posted on the children's birthdays.

The taking of physical measurements, when it is conducted in this way, also has an educational value. The children acquire orderly habits, and they become accustomed to observe themselves. (I can say parenthetically that little children take delight in being measured. As soon as a teacher looks at a child and says, "height," he will immediately kick off his shoes with a joyful laugh and run to the measure and take such a perfect position that the teacher has only to lower the horizontal bar and write down the reading.)

| | September | | | |
	1st week pounds	2nd week pounds	3rd week pounds	4th week pounds
Monday				
Tuesday				
Wednesday				
etc.				

(Each page of the register corresponds to one month.)

Name........................   Date of enrollment...............
Surname and name....................   Age.....................
Name of father......................   Age of mother.......................
Age of father........................
Profession.......................
Hereditary antecedents...............
Personal antecedents..................

In addition to the measurements which a doctor takes with his ordinary instruments such as callipers and tapes, he notes the pigmentation of a child's skin, his muscular tone, the condition of his lymph glands, his blood supply, and so forth. He also takes note of structural defects and occasional pathological conditions, such as rickets, infantile paralysis, eye defects, and so forth, and these have to be carefully described. Such an objective study will also enable a doctor to draw up questions to be submitted to a child's parents to complete the history of his case.

							Head			
Height Standing	Weight	Chest Measurement	Height Seated	Index of Height	Index of Weight	Circumference	Diameter Front to Back	Transverse Diameter	Cephalic Index

Physical constitution.......................

Muscle tone.......................

Skin coloring.......................

Color of Hair.......................

Notes

Moreover the physician makes the usual health calls, diagnosing cases of eczema, infections of the ear, conjunctivitis, feverish conditions, upset stomachs, and so forth. The ills are then treated in the infirmary connected with the house. This guarantees immediate attention to, and a constant watch for, sickness in the children. As a result of my work with the Children's Houses of the Association for Good Buildings I came to the conclusion that the usual case histories drawn up in the clinics are not suitable for a school. As a rule the family is perfectly normal. I therefore encouraged the teachers to obtain through talks with the children's mothers information of a social character, such as, the education of the parents, their habits, their earnings, expenses, and so forth, so that a family portrait might be drawn up after the manner of Le Play. But I believe that such a plan is only practical when the teacher lives near the families of her students.

At any rate, it would be very advantageous for the advice of the physician to be passed on to the children's mothers through their teachers, whether this be with respect to the health of a particular child or to children in general. Along with this advice, the teacher could also give her own suggestions on the education of individual children, but I cannot delay on this point which would take us into the hygienic and social aspects of the Children's Houses.

The Environment

There is only one basis for observation: the children must be free to express themselves and thus reveal those needs and attitudes which would otherwise remain hidden or repressed in an environment that did not permit them to act spontaneously. An observer obviously needs something to observe, and if he must be trained in order to be able to see and recognize objective truth, he must also have at his disposal children placed in such an environment that they can manifest their natural traits.

It was this part of the problem, which had not as yet been taken up by educators, that seemed to me to be most important and most pertinent to teaching since it has direct reference to a child's vital activities.

I therefore began by having school equipment made proportionate to the size of the children that satisfied the need they had of moving about intelligently.

The tables which I had made were of various shapes. They were strong but extremely light so that two four-year-olds could easily move them about. The chairs were light but attractive, some with seats of wood, others of straw. These were not miniature copies of adult chairs but were proportioned to a child's body. In addition to these I ordered little wooden armchairs with wide arms and others made of wicker. Small square tables for one child to sit at were also provided, and others of different sizes and shapes. These were covered with small tablecloths and decorated with vases containing flowers or plants. Part of the equipment consisted of a very low washstand that could be used by a child of three or four. The flat sides for holding soap, brushes, and towels were white and easily cleaned. The cupboards were low, light and very simple. Some were closed by a simple curtain, others had doors, each of which was locked with a different key. The safety lock was within reach of a child's hand so that he could open and shut it and place objects on their shelves. On the long narrow top of the cupboard was placed a bowl with live fish in it or other types of ornament. All around the walls, and low enough to be reached by little children, were arranged blackboards and small pictures representing pleasant family scenes or natural objects such as animals or flowers. Or there were historical or sacred pictures which could be changed from day to day.

A large colored picture of Raphael's Madonna of the Chair was then enthroned on a wall. We have chosen this painting as the symbol and emblem of the Children's Houses. As a matter of fact these houses represent not only an advance in society but also in humanity. They are closely connected with the elevation of motherhood, the advancement of women, and the protection of posterity. Raphael's idealized Madonna of the virgin mother with her adorable child is not only sweet and beautiful, but next to this perfect symbol of motherhood stands the figure of John the Baptist as a beautiful young child at the beginning of that rigorous life which was to prepare the way for Christ. It is the work of the greatest Italian artist, and if one day the Children's Houses become spread throughout the world, Raphael's picture will be there to speak eloquently of the country of their origin.

The children cannot understand the symbolic meaning of the Madonna of the Chair, but they see in it something greater than in the other pictures of mothers, fathers, grandparents, and infants, and they will enfold it in their hearts in simple piety. So much for the environment.

Practical Observations

We may begin with the first objection that rises up in the

minds of those who follow the old rigid systems: as they move about, the children will upset tables and chairs and thus create noise and confusion. But such an attitude is really the result of prejudice. People have also believed that they should wrap newly born children in swaddling bands and that children who are learning to toddle about should be shut up in walkers. We still believe that there should be heavy desks in school practically nailed to the floor. All of this is based on the conviction that children should grow up immobile and that education should depend upon a child retaining a special position.

The light and easily moved tables, chairs, and armchairs permit a child to choose the most convenient position. He can make himself comfortable rather than sit in his place, and this is at once an indication of his inner freedom and a further means of education. If a child's awkward movements make a chair fall over with a crash, he has an obvious proof of his own incapacity. A similar movement among desks would have passed unnoticed. A child thus has a means of correcting himself, and when he has done so he has proof positive of it: the chairs and tables remain silent and unmoved where they are. When this happens one can say that a child has learned how to move about. On the other hand, the exact opposite was attained under the old systems. The silence and immobility of the child himself was taken as a proof of discipline. But silence and immobility of this type actually keep a child from learning how to move about with ease and grace. The result is that when he finds himself in a place where there are no desks he starts knocking over light objects. But in our schools a child learns how to behave and how to move about with ease, and this will be useful for him outside the school as well. Even though he is still a child, he knows how to act freely and correctly.

The teacher in the Children's House in Milan had a long shelf built next to a window on which were set out the containers of metal inserts used in the first drawing lessons. (This material will be discussed later.) But the ledge, since it was too narrow, was awkward to use. When the children took pieces out of the containers they often sent one of them crashing to the floor, and this caused a great deal of noise as the metal pieces scattered about. The teacher decided to have the shelf altered, but the carpenter was slow in coming. In the meantime the children learned to lift the objects so carefully that the containers ceased to fall despite their precarious position.

The skill which the children had acquired in moving the objects counteracted the inadequacy of the place for keeping the equipment.

The simplicity or imperfection of external objects can therefore help in the development of a child's activity and dexterity.

All this is logical and simple, and now that it has been expounded and proved by experiments, it seems as obvious to all as the egg of Christopher Columbus.

Discipline and Liberty

Here is another easy objection raised by the followers of the common schools. How can one attain discipline in a class where the children are free to move about?

In our system we obviously have a different concept of discipline. The discipline that we are looking for is active. We do not believe that one is disciplined only when he is artificially made as silent as a mute and as motionless as a paralytic. Such a one is not disciplined but annihilated.

We claim that an individual is disciplined when he is the master of himself and when he can, as a consequence, control himself when he must follow a rule of life. Such a concept of active discipline is not easy to understand nor to attain. But it certainly embodies a lofty principle of education that is quite different from the absolute and undiscussed coercion that produces immobility.

A teacher must possess a special technique in order to be able to lead a child along this way of discipline, which he should follow all his life as he constantly perfects himself in it. Just as a child, when he learns how to move about instead of remaining fixed in one spot, is preparing himself not for school but for a well-ordered life, so he becomes accustomed to a discipline which is not limited to the school but which extends out into society.

A child's liberty should have as its limit the interests of the group to which he belongs. Its form should consist in what we call good breeding and behavior. We should therefore prevent a child from doing anything which may offend or hurt others, or which is impolite or unbecoming. But everything else, every act that can be useful in any way whatever, may be expressed. It should not only be permitted but it should also be observed by the teacher. This is essential. From his scientific training, a teacher should acquire not only an ability but also an interest in observing natural phenomena. In our system he should be much more passive than active, and his passivity should be compounded of an anxious scientific curiosity and a respect for the phenomena which he wishes to observe. It is imperative that a teacher understand and appreciate his position as an observer.

Such an attitude should certainly be found in a school for little children who are making the first revelations of their psychic lives. We cannot know the consequences of suppressing a child's spontaneity when he is just beginning to be active. We may even suffocate life itself. That humanity which is revealed in all its intellectual splendor during the sweet and tender age of childhood should be respected with a kind of religious veneration. It is like the sun which appears at dawn or a flower just beginning to bloom. Education cannot be effective unless it helps a child to open up himself to life.

In order to achieve this it is essential that a child's spontaneous movements should not be checked or that he be compelled to act according to the will of another. But he should not, of course, be allowed to indulge in useless or harmful activities. These must be checked and repressed.

The Difficulty of Discipline in Schools

In order to carry out my plans, I usually had to make use of teachers accustomed to the old methods of instruction in common schools. This convinced me of the radical difference between the new and the old systems. Even an intelligent teacher who has understood the principle finds it very difficult to put it into practice. She cannot understand her apparently passive role, which is like that of an astronomer who sits fixed at his telescope while the planets go spinning around. It is very difficult to assimilate and to put into practice the idea that life and all that is connected with it go on by themselves, and that it must be observed and understood without intervention if we wish to divine its secrets or direct its activities. The teacher has learned too well to be the only freely active person in the room. She has thought it her task to repress the activity of her pupils. When she fails to obtain silence and order in the classroom, she looks around in dismay as if she were asking the world to excuse her and calling on those present to testify to her innocence. In vain she is told that disorder at the beginning is unavoidable and then, when she is told to do nothing but watch, she asks herself if she should not send in her resignation since she is no longer a teacher.

Then when she begins to see that it is her duty to distinguish between acts which should be prevented and those which should be observed, she feels how empty she is and begins to ask herself if she is capable of performing such a task.

As a matter of fact, one who is unprepared for it will be helpless and bewildered for a long time. But, on the other hand, the more profound is her scientific knowledge and the wider her practical experience, the sooner will she come to appreciate the marvels of unfolding life and the more will her interest be aroused.

In his novel, *My Millionaire Uncle*, Notari has given a brilliant description of the old way of keeping discipline. The uncle in the story is obviously a very spoiled child, and after having caused enough mischief to upset a whole city, he is shut up, as a last desperate resort, in a school. Here Fufu, for that is the uncle's name, performs his first kind act and experiences his first emotion when, finding himself near the pretty little Fufetta, he notices that she is hungry and has nothing to eat:

He glanced around, looked at her, took his lunch basket and, without saying a word, placed it on her lap.

Then he withdrew a few steps from her and, without knowing why, hung his head and burst into tears.

My uncle could not himself understand the reason for this sudden outburst.

He had seen for the first time two gentle eyes filled with tears. His emotions had been suddenly stirred and, at the same time, he had felt ashamed to eat when there was one near him who was hungry.

Not knowing how to express his feelings, nor what to say

in excuse as he offered her his basket, he had been completely overcome by this first disturbance in his little soul.

Fufetta, all confused, at once ran up to him. With great gentleness, she drew aside the elbow with which he was hiding his face.

"Don't cry, Fufu," she said in a low and intriguing tone. Fufu was sad and ashamed, but she looked at him full of motherly concern, as if she were talking to one of her rag dolls.

Then she kissed him, and my uncle, yielding again to the impulse of his heart, threw his arms around her neck, pursed his lips, and without thinking or looking about, still silent and sobbing, kissed her on the cheek.

Then he drew a long sigh, passed his sleeve across his face to wipe his eyes and nose and recovered his serenity.

A harsh voice cried out from the far corner of the court, "Here, here, you two down there, hurry up! Inside, both of you!"

It was the guardian. She crushed that first gentle stirring in the soul of a rebel with the same kind of blind brutality she would have used if the two had been fighting. It was time to go back into the school, and everybody had to obey.

This incident illustrates the thoughtless manner in which my young teachers behaved at first. Almost unwillingly they reduced the children to a state of immobility without observing or distinguishing their movements. There was, for example, a little girl who gathered her companions in a group about her and then in the midst of them moved about speaking and waving her hands in grand fashion. Her teacher immediately ran over, stilled the waving arms, and urged her to be quiet. But as I was watching the child, I saw that she was pretending to be a teacher or mother to the other children and was teaching them their prayers with expansive gestures and invocations of the saints and the Sign of the Cross. She was already showing herself to be a leader. Another child, a small boy, constantly made awkward gestures, and was thought to be somewhat unstable and abnormal. One day with great attention he set about moving the little tables. At once they were on top of him and made him cease because he was making too much noise. But actually what he was doing was the first manifestation of coordinated movements for a definite goal. The child was revealing his inner desires, and consequently his actions should have been respected.

In fact, after this he began to be as quiet as the other children whenever he had a small object to move about on his table.

Sometimes it happened that when a teacher was replacing the objects that had been used in the boxes a child would draw near and take up the objects with the obvious intent of imitating her. The first impulse of the teacher was to send him back to his place with the usual admonition: "Leave it alone, go to your seat." Yet the child by his actions was really expressing a desire to be helpful. He would doubtlessly have carried out successfully some exercise requiring order and so forth. On another occasion the children were noisily gathered around a basin of water in the room in which some toys were floating. We had in the school a little fellow hardly two-and-a-half years old. He had been left behind alone and seemed obviously animated with intense curiosity. I observed him from a distance with great interest. He went up to the group, tried to push the children aside with his little hands, realized that he did not have the strength to make a way for himself, and then stopped and looked around. The thought reflected on his infant face was most interesting. If I had had a camera I would have captured that expression. His eyes spied a little chair and he evidently thought of carrying it up behind the group of children and mounting it. With a face lit up with hope he moved toward the chair, but at that moment the teacher brutally seized him (or perhaps gently, as she thought) in her arms, and, lifting him up over the heads of the other children, showed him the basin and said: "You poor little boy, take a look for yourself!" Certainly the child, while seeing the toys floating about, did not experience that joy which he would have felt at conquering the obstacle through his own efforts. The sight of those objects did him no good, whereas his own intelligent efforts would have developed his inner powers.

The teacher prevented the child from teaching himself without affording any compensation in return. He had been on the point of experiencing the thrill of victory, and he found himself borne aloft by two arms as if he were powerless. The expression of anxiety, hope, and joy which had interested me so much faded from his face, and was replaced by the stupid expression of a child who knows that others will act for him.

When the teachers became weary of my observations, they began to let the children do anything they pleased. I saw some of them with their feet on the desks and their fingers in their noses without the teachers correcting them in any way. I saw others pushing their companions about and drawing up their faces in expressions of violence without the teacher paying the slightest attention. Then I had to patiently intervene to make them see how absolutely necessary it is to check and little by little eradicate all those actions which the children should avoid so that they clearly discern between what is right and wrong.

This is the necessary starting point for discipline and the most trying time for the teacher. The first idea that a child must acquire in order to be actively disciplined is the difference between right and wrong; and it is the duty of the instructor to prevent the child's confusing immobility with good, and activity with evil, as happened with the old kind of discipline. It is our object to train the child for activity, for work, for doing good, and not for immobility or passivity.

It would seem to me that children are very well disciplined indeed when they can all move around in a room in a useful, intelligent, and free fashion without doing anything rude or unmannerly.

Arranging the children in lines, as is done in ordinary schools, and giving each one his own place, and expecting them all to remain still and keep an assigned order can come later as an exercise in collective education.

It also happens in ordnary life that people have to remain seated quietly together, when they are present, for example, at a concert or a lecture. And we know that this requires no small sacrifice on the part of us adults. Children may therefore be arranged in order in their proper places. The important thing is to get them to understand the idea in such a way that they learn and assimilate the principle of collective order.

If, after they have gained this concept, they get up, talk, change their positions, they do not do this as they did before without knowing what they were doing and without reflecting upon it, but they do it because they wish to rise, to speak, and so forth. In other words, they set out from that well-known state of repose and order to engage in some voluntary activity, and since they know that certain actions are forbidden, they are forced to remember the difference between right and wrong.

Starting from this state of order, the movements of the children daily become more perfect and coordinated. They learn to reflect upon their own actions. The book for the teacher, the book which inspires her own actions, and the only one in which she can read and study if she is to become an expert, is the constant observance of the children as they pass from their first disordered movements to those that are spontaneously regulated. Acting thus, a child in a way selects his own tendencies which were at first confused and disordered in his unreflected acts.

Every child reveals himself, and it is remarkable how clearly individual differences stand out if we follow this procedure.

There are those who remain fixed at their place, apathetic, and sleepy. There are others who stand up to shout, strike, and overturn various objects. And finally there are those who aim at completing some determined action, such as setting a chair on its side and attempting to sit on it, or moving a table, or looking at a picture. The children show that they are mentally slow or, perhaps, ill, or slow in developing their personalities or, finally, intelligent, amenable to their environment, able to express their tastes, their tendencies, their powers of concentration, and the limits of their endurance.

Independence

When we observe a child's freedom, we cannot do it in exactly the same way that we observe the growth of plants and insects. A child, because of his inherent weakness at birth and his status as a member of society, is surrounded by fetters which limit his activity.

A system of education that is based on liberty ought to aim at assisting a child in obtaining it, and it should have as its specific aim the freeing of the child from those ties which limit its spontaneous manifestations. Little by little, as a child proceeds along this way, he will freely manifest himself with greater clarity and truth and thus reveal his own proper nature.

This is why the first educational influence upon a child should have as its object the guidance of the child along the way of independence.

No one can be free if he is not independent, therefore, in order to attain this independence, the active manifestations of personal liberty must be guided from earliest infancy. From the time that they are weaned, children are making their way along the risky path of independence.

What does it mean to be weaned? The child becomes independent of his mother's breast. Leaving this source of nourishment, he will be able to choose a hundred different sources of food. This is the same as saying that his means of subsistence have been multiplied. He will be able to make a choice, where as at first he had to limit himself to one form of nourishment.

Nevertheless, he is still dependent since he cannot walk or wash and clothe himself, nor can he ask for what he wants in intelligible language. He is the slave of everybody. But by the time he is three years old, a child should have made himself to a great extent independent and free.

We have not yet really understood the lofty concept of independence since the social conditions in which we live are still servile. Where there are servants, social conditions cannot nourish the idea of independence, just as when slavery was prevalent, the idea of liberty was obscure.

Our servants do not depend upon us, rather we depend upon them. We cannot tolerate in society such a radical error without a general lowering of moral standards.

Very often we believe that we are independent because no one commands us and we command others. But a master who has need of a servant by this very fact indicates his own inferiority. A paralytic who cannot lift his shoes because of his infirmities, and a prince who cannot lift them because of social conventions, are practically in the same condition.

A race that accepts the idea of servitude and believes that it is an advantage for a man to be served in everything rather than to be helped by another regards servility as an instinct. In fact we readily rush to the service of others as if otherwise we were to fail completely in showing them perfect courtesy, kindness, and charity.

But actually, he who is served instead of being helped is in a certain sense deprived of his independence. Rather, his human dignity should make him say: "I do not wish to be served because I am not helpless, but we should assist one another since we are social beings." Such an attitude must become prevalent before men can feel themselves to be truly free.

If teaching is to be effective with young children, it must assist them to advance on the way to independence. It must initiate them into those kinds of activities which they can perform themselves and which keep them from being a burden to others because of their inabilities. We must help them to learn how to walk without assistance, to run, to go up and down stairs, to pick up fallen objects, to dress and undress, to wash themselves, to express their needs in a way that is clearly understood, and to attempt to satisfy their desires through their own efforts. All this is part of an education for independence.

We wait upon our children; and to serve them in this way is not less fatal than to do something that would tend to suffocate their own useful, spontaneous actions.

We believe that children are like puppets. We wash them and feed them as if they were dolls. We never stop to think that a child who does not act does not know how to act, but he should act, and nature has given him all the means for learning how to act. Our primary duty towards him is to assist him to perform useful acts. A mother who feeds her child without taking the least effort to teach him how to hold a spoon or to find his mouth, or who, when she is herself eating, does not at least invite him to watch how it is done, is not a good mother. She offends her son's human dignity by treating him as a puppet, whereas he is by nature a man that has been entrusted to her care. Everyone knows that it requires much more time and patience to teach a child how to eat, wash, and clothe himself than it does to feed, bathe, and clothe him by oneself.

The one who does the former is an educator, the latter performs the lower office of a servant.

But such service is dangerous as well as easy. It closes

outlets, places obstacles in the way of a life which is unfolding, and besides these immediate consequences it has others which are more serious for the future. One who has too many servants becomes increasingly dependent upon them and eventually their slave. His muscles become weak through inactivity and ultimately lose their natural capacity for work. Since such a one does not have to labor but simply to ask for what he needs, his mind becomes weak and atrophied. It is in this way that we infect children's souls with the vice of sloth.

If one day, through a flash of consciousness, one who has been constantly served would want to regain his own independence, he would perhaps find that he did not have the strength to do it. And this is something that wealthy parents should bear in mind.

The More Useless Help Is, the More It Is a Hindrance to the Development of Natural Powers

The danger of servitude does not lie simply in a useless waste of life which leads to a state of helplessness, but also in the development of reactions which are marked by weakness or perversion. They may be compared with the outbreaks of hysterical persons or to the compulsions of epileptics.

Their actions are unrestrained. This lack of self-control develops as a parallel to helplessness. Anger often accompanies sloth.

Let us imagine a skilled and prudent workman who is not only able to do his work perfectly but can also give advice in a shop because of the calmness with which he manages everything. He will often be a peacemaker and will smile when others are angry. However it would not surprise us in the least to discover that this same workman shouts at his wife if the soup is not good enough or is not ready on time. At home he is easily angered. There it is not he who is the skilled workman but his wife who waits upon him and pities him. Such a one shows us how a man may be calm where he has power and overbearing where he is served. If he learned how to make soup, he might perhaps become perfect. A man who acts by himself, who expends his strength on his own actions, conquers himself, increases his strength, and perfects himself. If men of the future are to be strong, they must be independent and free.

Rewards and Punishments for Our Children

We have only to apply these principles to see a calm come upon a child which characterizes and, as it were, illuminates all his actions. There is thus truly born a new child, a child that is morally superior to one who is treated as a helpless and incompetent being. This inner liberation is accompanied by a new sense of dignity. From now on a child becomes interested in his own conquests and remains indifferent to the many small external temptations which would formerly have been so irresistible to his lower feelings.

I must confess that this experience filled me with wonder. I had been subject to the delusion of one of the most absurd procedures of ordinary education. Like others I had believed that it was necessary to encourage a child by means of some exterior reward that would flatter his baser sentiments such as gluttony, vanity, or self-love, in order to foster in him a spirit of work and of peace. And I was astonished when I learned that a child who is permitted to educate himself really gives up these lower instincts. I then urged the teachers to cease handing out the ordinary prizes and punishments, which were no longer suited to our children, and to confine themselves to directing them gently in their work.

But nothing is more difficult for a teacher than to give up her old habits and prejudices.

There was one especially who was interested in improving upon my ideas when I was absent by introducing a little from the methods to which she had been accustomed. One day when I made an unexpected visit to her room I saw a child, one of the most intelligent, wearing a large silver Greek cross suspended from a beautiful white ribbon on his breast. Another child was seated in an armchair in the middle of the room.

The first had been rewarded, the second was being punished. The teacher, at least while I was present, did not interfere with the children, and things thus remained as I had found them. I kept quiet and set myself to watch. The child wearing the cross moved back and forth carrying objects from his little table to the table of the teacher. He was quite busy and intent on what he was doing. He passed many times in front of the boy in the armchair. His cross happened to fall to the floor, and the boy who was being punished picked it up, looked at it carefully on all sides, and then said to its owner: "Do you see what you dropped?" The child turned and looked at the object indifferently. His expression seemed to imply: "Don't interrupt me," and then he said, "What difference is it to me?" "It doesn't make any difference to you?" the culprit calmly asked. And then he added, "In that case, I'll put it on." The other answered, "Yes, yes, you put it on!" in a tone that seemed to say, "But don't bother me!" The boy in the armchair slowly put the cross upon his breast, looked carefully at it, then stretched out his arms and relaxed in his chair. This was the right ending for the little incident. The pendant could satisfy the one who was being punished but not the active child content with his work.

One day I brought a woman to visit another Children's House. She praised the children highly and, finally, in my presence opened up a box from which she took out many little bronze medals. They were all brightly shining and attached to red ribbons. "The teacher," she said, "will attach these to the breasts of the best and cleverest children." Since I was not obliged to instruct this woman on my methods I kept silent. The teacher took the box. Then a very intelligent boy of four years, who was sitting quietly at the first desk wrinkled his brow in protest and cried out several times: "But not to the boys! But not to the boys!"

What a revelation! The little fellow already knew that he was one of the cleverest in the room even though no one had told him as much, and he did not want to be offended by this reward. Not knowing how to defend himself, he appealed to the fact that he was a boy!

As far as punishments are concerned, we frequently found ourselves confronted with children who disturbed others, but who would not listen to our entreaties. We immediately had them examined by a physician, but very often they turned out to be normal. We then placed a little table in a corner of the room and there, isolating the child, we made him sit in an armchair where he could be seen by his companions and gave him all the objects he desires. This isolation always succeeded in calming the child. From his position he could see all of his companions, and their way of acting was an object lesson in behavior more effective than words of his teacher could have been. Little by little he came to realize the advantages of being with the others and to desire to act as they did. In this way we imparted discipline to all the children who at first had seemed to us to be rebels. For the most part an isolated child was an object of special care, as if he were sick or helpless. I myself whenever I came into the room would go first of all straight to him and address him as if he were an infant. Then I would turn to the others and interest myself in their work as if they were men. I do not know what happened within the souls of the isolated children, but certainly their conversions were always true and lasting. They became proud of their work and behavior, and they generally retained a tender affection for their teacher and for me.

Freedom to Develop

From a biological point of view, the concept of liberty in the education of very young children should be understood as a condition most favorable to their physiological and psychological development. A teacher who is urged on by a profound reverence for life, while she is making her interesting observations, should respect the gradual unfolding of a child's life. The life of a child is not an abstraction; it is something that is lived by each one in particular. There is only one real biological manifestation, that of the living individual; and education, that is, the active assistance required for the normal expansion of life, should be directed towards these individuals as they are observed one by one. A child has a body which grows and a mind which develops. Both his physiological and psychic development have a single source, life. We should not corrupt or suffocate his mysterious potentialities but wait for their successive manifestations.

The environment is certainly secondary in the phenomena of life. It can modify, as it can assist or destroy, but it can never create. The source of growth lies within. A child does not grow because he is fed, because he breathes, because he lives in suitable climatic conditions. He grows because his potentialities for life are actualized, because the fertile seed from which life comes is developing according to its natural destiny. An adult eats, breathes, experiences heat and cold, but he does not grow. Puberty does not come because a child laughs or dances, or engages in gymnastic exercises, or eats better than usual, but because of a physiological phenomenon. Life increases, becomes manifest, and perfects the individual, but it is confined within limits and is governed by insuperable laws.

Therefore, when we speak of the freedom of a small child, we do not mean to countenance the external disorderly actions which children left to themselves engage in as a relief from their aimless activity, but we understand by this the freeing of his life from the obstacles which can impede his normal development.

A child is constantly being pushed on by his great mission, that of growing up and becoming a man. Because a child is himself unaware of his mission and of his internal needs, and adults are far from being able to interpret them, many conditions prevail both at home and in school that impede the expansion of his infant life. The freeing of a child consists in removing as far as possible these obstacles through a close and thorough study of the secret needs of early childhood in order to assist it.

Such an objective demands on the part of an adult greater care for, and closer attention to, the true needs of a child; and, practically, it leads to the creation of a suitable environment where a child can pursue a series of interesting objectives and thus channel his random energies into orderly and well-executed actions.

In the gay environment described above, furnished according to the proportions of a child, there are objects which permit the child who uses them to attain a determined goal. There are, for example, simple frames which enable a child to learn how to button, lace, hook, or tie things together. There are also washbasins where a child can wash his hands, brooms with which he can sweep the floor, dusters so that he can clean the furniture, brushes for shining his shoes or cleaning his clothes. All these objects invite a child to do something, to carry out a real task with a practical goal to be obtained. To spread out carpets and roll them up after they have been used, to spread a tablecloth for dinner and to fold it up and replace it carefully after the meal is finished, to set the table completely, to eat correctly and afterwards to remove the dishes and wash them, placing each object in its proper place in the cupboard, are tasks which not only require increasing skills but also a gradual development of character because of the patience necessary for their execution and the sense of responsibility for their successful accomplishment.

In the Children's Houses these activities which I have just described are called "exercises in practical life" because the children lead a practical life and do ordinary housework with a devotion and accuracy that becomes remarkably calm and dignified.

Besides the various objects which the children are taught to use for their "practical life," there are many others which lend themselves to the gradual development and refinement of a child's intellect. These are, for example, various materials for the education of the senses, for learning the alphabet, numbers, and reading, writing, and arithmetic. These objects are called "materials for development" to distinguish them from those used in practical life.

When we speak of "environment" we include the sum total of objects which a child can freely choose and use as he pleases, that is to say, according to his needs and tendencies. A teacher simply assists him at the beginning to get his bearings among so many different things and teaches him the precise use of each of them, that is to say, she introduces him to the ordered and active life of the environment. But then she leaves him free in the choice and execution of his work. Children as a rule have different desires at any particular moment, and one keeps busy at one thing and another at another without quarreling. In this way they are engaged in an admirable social life full of activity. In peaceful delight the children solve by themselves the various social problems which their free and many-sided activities create from time to time. An educational influence is diffused throughout the whole environment, and both children and teacher have their roles to play in it.

4. Nature in Education

Itard, in his classic work, *Des premiers développements du jeune sauvage d l'Aveyron (The First Developments of the Young Savage, of Aveyron)*, describes in detail the extraordinary drama of an education aimed at dispelling the mental darkness of an idiot and rescuing a child from a state of savagery.

The Savage of Aveyron was an abandoned child that had grown up in purely natural surroundings. The child had been wounded in a woods by assassins, who believed that they had killed him. After he had been cured by natural means, he lived for many years naked and free in the forest. He was finally found by hunters and introduced to civilized life at Paris. Scars on his small body gave evidence of his encounters with wild beasts and of his falls from heights.

The child was found mute and remained so. Pinel diagnosed his mentality as that of an idiot, and he proved to be incapable of assimilating an intellectual training.

And yet scientific education owes its first advances to this boy. Itard, who was interested in philosophy and, as a physician, had specialized in the defects of deaf mutes, undertook the boy's education, using means that had already proved to be partially successful in restoring hearing to people who were almost deaf. He was of the opinion that the defects of the little savage were more the result of his lack of education than of functional disorders. He subscribed to the principle of Helvetius that "a man is nothing without the work of men," and he believed that education could do everything. He was opposed to the principle proclaimed by Rousseau before the French Revolution: *"Tout est bien sortant des mains de l'Auteur des choses, tout dégénère dans les mains de l'homme,"* in other words, education is harmful and injurious to man.

64

Itard's first conclusion was that the little savage proved experimentally through his actions the truth of Helvetius' statement. However, when, with the assistance of Pinel, Itard became convinced that he was dealing with an idiot, his philosophical theories gave way to admirable attempts at education through practical experimentation.

Itard divided the education of this boy into two phases. In the first he sought to bring him within the bounds of ordinary social life. In the second he attempted to educate the mind of the idiot. The boy, who had lived in terrible abandonment, had found his happiness in it. He had become almost a part of the nature which had absorbed him. He took his delight in rain, snow, storms, and boundless vistas, for these had been the object of his vision, his companions, and his love. Civil life means a renunciation of all this, but it brings with it a conquest that facilitates human progress. In the pages of his book Itard has described in vivid terms the efforts he made to bring the little savage to a civilized state. This means that the needs of the child, who was now surrounded with loving care, were multiplied. Itard was a patient worker and keen observer of his pupil's spontaneous acts. His patient work and abnegation, which may be seen in the following description, can be an inspiration to teachers who are preparing themselves to make use of experimental methods in their own teaching:

When for example he was observed in his room, he could be seen weaving back and forth in endless monotony with his eyes always turned towards the window staring out into empty space. If a gust of wind suddenly rose up, or if the sun broke through the clouds and filled the heavens with its light, the boy broke out in laughter as if he were convulsed with joy. At times these periods of joy gave way to a kind of frenzied rage. He twisted his arms, rubbed his eyes with his closed fist, ground his teeth, and threatened anyone who was near him.

One morning the snow was falling heavily. He was still in bed, but waking up he gave a cry of joy, leapt from his bed, ran to the window, and then to the door. Impatiently he went from one to the other, and finally dashed naked out into the garden. There, giving free rein to his joy in sharp cries, he rushed about, rolled in the snow, gathered up large handfuls of it, and ate it with incredible eagerness.

But he did not always show such a lively and boisterous attitude when he was stirred by the great spectacles of nature. At certain times he seemed to experience a kind of calm regret and melancholy. Thus, for example, when the weather was bad and everybody left the garden the little Savage of Aveyron would choose that time to go out. He would go around the garden several times and then sit down on the edge of the fountain.

I have spent whole hours of intense pleasure watching him in that position, noting how his face, which was without expression and twisted into grimaces, would gradually assume an expression of sadness and melancholy, and how his eyes would gaze fixedly at the surface of the water, upon which he would toss from time to time a few dead leaves.

When on a beautiful evening there was a full moon and a silver ray penetrated into his room, he would almost always wake up and go to the window. During a great part of the night he would remain there, motionless, with his head stretched forward, his eyes fixed on the moonlit landscape, immersed in a kind of esthetic contemplation, the silence and stillness of which was only broken at long intervals by a long breath that died away like a sigh of distress.

In other passages of his book, Itard relates how the boy could not walk in a normal fashion, but would only run; and he tells us how he himself used to run after him at first when he was taking him for a walk through the streets of Paris rather than put a violent check on him.

Itard's treatment of the little savage furnishes us with a combination of valuable educational principles that can be generalized and applied to the whole of child education. We may note in particular the gradual and gentle way in which he introduced the boy to the ways of social life, the manner in which he first adapted himself to his pupil rather than wait for the pupil to adapt himself to him, and how he made the new life attractive so that it won the boy with its charm rather than impose it harshly on the child in a way that would have caused him pain and oppression.

I do not believe that there is any writing that offers us so eloquent a contrast between the natural and the social life, and which shows so clearly how the latter is made up of renunciations and restrictions. It is enough to think of how running is reduced to a rhythmical walk, and how a shrill cry is brought down to the modulations of ordinary speech.

At the present time, however, and in the circumstances of modern society, children live very far from nature and have few opportunities of coming into intimate contact with, or having any direct experience of, it.

For a long time it was thought that nature had only a moral influence on the education of a child. Efforts were made to develop a sensible response to the marvels of nature, to flowers, plants, animals, landscapes, winds, and light.

Later an attempt was made to interest a child in nature by giving him little plots of land to till. But the concept of living in nature is still more recent in a child's education. As a matter of fact, a child needs to live naturally and not simply have a knowledge of nature. The most important thing to do is to free the child, if possible, from the ties which keep him isolated in the artificial life of a city. Today child hygiene contributes to the physical education of children by introducing them to the open air in public parks and by leaving them exposed to the sun and water of a beach. Some timid attempts at freeing children from the excessive burdens of city life may be found in the permission given to children to wear simpler and lighter clothes, to go about in sandals or barefooted. Experience has shown that the only means of curing children from tuberculosis and rickets in modern sanitaria is to expose them to nature and to make them sleep in the open air and to live in the sun. When we reflect on this, it should be clear that normal and strong children should not only be able to resist an exposure to nature, but that they would be greatly benefited by it. But there are still too many prejudices in the way. We have readily given up our own freedom and have ended up loving our prison and passing it on to our children. Little by little we have come to look upon nature as being restricted to the growing of flowers or to the care of domestic animals which provide us with food, assist us in our labors, or help in our defense. This has caused our souls to shrink and has filled them with contradictions. We can even confuse the pleasure that we have in seeing animals with that of being near a poor animal destined to die so that it may feed us, or we admire the beauty or the songs of birds imprisoned in little cages with a kind of hazy love of nature. We even think that a tray full of sand from the sea should be a great help to a child. The seashore is often thought to be educational because it has sand like that in a child's box. Imprisoned as we are in such a confused world, it is no wonder that we come to some absurd conclusions.

Actually, nature frightens most people. They fear the air and the sun as if they were mortal enemies. They fear the frost at night as if it were a snake hidden in the grass. They fear the rain as if it were a fire. Civilized man is a kind of contented prisoner, and if now he is warned that he should enjoy nature for his own health, he does so timidly and with his eyes on the alert for any danger. To sleep in the open, to expose oneself to the winds and to the rains, to defy the sun, and to take a dip in the water are all things about which one can talk but which one does not always put into practice.

Who does not run to close a door for fear of a draft? And who does not shut the windows before going to sleep, especially if it is winter or it is raining? Almost everyone believes that it is dangerous and requires a heroic effort to take very long walks in the open country in rain or shine and rely simply on the shelter which nature affords. It is said that one must become accustomed to such efforts, and so no one moves. But how is one to become accustomed to such activities? Perhaps little children should be so conditioned. No. They are the most protected. Even the English, with their enthusiasm for sports, do not want their children to be tried by nature and fatigue. Even when they are quite large, a nurse pushes them in carriages to some shady spot when the weather is good, and she will not let them walk far or act as they please. Where people engage in sports, these become veritable battles among the strongest and most courageous youths, the very ones who are called to arms to fight the enemy.

It would be too soon for us to say: Let the children be free; encourage them; let them run outside when it is raining; let them remove their shoes when they find a puddle of water; and, when the grass of the meadows is damp with dew, let them run on it and trample it with their bare feet; let them rest peacefully when a tree invites them to sleep beneath its shade; let them shout and laugh when the sun wakes them in the morning as it wakes every living creature that divides its day between waking and sleeping. But, instead of this, we anxiously ask ourselves how we can make a child sleep after the sun has risen, and how we can teach him not to take off his shoes or wander over the meadows. Where, as the result of such restraints, a child degenerates, and, becoming irked with his prison, kills insects or small harmless animals, we look on this as something natural and do not notice that his soul has already become estranged from nature. We simply ask our children to adapt themselves to their prison without causing us any trouble.

The strength of even the smallest children is more than we imagine, but it must have a free play in order to reveal itself.

In a city a child will say that he is tired after a brief walk, and this leads us to believe that he lacks strength. But his sluggishness comes from the artificiality of his environment, from ennui, from his awkward clothing, from the pain which his small feet suffer from their leather shoes as they strike the bare pavement of the city streets, and from the enervating example of those who walk about him silent, indifferent, and without a smile. A club which he might join, or attractive clothes which might bring him admiration, are nothing to him. He is on a leash. He is ensnared by laziness and would like to be dragged along.

But when children come into contact with nature, they reveal their strength. Normal children, if they have a strong constitution and are well nourished, can walk for miles even when they are less than two years old. Their tireless little legs will climb long steep slopes in the sunshine. I remember how a child of about six once disappeared for several hours. He had set out to climb a hill, thinking that if he arrived at its summit he would be able to see what lay on the other side. He was not tired, but disillusioned in not having found what he sought. I once knew a couple who had a child barely two years old. Wishing to go to a distant beach they tried to take turns carrying him in their arms, but the attempt was too tiring. The child, however, then enthusiastically made the trip by himself and repeated the excursion every day. Instead of carrying him in their arms, his parents made the sacrifice of walking more slowly and of halting whenever the child stopped to gather a small flower or saw a patient little donkey grazing in a meadow and sat down, thoughtful and serious, to pass a moment with this humble and privileged creature. Instead of carrying their child, these parents solved their problem by following him. Only poets and little children can feel the fascination of a tiny rivulet of water flowing over pebbles. A child at such a sight will laugh with joy and want to stop to touch it with his hands as if to caress it.

I would suggest that you take up in your arms a child that has not yet begun to walk. On a country road from which may be seen a great and beautiful expanse, hold him in such a way that his back is to the view. Stop there with him! He will turn around and enjoy the beauty of the scene even though he cannot yet stand upright on his own feet and his tongue cannot as yet ask you to pause.

Have you ever seen children standing seriously and sad about the body of a little bird that has fallen from its nest, or watched them run back and forth asking and reporting what has happened with deep concern? Well, these are the children who can soon degenerate to the point where they steal eggs from birds' nests.

Like everything else, a feeling for nature grows with exercise. We certainly do not communicate it by a pedantic description or exhortation made to a listless and bored child shut up within the walls of a room and who has become accustomed to see or hear that cruelty toward animals is just a part of life. But experience strikes home. The death of the first dove killed intentionally by a member of his family is a dark spot in the heart of almost every child. We must cure the unsuspected wounds, the spiritual ills that already afflict these charming children who are the victims of the artificial environment in which they live.

The Place of Nature in Education

Education in school can fix the attention of a child on special objects which will show exactly how far he has been able to stir up within himself a feeling for nature or will arouse within him latent or lost sentiments. Here, as in every other kind of activity, the function of the school is to supply him with interesting information and motives for action.

A child, who more than anyone else is a spontaneous

observer of nature, certainly needs to have at his disposal material upon which he can work.

Care for Others

Children have an anxious concern for living beings, and the satisfaction of this instinct fills them with delight. It is therefore easy to interest them in taking care of plants and especially of animals. Nothing awakens foresight in a small child, who lives as a rule for the passing moment and without care for the morrow, so much as this. When he knows that animals have need of him, that little plants will dry up if he does not water them, he binds together with a new thread of love today's passing moments with those of the morrow.

One should watch little children when, one morning, after they have for many days placed food and water with loving care near brooding doves, they see the results of their labors. On another day they see a number of dainty chicks that have come from the eggs which a hen has covered with her wings for so long. The children are filled with feelings of tenderness and enthusiasm, and there is born in them a desire to give further help. They collect little bits of straw, threads of old cotton cloth, or wisps of wadding for the birds nesting under the roof or in the trees in the garden. And the chirping that goes on about them tells them thanks.

The metamorphoses of insects and the care which mothers bestow upon their offspring are objects of patient observation on the part of children, and they often give rise to an interest that surprises us. Once a small child was so struck by the changes undergone by tadpoles that he could describe their development, reporting the various phases in the life of a frog like a miniature scientist.

Children are also attracted by plants. One Children's House did not have any land that could be tilled, so flower pots were set out all around a large terrace. The children never forgot to water the plants with a little watering can. One morning I found them all seated in a circle on the floor around a magnificent red rose that had opened up during the night. They were silent and peaceful, completely absorbed in contemplation.

Another time a little girl kept looking down from a terrace in obvious excitement. Her mother and her teachers had seen to it that she had grown up with a love for flowers and gardens, but now she was attracted by something more. "Down there," she told her mother, "there is a garden of things to eat."

It was an orchard, which did not strike the child's mother as being at all remarkable, but which had nevertheless filled her tiny daughter with enthusiasm.

Prejudices About the Gardens

Our minds are prejudiced even with respect to nature, and we find it very difficult to understand. Our ideas about flowers are too symbolic, and we try to mold a child's reactions to our own instead of following his lead in order to interpret his own real tastes and needs. This is why even in gardens children have been forced to imitate the artificial activities of adults. They find that it takes too long to place a seed in the earth and wait for a little plant to appear; and further the task itself is too small for them. They want to do something big and to bring their activities into immediate contact with the products of nature.

Children indeed love flowers, but they need to do something more than remain among them and contemplate their colored blossoms. They find their greatest pleasure in acting, in knowing, in exploring, even apart from the attraction of external beauty.

Their Favorite Work

Our experiences have led us to a number of conclusions different from those which I myself once had, and we have been led to these by children who have been left free to make their own choices.

1) The most pleasant work for children is not sowing but reaping, a work, we all know, that is no less exacting than the former. It may even be said that it is the harvest which intensifies an interest in sowing. The more one has reaped, the more he experiences the secret fascination of sowing.

One of the brightest experiences is that of harvesting grain or grapes. The reaping of a field of wheat, the gathering of the grain into sheaves to be bound with bright-colored ribbons, has been most successful and can become the occasion for beautiful farm festivals. The care of the vines, the cleansing of the grapes, and the gathering of the fruit into beautiful baskets can also give rise to various feasts.

Fruit trees provide similar types of work. Even the smallest children like to gather the olives, and they perform a truly useful work in the dilligent search they make for fallen fruit which they put in their baskets. A hunt for strawberries hidden under the leaves of the vines is no less pleasing than looking for fragrant violets.

From these experiments the children derive an interest in the sowing of seeds on a larger scale, as for example, the sowing of a field of wheat with all its various operations. Only an adult can lay out the furrows, but the children can pile up the little heaps of grain to be sown. They can then divide this into little baskets and scatter it along the rows. The growth of so many frail and tender plants gives great pleasure to the eye and to the mind. The uniform quality and the patterns made by the long parallel lines seem to emphasize their growth. Grandeur seems to come from the massing together of single items which are of themselves of little interest. The yellow stalks that toss about in the wind and grow until they are at the height of a child's shoulder entrance the little group waiting for the harvest. Although our small fields were sown for the making of altar breads, we were nevertheless able to conclude that a country life is more suitable for a child than philosophy and the symbolism of flowers.

Little plots of fragrant plants can also have a practical interest. A child's activity then consists in searching for, distinguishing, and gathering the plants with different scents. An exercise in distinguishing things that look alike and in seeking out a scent rather than a flower is exacting and affords the satisfaction of discovery.

Flowers are, of course, also interesting, but gathering them is more unnatural than gathering the fruits of the earth that grow from them. Flowers seem to call insects to themselves rather than men to assist them in carrying out their eternal mission. Actually, children who have been taught how to satisfy their spiritual needs often will sit down near flowers to admire them, but they will soon get up and go in search of something to do since it is their own activity that causes the buds of their charming little personalities to unfold.

Simplicity

Work for a child must possess some variety within itself. A child does not have to know the reasons for sowing or reaping to have his interest aroused. He will readily undertake very simple actions which have an immediate end or which permit him to use some special effort. He will, for example, gladly pluck weeds from paths or furrows, sweep up dried leaves, or carry away an old branch. In a word, to have a field of activity and occasions for new experiences and difficult enterprises bring satisfaction to the animating spirit which prompts a child to make its way in the world.

We have pictures showing small children walking without fear among cows and in the midst of a flock of sheep, and others showing them sifting earth and carrying it away in wheelbarrows or heaping up big piles of branches from a tree.

Because of the lack of a suitable environment, such works as the care of greenhouses, the preparation of water for aquatic plants, the spreading of nets to protect a pool from insects, and the like, are seldom practicable, but they would not be beyond the strength or will of a child.

Our Garden

A further conclusion which we reached from observing children in conditions where they could freely manifest their needs was that of limiting the field or garden to their spiritual needs. The opposite conviction, however, is common, namely, that it is good to give children a limitless space. Such an attitude is due to an almost exclusive regard for a child's physical life. The limits seem to be indicated by the swiftness of his feet. Nevertheless, even if, to be specific, we were to take a racetrack as a spatial limit, we would find it to be considerably more restricted than we had thought. Even in a large field, children always run and play in one spot, in a corner or some narrow space. All living beings tend to find a place for themselves and to keep within its boundaries.

This same criterion is also applicable to the psychic life. Its limits must be found in a mean which lies between an excess and an insufficiency of space or anything else. A child does not like one of the so-called "educational playgrounds" since it is too small for him. It is a wretched piece of property not even big enough for himself. A child whose needs are satisfied does not care whether something belongs to him or not. What he wants is precisely a sense of satisfaction. He should be able to watch over as many plants as he can come to know, as many as he can remember, so that he really knows them.

Even for us a garden that has too many plants and too many flowers is a place full of unknowns that are foreign to our consciousness. Our lungs will breathe well there, but the soul is not affected. But neither can a tiny flower bed satisfy us. Its contents are trivial and not sufficient for our needs. They do not satisfy the hunger of the spirit which longs to come into contact with nature. The limits, then, are those which make it our garden, where every plant is dear to us and sensibly helps us to support our inner selves.

The criterion for judging the limits of a child's activities has created a great deal of interest. In many countries attempts have been made to interpret it practically as a garden which corresponds to a child's inner needs. Today, plans for a garden run parallel with those for the building of a Children's House.[1]

---

[1] As the result of further experiments by Dr. Mario Montessori the scientific education of children in nature studies has been further elaborated. It is impossible here to take into account the mass of work and the surprising amount of material that has been suggested solely by the interests and activities of the children themselves. It is enough to note that this includes much with respect to the shape and classification of animals and plants, and this prepares them for further study in physiology. Careful attention has also been given to the preparation of aquaria and plots for the growing of vegetables, which should be present in every school. These means for study have led to a spontaneous and purposeful exploration of nature and to a number of discoveries made by the children themselves. They have satisfied the need which children have to exercise their senses and their powers of motion and have laid the foundations for further far-reaching developments in elementary schools. It provides an answer to the problem of satisfying the interests of older children without forcing them to reluctantly assimilate ideas and terms when their interest in these has already disappeared. A younger child readily and enthusiastically lays the foundations which the older child then uses to satisfy his own higher interests.

5. Education in Movement

The Red Man and the White Man

One point which I think it would be well to clarify for teachers is the distinction between the vegetative and the sensitive lives of the body. The former is connected with the circulation of the blood and the latter with the nervous system.

The nervous system can be divided into the sympathetic nervous system, which largely controls the organic functions of the body and is closely connected with the emotions, and the central nervous system with its countless ramifications which put the sense organs in contact with the external world and subject the voluntary muscles to the control of the will. The presence of both emotions and the will indicate that the sympathetic system is both subordinate to, and dependent upon, the central nervous system. And this must be carefully taken into account by anyone interested in education.

The matter of particular concern to us at present is to direct our attention for a moment to two different systems in a summary fashion. One of these is the circulatory system, with the heart at its center and spreading out to the surface of the body in a very minute system of capillary vessels. The other is that of the nervous system, which has the brain as its principle center sending out countless branches which finally reach microscopic proportions in the nerves on the body's periphery.

Capillary vessels and nerve endings, as we all know, are to be found everywhere in the body. They supply blood for nourishment and preserve the vital tone of all the tissues. To have a clear idea of the extent of the capillary and peripheral nervous systems, it is sufficient to recall that a pin prick on any part of the body whatever, whether external or internal, causes bleeding and pain. If by some means or other we could remove from a body a complete sanguinary and a complete nervous system, we would have the body itself reproduced in all its details, first as a "red" man and second as a "white" man. To the red man belongs the vegetative life. In him may be found linked together the various means that enable him to gather what he needs to survive from his environment, that is, food and oxygen, and also the organs for expelling wastes. On the other hand, the white man has relations with the sense organs, which receive impressions from the external environment, and with the muscular system which carries out his movements. Although the two "men" are quite distinct from each other and clearly divided in their functions (one assimilates material for the body, the other for the spirit), they are so closely interlocked, and so closely related to each other, that no part of the total organism can function without their mutual cooperation. The heart beats and circulates the blood because it is connected with the nervous system, and the nerves and nerve centers function because they are fed with blood.

Muscles make up the greater portion of a person's body. They are attached to the skeleton which acts as a support for them and as a protection for the centers of the nervous and circulatory systems. It is through his muscles that a man can act on the external world and give expression to his thoughts. The tiny sense organs might be compared with pores through which the soul takes in the images necessary for its psychic development, but the practical work of life depends upon the muscles. The will carries out its desires through these marvelous instruments of motion. The mind must have all these means of expression by means of which its concepts are changed into action and its feelings are carried out in works.

Though the muscles have such an important goal to accomplish, and must carry out very complicated operations to achieve it, they at the same time assist the circulation of the blood and are of greatest assistance to the heart. But all this happens as a corollary of their primary function of providing motion and thus coming into relationship with other beings.

It has happened, however, that men, and particularly children, have been compelled to lead an inactive life, to carry on mental work that has been artifically separated from the organs which ought to remain connected with it; and these include not only the brain but muscles and sense organs. This has resulted in a physical degeneration, since even a man's vegetative life is a part of his individual being. In the area of teaching, this has led to demands for an active life, that is, for an increase of physical activity, with the primary hope of reviving and intensifying the vegetative life which, when it is not properly functioning, is marked by a lack of energy and physical weakness, the lowering of the metabolism, and the consequent weakening of resistance to disease. The muscular system, therefore, which is intimately connected with the life of relationships has been degraded to the point where it simply assists the blood to flow more quickly in its difficult and complicated journey. The organs that have been given to us to express our minds have thus become simply a help to circulate the blood.

Such a reversal of functions obviously cannot bring a man back to a normal state of activity. This apathy has led to a functional error. One mistake has tried to remedy another. And this has led to a continued detriment of man's intellectual and moral life. Because of their emphasis on what is purely physical, games and athletics and similar activities dissipate man's higher energies.

When a joint is dislocated it causes pain, anguish, and physical deformities. But when a bone is set, the limb regains its normal functions, and all the painful side effects disappear. Teachers erred in letting the senses and muscles of their pupils remain unused and inert while their thoughts wandered about in idle fancies. And yet the muscles, nerves, and senses all constitute a whole. If the disorder is to be corrected, the organs connected with the psychic life must be activated. Mental work should be accompanied by an appreciation of what is true and beautiful which will animate it, and by movements which bring ideas into play and leave their traces on the external world, where men should help each other. The actions of the muscles should always be at the service of the mind and should not stoop to make themselves servants of what is known as the "vegetative" or "physical life" of man.

We can illustrate this by noting that work is a physical exercise in the service of the mind, and that, when a man works, his work indirectly assists in the circulation of the blood and respiration.

A problem of health is, therefore, also a problem of work.

Health and a normal life are as a rule obtained by eating properly and working in the open air in a way that will give free reign to the higher functions of the mind.

Discipline and Gymnastics

In the ordinary schools the term "gymnastics" is given to a kind of group activity which aims at disciplining the muscles of a whole class in unison. There is also a more formal type of gymnastics which tends toward acrobatics.

These different types of movement have been found useful to counterbalance the muscular inertia of pupils who have to lead a sedentary life and keep a regularly ordered position in class by remaining seated at their wooden desks. Gymnastics thus represents an enforced remedy against an imposed evil; and nothing is more characteristic or symbolic of the old regime than his action and reaction imposed by the teacher, who tyrannically increases evils and remedies for the passive, disciplined child.

There is a modern tendency to allow a greater variety in gymnastics. We have, for example, borrowed open air games from the English and have introduced rhythmical gymnastics that were started by Dalcroze. These are more humane. They give a child the opportunity to loosen up his muscles from the rigid position in which they have been kept and take his personality more into account. But all these methods are reactions to a life that has been wrongly understood and do not have any modifying influence on life itself. Like amusements, they lie outside the pale of ordinary existence.

One of the most important practical aspects of our method has been to make the training of the muscles enter into the very life of the children so that it is intimately connected with their daily activities. Education in movement is thus fully incorporated into the education of the child's personality.

Everybody admits that a child must be constantly on the move. This need for movement, which is irresistible in childhood, apparently diminishes with the development of inhibiting forces at the time when these, by entering into a harmony with the motor impulses, create the means for subjecting them to the will. Thus the more developed a child is, the more obedient are his instruments of motion to his will; and if he experiences the pressure of an outside will he can resist it. But movement always remains as the basis for a life of relationships, for it is precisely this capacity to move that distinguishes man and in fact the whole animal kingdom from the vegetable world. Movement is therefore an essential part of life, and education cannot be conceived as moderating or, what is worse, inhibiting it. Rather it should permit a child's energies to develop normally and assist him to exert them more profitably.

Nature is a guide that teaches children how to move about. This hardly needs to be demonstrated. An infant's movements are constant and uncoordinated like those of a puppet. A child of three is always on the move, he throws himself frequently to the ground, runs about, and touches everything. A child of nine walks and no longer feels the need of stretching himself out upon the ground or of grasping everything he meets. These changes in attitude come by themselves and are independent of any educational influence. Connected with them is a change in the proportions of the body, between the length of the trunk and that of the lower limbs. The length of a newly born child from the top of its head to its groin is equal to 68% of the whole length of its body. This means that its legs are 32% of its total height, whereas in an adult the length of the trunk and of the limbs are about equal. This change in proportions is a part of the growth. When a child enters one of our schools at the age of three, his legs make up 38% of his height, and then they grow relatively to his trunk until they greatly excede the proportions of an adult. By the time a child is seven, his limbs make up 57% of his height. However after puberty, the trunk increases in size until it attains the usual adult proportions. Such an elementary factor with respect to growth should be enough to make us understand that children have a different need for moving, and that it is necessary to observe their spontaneous movements in order to help them to grow up to their full potential. Here it will be enough to note some fundamental facts. Standing on their short legs, children make great efforts to keep perfectly balanced, and they conceal the difficulty they have in walking by running. When they feel the need to rest, they stretch themselves out on the ground and lift up their legs. But where an infant takes an almost natural position on his back with his feet and hands meeting each other in the air, a child from three to five years of age rests with his stomach on the ground and the lower part of his limbs upturned, often raising his shoulders by resting on his elbows. He also finds a position in which to rest different from that of sitting on a chair. Children love to sit upon the ground resting their weight upon the whole length of their crossed legs or upon the length of one leg placed to the side. This gives them a wider base of support. Since children have a natural need for a period of rest that breaks their continual movements, we have equipped the Children's Houses with small rugs which are usually rolled up and kept in a part of the room destined for this purpose. Children who wish to work on the floor instead of seated at a little table must first get one of the little carpets, spread it out on the floor, and then work upon it. No adult dictates the change of positions, and the child thus peacefully follows the dictates of nature.

Work and Gymnastics

If we would but think of it, the carrying out of a practical life affords an abundance of exercise, and the gymnasium for perfecting one's actions is the very environment in which he lives. This is something different from that type of manual labor which produces something new. Instead, we are continually moving objects around at the bidding of our intellect which foresees the goal to be obtained. Rolling up a carpet, polishing a pair of shoes, washing a basin or the floor, setting the table, opening and shutting boxes, doors, and windows, arranging a room, putting chairs in order, drawing curtains, carrying furniture, and so forth, are all exercises that engage the whole body and exercise and perfect now one movement and now another. By a habit of work a child learns how to move his hands and arms and to strengthen his muscles more than he does through ordinary gymnastic exercises. Nevertheless the exercises of practical life cannot be regarded as a simple kind of gymnastics; they are "work." But the work is refreshing and not tiring because of the interest which one takes in all his movements. It is a natural exercise, since man ought to have some object in view when he moves. The muscles should always serve the intellect and thus preserve their functional unity with the human personality. If a man is an intelligent creature and muscularly active, then his rest lies in intelligent activity, just as the rest of every being lies in the normal exercise of its proper functions. We must therefore provide a child in his environment with means for exercising his activities. We must remember, however, that a Children's House is open to children of different ages from three to six years, who all live together as members of a family and who, therefore, have need of different occupations.

The objects that are used for practical life have no scientific purpose. They are the objects used where a child lives and which he sees employed in his own home, but they are especially made to a size that he can use. The number of these objects is not determined by our method, but depends upon the resources of a school, and especially upon the length of time that a child spends in the school each day. If the school has a garden attached to it, the care of the paths, the weeding of plants, or the gathering of ripe fruit, and so on, will make up a part of a child's practical occupations. If the daily schedule is very long, dinner will also form a part of them. Of all the exercises of practical life this is the most difficult, exacting, and interesting. It includes such things as setting the table with great care, serving the meals, eating properly, washing the cups and plates, and putting away pots and pans.

Work

When a child comes to school he takes off his own coat and hat. He has at his disposal little hooks fixed to the wall low enough for a child of three to reach them easily. The washbasins are so low that they would not even reach the knee of an adult, and they are equipped with little pieces of soap, small brushes for the nails, and little towels, all within the reach of a child. Or, if there is no regular washbowl, there will be at least a basin on a low table with a small pitcher and a receptacle for used water. Other practical objects are a box containing two brushes and a few bags attached to the wall containing clothesbrushes so small that they can be easily grasped by a tiny hand. Where it is possible, a small table should be set up with a mirror, but this should be so low that it will scarcely reflect more than the space between the feet and knees of an adult. A child can look at himself in the mirror while seated, and if his hair becomes disheveled from taking off his cap or because of the wind in the street, he can straighten it out. On the table there is a small hairbrush and comb. The child next puts on an apron and blouse for work and is then ready to make his entry.

If the classroom is not in order, there is work to do. Perhaps there are vases of somewhat faded flowers which it would be well to throw away. Or the water needs to be changed. There are variously colored dustcloths hanging from hooks and amidst them a brightly colored feather duster. The object most suited for the task is chosen and the work of cleaning is begun. One table has a spot on it! It must be washed with soap and water. Then if a little water has fallen on the floor it must be promptly wiped up, or if bread crumbs or dried leaves have fallen on the floor, a small white broom is at hand to sweep them up. Its pretty colors and the pictures which adorn its shining varnished handle invite the children to use it. What is more pleasing than a green dustpan covered with red spots, or what is so white as a washcloth? As often as the occasion arises, the children engage in similar occupations. There is no timetable for the morning or the afternoon. A child is constantly inspecting his surroundings, his "house"; and when a chair is out of place, making the room look disorderly, we can be certain that it will be the smallest children who notice it. Before a child reaches the age of three, the highest form of work and the most enobling that engages him is that of arranging furniture and putting things in order, and it is also the one that calls for the greatest activity.

Voices

It is true that the teacher supervises the children, but there are various things that "call" the children at different ages. Indeed, the brilliancy, the colors, and the beauty of gaily decorated objects are nothing more than "voices" which attract the attention of a child and encourage him to act. These objects possess an eloquence that no teacher could ever attain. "Take me," they say, "keep me unharmed, and put me back in my place," and a child's action carried out in response to this invitation gives him that lively satisfaction and that awakening of energy which predispose him for the more difficult task of developing his intellect. Very often, however, there is more than one voice that is calling him or there is a complicated order that is given. Some important works require the attention of an organized band of children rather than of one alone, and this requires a long training and preparation. Among such tasks are those of setting a table, serving dinner, and washing pots and pans.

Talents

It would be a mistake to attempt to estimate a child's capacity for work according to his age before testing him, or to exclude any from a task to be done on the grounds that they could not be of any assistance. A teacher should always open up the way, and should never discourage a child through lack of confidence in him. Even the littlest children are anxious to do something and are more anxious to exert themselves than those who are older. A good teacher will therefore look for some way in which even the tiniest child can be of help. A little fellow of two-and-a-half may perhaps be able to carry the bread, while a child of four-and-a-half can manage to carry the kettle of hot soup. The importance of the works does not bother children, they are satisfied when they have done as much as they can and see that they are not excluded from an opportunity to exert themselves in their surroundings. The most admired work is that which offers the greatest opportunities to each one. They have a kind of inner ambition which consists in bringing into full play the talents which God has given them, as in the gospel parable; and when they succeed in this, they arouse the admiration of many others. When the children are invited to dinner, they do not simply eat but are delighted by this fine opportunity to exercise their inner powers and higher aspirations (as in waiting for their companions or saying their prayers). They do not waste their time, and they know full well how to take advantage of their opportunities. You can see a tiny waiter wearing a white apron, standing in deep thought before the table on which he has just now carefully spread the tablecloth. He is reflecting on the number of guests and the best way of setting the places. You can also see a little girl with a smile slowly pouring water into the glasses, taking care that the bottle does not touch the edge of the glass or that any drops fall upon the tablecloth. And here is a little band of serving girls coming up quickly with stacks of plates which will be used for the different tables. The satisfaction which they find in their work has given them a grace and ease like that which comes from music.

Precision

Anyone who spends some time with these children notices that there is a special secret which enables the children to carry out their practical activities with success. It is the precision, the exactness with which the acts must be performed. They are much less interested in filling a glass with water than in pouring it out of the bottle without touching the edge of the glass and without spilling any of it upon the tablecloth. Washing one's hands becomes more attractive if one has to remember the exact place for the soap, and where the towel must be hung.

Of itself movement is something unrefined, but its value increases when one attempts to perfect it. Hands, for example, are then no longer washed simply to make them clean, but in order to be able to wash them perfectly. When hands are washed in this manner, they are not only clean but the child himself becomes more skilled, and acquires a certain refinement which sets him above a child with unwashed hands. When children experience pleasure not only from an activity leading towards a special goal but also in carrying it out exactly in all its details, they open up a whole new area of education for themselves. In other words, preference should be given to an education in movement: practical activities are simply an external incentive to the educational process, they provide a motive and urge the child on to organize his movements.

The Sensitive Age

Children are therefore at an age when they are greatly interested in movements and seem to be anxious to learn how they should move about. They are passing through that epoch of their lives when they must become masters of their own actions. Physiologically we may say that their muscles and nerves are passing through a period when they are learning how to work harmoniously together. Successful passage through this period is of utmost importance for an individual's ultimate perfection. A good beginning here is most important for a child's future. After employing a minimum of effort in sowing the seed, a teacher sees an immense harvest. She is teaching those who are very eager to acquire definite knowledge.

When a teacher acts in this way she gets the impression that she is not so much teaching as giving, as performing an act of charity. When she sows the seed necessary for their particular age among a crowd of little children, she feels that she is doing one of the most valuable works of mercy, one that is much like feeding the hungry. Later on the children themselves will tend to become careless in the exact performance of their movements. Their interest in developing the coordination of the muscles will begin to decline. The mind of the child will press on, he will no longer have the same love that he had before. His mind must move along a determined path which is independent both of his own will and that of his teacher. Later on a sense of duty will make him persevere in doing through voluntary effort that which at a certain period he largely did through love, that is, at a time when he had to create within himself new attitudes. At such a period, then, it is possible to teach even the littlest children how to analyze their movements.

Analysis of Movements

Every complex action comprises a series of distinct movements; one act follows the other. The analysis of movements consists in trying to recognize and to carry out exactly these separate and distinct acts.

Dressing and undressing oneself, for example, are highly complex acts which we adults, except on special occasions, carry out rather imperfectly. The imperfection consists in carrying out at the same time and confusing various movements that should follow each other. It resembles the mispronunciation of long words, where different syllables are run together in a way that is at times incomprehensible. A person speaks poorly because he does not analyze the sounds that make up a word. The dropping or confusing of sounds has nothing to do with rapidity or slowness of speech. One can speak clearly and rapidly. And, on the other hand, one who mispronounces words is often slow in speaking. Therefore it is not a question of speed but of exactness. In general, we are inexact in many of our movements. This comes from a lack of education and it remains with us, even though we may be unaware of it, as a mark of inferiority. Let us imagine, for example, that we wish to button up a jacket. After we have more or less completely pushed the botton through the buttonhole, we begin to insert our thumb through the hole and grasp the opposite side as we search for the button unconscious of the fact that we have already pushed the button into the button hole. What we should do first of all is to place one edge of the jacket next to the other and turn the button in the direction of the buttonhole, pass it through, and then straighten it up. As a matter of fact, this is what servants or tailors do when they dress their patrons or clients. Clothes are thus preserved intact for a long time, whereas when clothes are buttoned three or four times in the other way they get out of shape. With similar clumsiness we spoil locks by blindly inserting keys and mixing up the two successive acts of turning the key and pulling the door. Often we draw a door half shut with the key even though it was not meant for that purpose, as is quite obvious from the handle on the door. And in the same way we ruin our best books as we awkwardly turn over the pages. Our abuse of external objects redounds upon ourselves: our movements are so crude and clumsy that they destroy the harmony of the body.

Economy of Movement

An analysis and economy of movement are bound together: to carry out no superfluous movements in the attainment of a goal is, in brief, the highest degree of perfection. This is the source of aesthetic movements and artistic attitudes. Greek movements, and those that resemble them today, like Japanese dancing, are simply a selection of the absolutely necessary movements in a succession of acts. But this is not simply a matter of art; it is a general principle for every vital act. A clumsy, awkward action is in general weighed down with movements that are not pertinent to the desired goal. If one, when getting out of a carriage, opens the door a little before the carriage has come to a halt or points his foot towards the step, he unconsciously does two or three useless acts since he cannot as yet descend. But all this is not simply useless as far as getting out of a carriage is concerned. It is also a sign of vulgarity.

These things may seem to be complicated and difficult to teach, but there is an age when movements possess a fascinating interest, when muscles and nerves respond to exercise, and when a person acquires those habits which will mark him in future life as a cultured or uncultured individual. And this is the period of childhood.

Fastening Frames

Exercise in the analysis of their movements is afforded to the children through fastening frames. These consist of wooden frames, each of which has two rectangular pieces of cloth that can be fastened together. Each one of the frames offers a different kind of fastening: buttons, hooks, laces, ribbons, buckles, hooks and eyes, and so forth. All of these various items are used in dressing oneself. The two pieces of cloth must first be placed edge to edge so that the objects to be used in joining them together lie opposite each other. These may be eyelets, which have to be threaded with a lace, or buttons and buttonholes, or ribbons to be tied. These various types of fastenings require sufficiently diverse and complicated maneuvers to enable a child to distinguish his successive acts, each of which must be completed before he can go on to the next. For example, a button must be tilted with one hand while the other hand moves the buttonhole so that it comes over the button; he then passes the button through the hole and flattens it out. After a teacher has shown a child exactly how it should be done, he keeps constantly at the task buttoning and unbuttoning the frame until he has acquired speed and dexterity.

Other Means

The following list can provide examples of similar activities: locking or unlocking desks or doors, distinguishing the acts of holding a key horizontally, inserting it, turning it, and then drawing out the drawer or opening the door; opening a book correctly and turning the pages one at a time with a gentle touch; rising up from a chair and sitting down on it; carrying various things, stopping, and then putting them down; avoiding obstacles while walking around, that is, by not bumping into people or furniture. All of these are examples of exercises frequently used in Children's Houses.

In addition to these, another series of acts is introduced relating to the formalities of social life, such as greeting each other, picking up and presenting an object dropped by another, the avoidance of passing in front of another, giving way to others, and so forth.

The Line

One single idea runs through every complex activity, and this single idea must be sought as the key to any general problem. There is also a secret key to the perfecting of the most varied types of movements. And this key is balance. We have therefore devised a means which can assist small children to secure their balance and at the same time perfect their most fundamental movement, that is, walking.

A line in the shape of a long ellipse is drawn in chalk on the floor, or painted to make it more durable. A child is then shown how to walk on this line, placing his foot completely on it, that is, covering it with the axis of his foot. The first thing that a child has to be shown is how to place his foot exactly upon the line so that his heel and toe are both on it. When a child moves forward with his feet in this position, he gets the impression that he is falling, as experience will easily show. This means that he has to make an effort to keep his balance. When a child begins to walk confidently, he is then taught how to overcome another difficulty. He has to walk in such a way that the forward foot is placed with its heel in contact with the toe of the rear foot. This exercise not only demands an effort on the part of a child to keep his balance, but it requires close attention so that he places his feet in their required positions. This satisfies the ordinary instinct of children, which everyone has noticed, to walk on a plank or narrow bar. It also explains the keen interest which the children take in performing this exercise on the line, and the use which we have made of it in our schools.

A teacher plays the piano or a violin, or a little organ, not to get the children to walk to the rhythm of the music, but to assist them by animating their movements.

Concurrent Exercises

Today there is in our schools as part of the standard equipment a rack holding many different little flags. These are attractive because of their bright colors, and the children love to hold them in their hands. As soon as the children have overcome their first difficulties in walking on the line and have secured their balance, they may take one of these little flags if they can hold it aloft. If they do not pay great attention to the way they hold their arms, the flags will gradually droop. They must therefore pay attention not only to the way in which they place their feet on the line but also how they hold the flag in their hands.

The following exercises are more difficult and require an ever increased control of movements. A series of glasses containing colored water is set out, and they are almost filled to the brim. A child has to walk carrying the glass upright so that the water does not spill. Through the same will-act he has to walk properly on the line and control the movements of his hands.

Bells are other objects which a child must carry upright while walking. As he walks down the line, he should not make a sound. If his mind wanders, it is immediately indicated by a sound from the bell.

At this stage a child becomes interested in overcoming ever greater difficulties. He enthusiastically engages in activities which little by little make him master of all his movements. His self-confidence is often audacious. I have seen children hold in their hands a column of blocks stacked one upon the other and carry them around like this without letting them fall. Others cautiously move about with baskets on their heads.

Immobility and Silence

A very different type of controlled movement is that which makes it possible for the children, as far as they can, to create an absolute silence. This is not the quasi-silence obtained by sitting still and saying nothing but a perfection that is attained only gradually. It consists in not uttering a single sound, in not causing the slightest noise, such as is made by a movement of the feet or stroke of the hand or heavy breathing. Absolute silence resembles complete immobility. But we shall discuss silence when we take up the exercises of the senses. We have simply mentioned it here in order to round out our discussion on the analysis and coordination of movements.

Open Roads

The final object of such exercises is the perfecting of the individual who performs them. But there are many ways which an individual can take. One who has advanced on the way to perfection is capable of doing many things, and the perfection of his activities leads to some practical results.

A child who has become master of his acts through long and repeated exercises, and who has been encouraged by the pleasant and interesting activities in which he has been engaged, is a child filled with health and joy and remarkable for his calmness and discipline.

He has also acquired in a natural way many practical skills. His body is attuned to musical rhythms, and he is ready for gymnastic exercises. Music is no longer a simple stimulus to his efforts, but it becomes an inner guide of his movements, which have become obedient to its rhythms.

Let us now consider something quite different. Our little children are about to enter into a sacred place, where silence and stillness are required of those who enter. They are actively attentive in every fiber of their being. They can walk without making a noise, they can stand, sit, and move their chairs about without disturbing the peace of the church. All this is not yet inspired by a religious sentiment, but nevertheless it shows that a small child can enter a place destined for worship with dignity. A refined and perfect child is capable of entering upon any path that helps him to advance.

The Free Life

These conquerers of themselves have also attained freedom since they have rid themselves of those many disorderly and unconscious tendencies that necessarily place children under the strict and continuous control of adults. They can cheerfully walk into a garden without damaging the paths or flowers, or run about on a meadow without acting improperly. The grace and dignity of their behavior and the ease of their movements are the corollaries to what they have gained through their own patient and laborious efforts. In a word they are "self-controlled," and to the extent that they are thus controlled they are free from the control of others. Anyone who makes a theoretical study of our method gets a first impression that is opposed to his own previous conception of it: "A child is free to do what he wishes." But then he begins to fear for this child, thought to be free, who instead is obliged to walk in a certain way upon a line, who tries to reduce his little body to a complete stillness, who patiently waits on others like a servant, and who analyzes his every movement. Only immediate contact with these children will show him that they are happy to make these sacrifices and convince him that the basic need of growing children is to submit themselves to this process of maturing.

Reality

Exercises in keeping their balance and in analyzing their various movements help the children to perfect all their acts. They force a child to use his organs of balance and accustom him to pay attention to his every move. Exercises in practical living alert a child to the many actions he carries out during the day. The two assist each other: analysis helps synthesis and its practical results, and vice versa.

Repetition is the secret of perfection, and this is why the exercises are connected with the common activities of daily life. If a child does not set a table for a group of people who are really going to eat, if he does not have real brushes for cleaning, and real carpets to sweep whenever they are used, if he does not himself have to wash and dry dishes and glasses he will never attain any real ability. And if he does not live a social life based on proper education, he will never attain that graceful naturalness which is so attractive in our children. Just as friction eventually stops even the smoothest and most polished sphere from rolling along a level surface, so even one who knows what he should do must constantly struggle to keep himself from falling into that depth of indolence which invites him to stop on the way to perfection. It is of no advantage to one to have reached the highest degree of refinement if this is not carried over in some way into daily life, which furnishes various motives for not relaxing, and where acquired skills have a reciprocal influence. Carelessness and crudity are like weeds which grow even on an arid rock which, by its very nature, would seem to be protected from them.

The Arrangement of Actions

One detail that is commonly little understood is the distinction between teaching a child how he should act, but leaving him free in the practical application of this freedom, and that which is followed in other systems of education, namely, of imposing the will and power of an adult upon the child and thus guiding him in all his actions. Those who subscribe to the older concepts imagine that we, when we defend a child's freedom, want it to remain without power and without a will, since we deprive it of that special supervision of an adult's will. But, as a matter of fact, we do not have such a simplistic attitude. Our education is not negative nor does it deprive a child of anything, but rather changes, intensifies and refines.

Everything must be taught, and everything must be connected with life; but this does not mean that the actions which children have learned to perform and to integrate with their practical lives should be suppressed or directed by us in every detail. This integration of his actions is one of the highest efforts that a child can make. A child has learned not only how to keep silent, but when he should be silent. He has not only learned various kinds of greetings, but he has also learned which one to use with another child, with his mother or father, with a stranger, or with one who is old and respected. In other words, he must use according to time and circumstances the many things which he has learned perfectly. But it is he who makes the decision. How he is to use what he has learned is a task for his own conscience, an exercise of his own responsibility. He is thus freed from the greatest of all dangers, that of making an adult responsible for his actions, of condemning his own conscience to a kind of idle slumber.

The new education does not consist in merely providing means for the development of individual actions, but also in giving a child the freedom of disposing of these actions himself.

This is what transforms a child into a little, but thoughtful and diligent, man who makes decisions in the secrets of his heart and chooses things quite different from what would have been expected, or who, with the swiftness of a generous impulse or with a delicate perfection, performs actions that are suddenly bidden by his inner ego. And it is especially in this way that he exercises himself. Thus it is that with surprising confidence he travels along the way chosen by his own intelligence.

A child's inner toil has a kind of modest sensibility, and it finds expression only when an adult has not intervened with his advice, exhortations, orders, and questions. We should leave a child free to activate his potentialities. He will show us that he is aware of the fact that he can always do better than he is doing at present. He will be scrupulous in carrying out every activity in perfect order, just as a younger child (that is, one who is about two years old) takes pride in knowing how to place each object in its proper place.

When he meets some dignitary who is visiting his school, he feels that he not only knows how to greet him, but how to extend the proper form of greeting as well. When he sits down in school or kneels in church he performs the actions which he has learned and perfected in the proper order. And this adds both knowledge and power to his intellect. A child who has finished his first bowl of soup does not ask for another if he has learned that he should not do this and that for the time being he should check his desire for more; and he will practice patience until the waiter, who is an anxious as he is himself to do everything well and in proper order, begins his second round and invites those who have finished to have their bowls refilled.

The inward satisfaction of a child, whether as a guest at table or waiter or artist or student, consists in consciously doing what is right according to principles.

Gymnastics and Games

What should our attitude be towards ordinary gymnastics

and games in the open air? They are a means of using up excessive energy, that is, energy not yet expended. There should be a carefree use of the forces which the daily order of work has not used up. This is something quite different from looking upon games and gymnastics in themselves as merely a means of physical exercise, as a kind of reaction to the dangers of inertia.

Much is said today of the moral advantages of sports, not simply because they expend pent-up energies which constitute a danger to a child's equilibrium, which should always be maintained, but because oragnized games, and this is most important, demand an exact use of objects and consequently concentration and a complete control of one's movements. Games thus lead to a feeling of rivalry and animate the participant with a spirit of competition. And this, in comparison with aimless play, represents moral progress.

But the demands of practical life share in these advantages, for example, exactness in the use of objects, the focusing of attention, and the ultimate perfection attained through movements. The moral object, however, is different since these exercises are not prompted by a feeling of rivalry or accomplishment but by a love of the children for their environment. Through practical exercises of this sort the children develop a true "social feeling," for they are working in the environment of the community in which they live, without concerning themselves as to whether it is for their own, or for the common good. As a matter of fact they correct all errors, whether their own or others, with the same readiness and enthusiasm without stopping to look for the culprit to make him repair the evil done.

All of us, and not simply children, should exercise our muscles by working and choose this kind of activity as the primary and most natural way of expending our energies. Work not only identifies one as an individual, but it also unites him with society, which is bound together by men's labor. Until now there has been no ruler who has been able to boast that he derived from sports the same assistance that Cincinnatus derived from his work in the fields; and no young sportsman will obtain from his exertions the moral advantages that a young monk derives from his daily labors as a novice in order to arrive at a state of peace.

Freedom of Choice

We can now take a look at the school, and the practical carrying out of our principles. The material used for the training of the senses, which has been determined on the basis of research, is a part of the environment.

Following the norms established through experience, a teacher gradually presents now one object and now another to a child according to his age and the progressive difficulty of the materials.

But the presentation of these materials is only the first step. It introduces the child to them but nothing more. The important activities begin only later. As he is attracted by the various objects, a child will go and freely choose any of the objects which he has come to know and which has been already presented to him.

The material is set out for him; he has only to stretch out his hand to take it. He can carry the chosen object wherever he chooses, to a table, to a place near the window, to a dark corner, or to a pretty little carpet spread out on the floor, and he can use the object over and over again as often as he feels like it.

What makes him choose one object rather than another? It is not imitation since there is only one example of each object, and if one child is using it at the time no other child can use it.

Therefore it is not imitation. This may be shown even in the way that the child uses the material: he becomes so attentive to what he is doing and so immersed in his work that he does not notice what is going on about him but continues to work, repeating the same exercise dozens of times over. This exemplifies that phenomenon of concentration and the repetition of an exercise which is connected with a child's inner development. No one can concentrate through imitation. Imitation, in fact, binds us to the external world, but here we are dealing with a diametrically opposed phenomenon, that is, with a withdrawal from the external world and the closest kind of union with that secret inner world lying within a child. He is not interested in learning or in attaining an external goal. Nothing of this sort can be connected with his moving of objects which are constantly being replaced in their original positions. It is therefore something completely interior connected with the current needs of a child and with the conditions characteristic of his age. As a matter of fact, an adult would never have such a great interest in these simple objects as to place and replace them dozens of times over and be pleased in the process, and still less would the inner faculties of an adult be able to concentrate so intently upon what was being done as to make him insensible to what was going on round about. Since a teacher is on quite a different psychic plane than a child, she cannot have the slightest influence on such a phenomenon. We are therefore faced with a real revelation of the inner world. An external stimulus, such as some great calamity, can draw out a revelation from the depths of the soul. But here we find ourselves confronted with a pure and simple phenomenon of growth.

The fact becomes evident when we observe the behavior of children still considerably younger. They show at times a similar kind of activity, although one that is limited to the field of motion. It consists in carrying objects that are alike from one place to another one by one. Only later does a child like to carry objects with some exterior end in view, such as setting a table, replacing objects in a cupboard, and so forth. There is therefore a formative period in which the actions have no external scope or application. We find analogous facts connected with the attainment of speech when a child for a long time repeats sounds, syllables, or words without actually speaking, much less applying the words to external objects.

This phenomenon, so commonly seen in the development of the psychic life, is therefore of the greatest interest. It means that a child should be left free to choose the objects he wishes. The more the obstacles that stand between a child and the object to which his soul unconsciously aspires are eliminiated, the better it will be for the child.

Every external object and still more every external activity which hinders that frail and hidden vital impulse which, even though it is still unknown, acts as a guide to a child will be an obstacle. A teacher can therefore become a child's main obstacle, since her activities are more conscious and energetic than his. A teacher, after she has shown the sensorial stimuli to the children and taught them their use, should seek to withdraw herself from the environment to which they are exposed. A child is urged on to act by his own interior drives and no longer by the teacher.

6. The Material for Development

The material we use for the development of the senses of a child has a history of its own. It has been drawn partly from the material used by Itard and Seguin in their attempts to educate retarded and mentally deficient children, partly from objects used in psychological tests, and partly from the materials which I earlier designed in my own experimental work. The reactions of children to various objects, the way in which, and the frequency with which, they used them, and the advantages which they derived from them, all gradually built up reliable criteria for the elimination, modification, and acceptance of apparatus to be used in our schools. Everything about these various objects—color, size, shape, and so forth were all determined by experience. Since we are not treating of this period of our work in the present volume, it is worth the trouble to at least mention it.

To prevent misunderstandings and to refute criticisms which were leveled at our method after it became widely known, it will also be useful to state our aim in training the senses. The training and sharpening of the senses has the obvious advantage of enlarging the field of perception and of offering an ever more solid foundation for intellectual growth. The intellect builds up its store of practical ideas through contact with, and exploration of, its environment. Without such concepts the intellect would lack precision and inspiration in its abstract operations. It is true that there are only certain professions that require great precision in the use of the various senses. Nevertheless, if they can be trained and refined, even if this is only a temporary achievement in the lives of many, this will be of great value since it is at this period of development that basic ideas are conceived and intellectual habits are formed.

There is also another important aspect to this training of the senses. A child of two-and-a-half or three who comes to one of our Children's Houses has, during the previous years, when his physical and mental powers were developing, accumulated and absorbed a host of impressions. This remarkable achievement, the importance of which can hardly be exaggerated, has, however, been accomplished without any outside help or guidance. Accidental and essential impressions are all mixed together, creating a confused but significant wealth in his subconscious mind.

With the gradual emergence of knowledge and volition, it becomes imperative to establish some order and clarity within the mind and to distinguish what is essential from what is accidental. A child at this time is ready to rediscover his own environment and the inner wealth of impressions which he has of it. To satisfy this need, he should have an exact, scientific guide such as that which is to be found in our apparatus and exercises. Such a child may be compared with one who does not have the knowledge he should of the treasures he has inherited, but is anxious to evaluate them with the help of a professional and to catalog and classify them so that he can have them under his immediate and absolute control.

If there can be any doubt about the lasting value of a refined sensory perception in certain walks of life, this second factor certainly seems to be a permanent acquisition. As a general rule, the first of these two goals has been assumed to be the reason we have stressed so much the training of the senses in our method, whereas the second is no less important and is actually the principal motive. Our experience and that of our followers have only confirmed us in this conviction.

In conclusion, we may mention the great assistance given by our sensorial materials and the exercises done with them in the detection of functional defects in the senses at a time when much can be done to correct them.

The sensorial materials comprise a series of objects which are grouped together according to some physical quality which they have, such as color, shape, size, sound, texture, weight, temperature, and so forth. There are thus, for example, a group of bells which reproduce musical tones, a series of tablets which present different shades of colors, groups of solid objects which have the same shape but different dimensions, or which have different shapes, or which have the same size but different weights, and so on.

Every single group of objects represents the same quality but in different degrees; there is consequently a regular but gradual distinction between the various objects and, when this is possible, one that is mathematically fixed.

The general rules, however, are subject to modifications, which may be determined by the mentality of the child. Experience will show how only that material which really interests a small child and which he will freely choose and regularly employ is suitable for a child's education.

Every series of objects, whether they produce sounds or represent different colors, and so forth, is graded so that there is a maximum and a minimum, which determines its limits, or which, more properly, are fixed by the use which a child makes of them. When the two extremes are brought together, they clearly demonstrate the difference that exists within the series and therefore determine the most striking contrast that can be achieved with the material. A sharp contrast between the extremes makes their differences evident and arouses the interest of a child before he has even had a chance to use them.

The Isolation of a Single Quality in the Material

Any object that we wish to use for the education of the senses must necessarily present many different qualities such as weight, texture, color, form, size, and so forth. How are we to isolate from many qualities one single one so that attention may be focused on it? This is done by a series and its gradations; the objects are identical among themselves with exception of the variable quality which they possess.

If, for example, we want to prepare objects to be used in distinguishing colors, we must make them of the same material, size, and dimensions, but then see that they are of different colors. Or, if we wish to prepare objects that will point out the various tones on the musical scale, it is necessary that they be perfectly alike in appearance, as are the bells which we use in our system. These have the same size and shape and are mounted on identical supports, but when they are struck with a small mallet, they give off different sounds, and these sounds are the only differences perceptible to the senses.

This illustrates the fact that the small instruments which

are usually given to children as musical toys do not lend themselves to a real exercise in musical perception that would differentiate sounds. These toys are made of longer or shorter rods, or tubes, of different lengths arranged like the pipes of an organ. This means that a child's eyes assist him in making distinctions, whereas his ears should be the sole judge of sounds.

A procedure of this sort succeeds in pointing up distinctions, and it is obvious that clarity is the principle factor in arousing an interest in making these distinctions.

Psychological studies have shown that it is necessary to isolate the senses as far as possible if some single quality is to be brought out. The sense of touch is more acute if it is directed toward an object that does not conduct heat, that is, at one that gives at the same time a feeling of heat or cold, and if the subject is placed in a dark, silent room where there are no sights or sounds to distract the impressions received from the sense of touch. There can thus be a twofold kind of isolation, one in the subject, who is isolated from every other impression that might come from the surroundings, and the other in the material, which is systematically graded according to a single quality.

The perfection of this exercise consists in removing as far as possible all distracting factors. It enables a child to engage in an inner and external analysis that can help him acquire an orderly mind.

A child is by his nature an avid explorer of his surroundings because he has not yet had the times or means of knowing them precisely. He willingly shuts his eyes, or is blindfolded, to shut out the light when he explores various shapes with his hands or when he gladly accepts darkness in order to be able to listen to the slightest sounds.

Fundamental Qualities Common to Everything in the Educational Environment Surrounding a Child

To the many characteristics mentioned above, many others should be added. These, however, do not have special reference to sense objects, but should be extended wherever possible to everything that surrounds a child. They are as follows:

1) *The control of error*. Every effort should be made to see that the materials offered to a child contain in themselves a control of error. An example of this may be seen in the solid insets. These consist in wooden bases with holes to receive cylinders of graduated dimensions, from thin to thick, or from short to tall, or from small to large. Since the holes in the wooden base correspond exactly to the cylinders, these latter cannot all be wrongly replaced. At least one would be left over, and this would betray the fact that an error has been committed. The same is true in buttoning. If one button is forgotten or is buttoned in the wrong hole, the mistake is revealed in the end by an empty hole. Mistakes are noticed in the use of other materials, such as the three series of blocks, by their size, and color, and so forth, and by the fact that a child has already accustomed himself to spotting errors.

The control of error through the material makes a child use his reason, critical faculty, and his ever increasing capacity for drawing distinctions. In this way a child's mind is conditioned to correct his errors even when these are not material or apparent to the senses.

But it is not simply the objects used for the training of the senses and developing habits but the whole environment that is designed to make it easy to correct mistakes. Everything in the room, from the furniture to the special material for the children, is an informer whose warning voice cannot be ignored.

Bright colors and shining surfaces reveal stains. The light furniture, when it is tipped over or noisily dragged over the floor, tells of movements which are still clumsy and imperfect. The whole environment thus becomes a kind of instructor or sentinel always on the alert. And each child hears its admonition as if he alone stood before this inanimate teacher.

2) *Aesthetics*. Another characteristic of the objects is that they are attractive. Color, brightness, and proportion are sought in everything that surrounds a child. Not only the sensorial material but also the whole environment is so prepared that it will attract him, just as in nature colored blossoms attract insects to drink the nectar which they conceal.

"Use me carefully," say the bright shiny tables. "Do not leave me idle," say the little brooms with their handles painted with tiny flowers. "Dip your little hand in here," say the clean wash basins, all set for use with their little brushes and little bars of soap.

The pieces of cloth to be joined together are green with silver buttons. The blocks are red. The tablets are graded into sixty-three different colors. The beautiful colored letters of the alphabet lie in their proper bins. All these are so many invitations to a child.

At any particular moment a child is attracted to the object that corresponds to his greatest need at the time. In the same way the petals of all the flowers in an open field are calling other living beings to themselves with their colors and perfumes, but each insect chooses the blossom that was made for it.

3) *Activity*. Another characteristic of this material for a child's development is that it must lend itself to a child's activity. The ability of a thing to attract the interest of a child does not depend so much upon the quality of the thing itself as upon the opportunity that it affords the child for action.

This is the same as saying that it is not enough that a thing should be interesting in itself but that it must lend itself to the motor activity of the child if it is to be interesting to him. There must be, for example, small objects that can be moved from their places. It is then that a child begins to move his hand rather than the objects. A child is delighted to make and unmake something, to place and replace things many times over and continue the process for a long time. A very beautiful toy, an attractive picture, a wonderful story, can, without doubt, rouse a child's interest, but if he may simply look at, or listen to, or touch an object, but dares not move it, his interest will be superficial and will pass from object to object. This is why the environment is so arranged that it lends itself to a child's desire to be active. It is beautiful, but this of itself would only interest a child for a day, whereas the fact that every object can be removed, used, and taken back to its proper place makes the attractions of the environment inexhaustible.

4) *Limits*. Finally, there is another principle that is common to all the material devised for a child's education. It is one that has been little understood till now and yet is of the greatest importance, namely, that the material should be

limited in quantity. Properly understood, this principle is clear and logical. A normal child does not need stimuli to awaken him or to put him in contact with the material world. He is already awake, and already has constant, countless relations with his environment. He needs rather to bring order into the chaos created in his mind by the host of sensations coming to him from the outside world. He is not mentally asleep like a retarded child, but an ardent explorer of a world that is new to him. And, what he needs, as an explorer, is a road (that is something which is straight and limited) which can lead him to his goal and keep him from wandering aimlessly about. He then passionately attaches himself to those things, limited and direct in scope, which bring order into the chaos that has been created within him; and with this order, they provide light for his exploring mind and a guide for his researches. The explorer who was at first abandoned to himself then becomes an enlightened man who makes new discoveries at every step and advances with the strength which he receives from his inner satisfaction.

Evidence of this kind should certainly modify the notion still held by many that a child is helped in proportion to the number of educational objects that are placed at his disposal. It is a common, but false, belief that the child who has the most toys, the most help, should also be the most developed. Instead of that, the confused multitude of objects with which he is surrounded only aggravate the chaos of his mind and further discourages him.

The number of aids which should be given to a child to bring order to his mind and facilitate his understanding of the infinite number of things which surround him should be determined by the need he has to preserve his strength, but which will at the same time enable him to advance safely along the difficult way of development.

7. The Exercises

How a Teacher Should Give a Lesson: Comparison with the Older Systems

When a child is ready to start the training of his senses, the lessons are given individually. A teacher makes an almost timid attempt to approach the child whom she believes is ready to learn the lesson. She sits down by his side and picks up an object which she thinks will interest him.

Here she reveals the extent of her own preparation. She should have been trained simply to make experiments. The answer she expects from the child is that he should be interiorly moved to use the material presented to him.

The lesson is a call to attention. If the object meets the inner needs of the child and is something that will satisfy them, it rouses the child to prolonged activity. He masters it and uses it over and over again.

Words are not always necessary. Very frequently all one has to do is to show the child how the object is used. But when the teacher has to speak and show the child how to employ material for his growth and development, the instruction should be brief. The best instruction is that which uses the least words sufficent for the task.

The fewer the words, the more perfect will be the lesson. Special care should be taken in preparing the lesson to counting and picking out the words to be used.

Another characteristic of a lesson is its simplicity. It should not have anything about it that is not the absolute truth. Since the avoidance of empty words is included the first characteristic of the lesson, the second also must be included under the first. The counted words should be of the simplest kind and they should represent nothing but the truth.

The third characteristic of a lesson is its objectivity. This means that the teacher forgets herself and focuses the attention of the child entirely upon the object. For the most part, the short and simple lesson should consist in an explanation of the object and of the use which the child can make of it.

The teacher will note whether or not the child is interested in the object, how he shows his interest, how long he is interested in it, and so on, and she will take care not to force a child's interest in what she is offering. If the lesson prepared with the necessary brevity, simplicity, and truth is not understood by the child as an explanation of the object, the teacher should be careful about two things. First, she should not insist on repeating the lesson. Second, she should refrain from letting the child know that he has made a mistake or has not understood, since this might arrest for a long time the impulse to act, which constitutes the whole basis for progress.

Let us imagine, for example, that a teacher wants to show a child the difference between the two colors red and blue. Attracting the attention of the child to the objects, she says: "Look, pay attention!" If she wants to teach him the names of the colors she says, showing him the red object: "This is red," raising her voice and pronouncing the word "red" very slowly. Then she shows him the other color saying, "This is blue." To see if the child has understood or not, she says: "Give me the red, give me the blue." Suppose the child makes a mistake; the teacher neither repeats the lesson nor insists any further. She smiles and puts away the colors.

Ordinary teachers as a rule marvel at this simplicity. They usually say: "Anyone can do that." But we are again confronted with something like the story of the egg of Columbus. The fact is that they cannot do it at all. In practice it is extremely difficult to evaluate one's own actions, and this is all the more so in the case of teachers who have been trained in the older methods. They overwhelm a child with a deluge of useless words and misinformation.

For example, if we were to take the case just mentioned, an ordinary teacher would attempt to teach the colors to a group, attributing excessive importance to the simple task at hand and compelling all of the children to follow her when perhaps not all were so inclined. She would probably begin the lesson as follows: "Children, can you guess what I have in my hand?" She knows perfectly well that the children cannot guess, and she thus attracts their attention with a falsehood. Then she would likely say: "Children, do you ever look up at the sky? Have you ever seen it? Have you ever looked at it at night, when it is all shining with stars? No? Look at my apron. Do you know what color it is? Does it look to you as if it has the same color as the sky? Well, now, look at the color which I have here. It is the same as that of the sky and of my apron. It is blue. Look about you. Do you see any other things that are blue? And do you know the color of cherries? Of glowing coals?" And so on and so on.

Thus it is that the child's mind, after being confused by questioning, is overwhelmed by a mass of ideas—sky, aprons, cherries, and so forth; and in all this confusion he finds it difficult to identify the subject, the aim of the lesson, which is to identify two colors, blue and red. Further the child's mind is incapable of making a choice, especially since he is unable to follow a long discourse.

I remember once being present at a lesson in arithmetic when the teacher was trying to show the children that two and three are five. To do this she was using a checkerboard so constructed that little balls could be inserted in corresponding holes. For example, two balls could be placed high on the board, three below these, and beneath these five more. I do not recall exactly how the lesson went. I know, however, that the teacher had to place near the two upper balls a paper doll representing a dancer. The doll was wearing a blue dress and it was now and then called by the name of one of the children of the class: "This is Mariettina." Then, next to the other three balls was placed another dancer dressed in a different way, who was called "Gigino." I do not know precisely how the teacher came to demonstrate the total, but she certainly chattered a long time with the dancers, moving them about, and so on. If I remember the dancers better than the process of addition, what must have remained in the minds of the children? If they did not learn by this means that two and three are five, they must at least have made a great mental effort. The teacher must have chattered with the dolls for a good many hours.

In another lesson a teacher wanted to demonstrate the difference between a noise and a musical sound. She began by telling the children a rather long story. Suddenly someone who was working with her knocked loudly on the door. The teacher broke off her story with a shout: "What is it? What's happened? What have they done? What is it, children? I have lost the thread of my thoughts, I cannot continue my story, I don't remember anything, I'll have to let it go. Do you know what happened? Did you hear? Did you understand? It was a noise! That's a noise! I would rather cradle this infant." (She took up a mandolin wrapped up in a blanket.) "Dear baby boy, I'd rather play with you. Do you see him? Do you see this baby I am holding in my arms?" One of the children cried out: "That's not a child!" And others joined in: "It's a mandolin." The teacher replied: "No, no, it's a baby, a real baby. You want me to prove it? Oh, do be quiet! He seems to me to be weeping, to be crying. Is he perhaps saying 'Papa' and 'Mama'?" She touched the strings of the mandolin under the blanket. "Did you hear? Did you hear what he did? Did he weep or cry?" Some of the children said: "It's a mandolin. You have plucked its cords." The teacher replied: "Keep quiet. Listen carefully to what I am doing." She uncovered the mandolin and lightly plucked the strings: "That's a musical sound!"

It is hopeless to imagine that a child as a result of such a lesson would understand the intention of the teacher, that is, to show the difference between a noise and a musical sound. A child would think that the teacher wanted to pull a joke and that she was rather stupid to have lost the thread of her thought because of a mere noise and had confused a mandolin with a baby. The person of the teacher would certainly be fixed in a child's mind, but not the object of the lesson.

It is very difficult to find a teacher prepared according to the usual method who can give a simple lesson. I remember that once, after I had explained the matter at length, I asked one of my teachers to teach the difference between a square and a triangle by the use of insets, as we shall show later. All she had to do was to put a square and a triangle made out of wood into corresponding empty spaces and make the child trace with his finger the outline of the insets and the empty spaces and say: "This is a square. This is a triangle." The teacher had them touch the edges of the insets and said: "This is a line, this another, this another, and this another. There are four of them. Now count with your fingers how many there are. And the corners. Count the corners. Touch them with your fingers. Press them. There are four of them also. Look carefully at it. It's a square!" I corrected the teacher pointing out to her that she was not teaching the child how to recognize a shape but was giving him ideas about size, corners, and numbers, something quite different from what she whould have been teaching. But she defended herself, saying: "It's all the same." But it is not all the same; she had been giving a geometrical and mathematical analysis of the object. One could have grasped the idea of a square without being able to count to four, that is, without learning the number of sides and corners. These are abstractions which do not exist of themselves. What does exist is a piece of wood of a definite shape. The explanations of the teacher not only confused the mind of the child but leapt over the abyss separating the concrete from the abstract, the shape of an object from mathematics.

Suppose, I said to the teacher, that an architect was showing you a beautifully shaped cupola that attracted you. He could give you two pictures of it. He could point out the beauty of the surroundings, the harmony of its parts. He might make you climb up and walk about the cupola itself in order to make you appreciate the relative proportions of its parts so that you might have an appreciation and knowledge of the whole. Or he could make a count of the windows, the wide or narrow cornices, and finally draw a sketch of the structure to illustrate the laws of stability and teach the algebraic formula to be employed in making calculations for its construction. In the first case you would take into account the shape of the cupola; in the second, you would understand nothing, and instead of getting an impression of the cupola, you would get one of the architect, who imagined that he was speaking to a fellow engineer instead of to a lady on a pleasure trip. We have an exact parallel to this in the case of a child if, instead of saying to him: "This is a square," and simply making him touch it and note its material outline, we should proceed to make a geometrical analysis of it for him. We believe that it is too early to teach a child the forms of plane geometry simply because we associate them with mathematical concepts. But a child is not incapable of appreciating simple forms. In fact, we can see square windows and tables without any effort. His eye is attuned to all the various forms about him. To direct a child's attention to a particular shape, one must make it stand out clearly so that it becomes impressed upon his mind. It is just as if we were standing on the edge of a lake, looking without much attention at the shore, when suddenly an artist came up and exclaimed: "What a beautiful curve the shore makes in the shadow of that cliff!" Then that hitherto dull scene comes to life within our minds, just as if it had been illuminated by a ray of the sun, and we experience the joy of fully appreciating what we had only imperfectly felt before.

This is our mission: to cast a ray of light and pass on.

The effects of these first lessons might be compared to the impressions which a lonely wayfarer experiences as he walks along, happy and peaceful, in the shade of a grove, leaving his inner thought free to wander in quiet meditation. Suddenly he is called to himself by the pealing of a church bell in the vicinity. Then he feels even more keenly the blessed peace which already possessed him, but of which he was not conscious.

This then is the first duty of an educator: to stir up life but leave it free to develop.

For such a delicate mission there is need, however, of a great art which will suggest the proper time and limits of one's interventions. This will prevent the teacher from disturbing or misdirecting, instead of assisting, a soul which is coming to life and which will live by virtue of its own efforts.

This art must accompany the scientific method, since the simplicity of our lessons bear a great resemblance to the experiments of experimental psychology.

Just as soon as a teacher has touched the hearts of each one of her pupils in turn, awakening them and calling them to life as if by a magic wand, she will have possession of those hearts, and a sign or word from her will be sufficient since they are all aware of her presence and listen to her.

There will come a day when the teacher, to her own great surprise, will notice that all the children obey her like gentle little lambs, not only prompt to respond to any suggestion from her, but even waiting for it. They regard her as one who gives them life and from whom they instinctively hope to receive ever more and more.

Experience has revealed this to us, and this collective discipline, attained almost as it were by magic, is the cause of the greatest wonder of those who visit the Children's Houses. Fifty or sixty children, from two-and-a-half to six years of age, all togehter, at a single sign, become so absolutely silent, that their silence resembles that of a desert. And if a teacher in a low voice gives a gentle order to the children, "Stand up, walk about for a minute on tip-toe, and then return to your seats in silence," they all, as if they were a single individual, rise and execute the movements with a minimum of noise. The teacher has spoken to each one with her voice, and each one hoping to receive from her intervention some little light and inner joy goes on attentive and obedient like an earnest explorer who has his own path to follow.

Here again we may recall the egg of Columbus. A concert director must train his musicians one by one if he wishes to obtain from their collective efforts a noble harmony, and each one of the musicians must make himself perfect before he can properly obey the silent direction of the conductor's baton. In the ordinary schools, on the contrary, we place a person in charge who teaches the same monotonous and even discordant melody to instruments and voices of the most diverse character.

The same happens in society: the most highly disciplined men are also those who are most perfect, provided that their conduct is not heavy, brutal, and authoritarian.

As far as child psychology is concerned, we are more prejudiced than wise. Up till now we have wanted to dominate children externally with the rod instead of trying to subdue them by guiding them inwardly like human beings. This is why they have passed close by us without our being able to get to know them.

But if we set aside the tricks with which we have tried to ensnare them and the violence which we took for discipline, they reveal themselves to us under another aspect. Their gentleness is sweet and absolute, and their love of knowledge is such that it enables them to overcome obstacles which we might have thought would have deterred their efforts.

How to Initiate a Child into the Exercises with the Sensorial Materials—Contrasts, Identities, and Gradations

One should begin the process with a very few contrasting stimuli so that the child can later pass on to a large number of similar objects but with always finer and less perceptible differences. Thus, for example, when there is a question of recognizing tactile differences, one will begin with only two surfaces, one perfectly smooth and the other very rough. When there is an experiment dealing with the weight of different objects, first the lightest of the whole series of tablets is given to a child and then the heaviest. The same is done with sounds. The two extremes of the graded series are the first to be offered. When it is a question of colors, the brightest and most contrasted colors are chosen, such as red and yellow. When it is a question of shapes, it is the circle and the triangle, and so on.

In order to give an even more complete idea of the differences between objects, it is well to include identical objects along with those which are strongly contrasted. There would thus be, for example, a double series of objects mixed together in confusion—two sounds equally loud and two equally faint, two objects of the same yellow color and two of an identical red. The exercise of looking for similarities among contrasts brings out the differences in a striking manner by rendering them prominent.

The last exercise, that of grading objects, consists in placing a series of similar objects that have been mixed together at random into a graded order. For example, a series of cubes of the same color but of different sizes according to a fixed scale, for example having a difference of half an inch on the sides. Similar to this is the presentation of a series of yellow objects whose shades run gradually from bright to dark, or a series of rectangles having one pair of sides of equal length but the other regularly decreasing. Such objects must be placed next to each other according to the position they have in a graduated series.

How to Begin the Tactile Exercises

Although the sense of touch is spread throughout the surface of the body, the exercises given to the children are limited to the tips of the fingers, and particularly, to those of the right hand.

Practical considerations make such a limitation necessary, but it also has a useful educative function insofar as it prepares a child for his ordinary life, for it is precisely these areas that he uses most for touching.

In our system, it is particularly useful, since, as we shall see, the various exercises which the children perform with their hands prepare them indirectly and remotely for writing.

I therefore have a child wash his hands well with soap in a basin and then rinse them in a nearby basin of tepid water. I next make the child dry his hands, and rub them gently together. This completes the preparatory work. I then teach the child how to touch, that is, the manner in which he should touch surfaces. To do this it is necessary to take the fingers of the child and draw them very, very lightly over the surface. Another detail of the technique is to teach the child to keep his eyes closed while he is touching something, encouraging him by telling him that he will feel the differences better and will be able to distinguish changes in the surface without seeing them. The child learns quickly and shows that he enjoys the process immediately. This is so true that, after these exercises have been taken up, when we enter into a Children's House the children will run up to meet us and, shutting their eyes, will touch with the greatest delicacy the palms of our hands, trying to find where the skin is smoothest, or they will touch our clothes especially the silk or velvet trimmings. The children truly exercise the sense of touch. They never seem to tire of touching smooth surfaces, such as satin, and they become very adept in distinguishing the differences in pieces of sandpaper.

The material for the first exercise consists of the following:

(a) a long rectangular plank divided into two equal rectangles, one covered with very smooth, and the other with rough, paper.

(b) another board of the same shape as the first, but covered with alternating strips of smooth and rough paper.

(c) another board like the former, having strips of emery- and sandpaper in decreasing grades of coarseness.

(d) a board on which are placed pieces of paper of the same size, but of different grades of smoothness, varying from parchment to the very smooth paper of the first plank.

These boards, which keep the various objects to be touched in a fixed position, serve to prepare a child's hand for touching things lightly, and they also teach him how to make systematic distinctions.

A child, with his eyes closed, touches the different areas of the board in turn and begins to measure differences by the movement of his arm.

As in many of the exercises, which we call sensorial, the sensitive stimulus is a means that leads to the determination of movements.

I have prepared movable material to be used after this. This material is gathered into separate groups, each for a specific exercise.

There are collections of the following:

(a) cards of varying grades of smoothness;
(b) sandpaper cards of graded coarseness;
(c) different kinds of fabrics.

This material is used in the usual way, that is, by mixing up the objects of a single series, to be arranged sometimes according to pairs, sometimes according to a series.

The fabrics consist of pairs of pieces of material kept in a special cabinet containing velvet, silk, wool, cotton, linen, knit, and so forth. The children can learn names of the various materials.

All the above exercises are carried out with their eyes blindfolded.

Impressions of Temperature

For this exercise I use various small metal receptacles. They are ovoid in shape and are water tight. I put a different quantity of water heated to 167° in each one of the receptacles. I then fill them up with cold water at 69°F, or I prepare the receptacles in pairs. Although the temperatures change rapidly as the objects are handled, the operation is still able to give a certain amount of exactness to the exercise.

A series of materials which differ in their condition of heat, such as wood, felt, glass, marble, and iron are used for more delicate exercises.

Impressions of Weight

For the education of the baric sense, that is, the impression of weight, rectangular tables of wood are used. These are ¾ inch long, ½ inch wide, and ⅛ inch thick. They are made of three different kinds of wood—wisteria, walnut, and fir. They weigh 1, ¾, and ½ ounch respectively, and thus differ from each other by ¼ ounce. They should be very smooth and varnished and polished so that any roughness disappears, though the actual color of the wood remains. A child, seeing the color, knows that they are of different weight. He can therefore have a control over his exercise. He takes in his hand two tablets, places them on his palms with his fingers extended and lifts his hand up and down to judge their weight. With practice the movement of his hand becomes almost imperceptible. The child is advised to make comparisons with his eyes closed. He is advised to do this by himself and becomes greatly interested in seeing if he is guessing.

The method just described provides one with the necessary technique for judging with sufficient accuracy different weights. The object has to be placed lightly on the skin and differences of temperature have to be avoided (and this is why the materials are made of wood), if one is to obtain a true impression of an object's weight. Moving the hand up and down changes the weight because of the resistance of the atmosphere. Such a movement is instinctive, but it should be made as small as possible if we want to obtain a more exact estimation of the object's weight.

The technique enables one to reach a degree of exactitude which is of itself quite interesting.

Impressions of Forms Through Touch Alone
(The Education of the Stereognostic Sense)

The recognition of the shape of an object by touching it all over with the tips of the fingers, as the blind do, is not simply an exercise of the sense of touch. As a matter of fact, only the superficial qualities of smoothness and roughness are perceived through the sense of "touch."

But when the hand and arm are moved about an object, an impression of movement is added to that of touch. Such an impression is attributed to a special, sixth sense, which is called a muscular sense, and which permits many impressions to be stored up in a "muscular memory," which recalls movements that have been made.

We can move without touching anything and remember and reproduce the movement made with respect to its direction, extent, and so forth. This results from the muscular sensations we have experienced. But when we touch something as we move, two sensations, tactile and muscular, are mixed together, and give rise to that sense which psychologists call the "sterognostic sense."

In such a case, there is not simply an impression of a completed movement, but "knowledge" of an external object. This knowledge can be integrated with that obtained through sight, thus giving greater exactness to the perception of an object. This is particularly noticeable in little children, who seem to recognize things more certainly and, especially, to remember them more easily, when they touch them rather than when they see them. A child's nature reveals this fact very early. Little children, in fact, touch everything they see, thus obtaining a double image (visual and muscular) of the countless different objects which they encounter in their environment.

But this habit of touching everything, as we have discovered from experience, is much more than a simple verification of what a child has seen. It is the obvious expression of a very keen muscular sensibility which a small child possesses at the period in his life in which the basic coordination of his movements is being fixed.

It is not therefore simply a verification of what has been seen, but the carrying out of a movement itself and the building of that physiological edifice and that coordination of movements needed to make the organs of expression effective.

Moreover, the fact that practically all the sensorial exercises are accompanied by movements shows that kinesthetic perceptions have a prominent role even at a very early age. This is why we have made extensive use of the stereognostic sense in our method of education. But this sense is also culturally important in that it is a necessary means for expressing oneself through drawing, writing, and so forth. Since these sensations are most useful for the attainment of the goal we have set for children, we have paid particular attention to their development in the formative period of early childhood.

The great success which we have had with experiments of this kind deserves to be described for the help of teachers.

The first material used were Froebel's blocks and bricks. Having called a child's attention to the shapes of the two solids, we had him feel them carefully with his eyes open. At the same time we gave him a brief description of them to keep his mind fixed on the details. We then told the child to place the blocks on the right and the bricks on the left, making the division by feeling and not by looking at the objects. Eventually the child did this blindfolded. Almost all the children succeeded in carrying out the exercise, and after a few repetitions all errors were eliminated. A child's attention could be kept fixed for a long time on this kind of game since altogether there were twenty-four bricks and cubes. Doubtlessly a child's attention to his work was encouraged by the fact that he knew he was being watched by curious companions ready to laugh at his mistakes, and he was further motivated by his own pride in guessing.

One of the teachers once brought me a three-year-old girl, one of the smallest in the class, who habitually repeated the exercise perfectly. We placed the girl comfortably in her armchair close to the table and put the twenty-four objects on the table, mixing them up together. After we had called her attention to their shapes, we asked her to place the cubes on the right and the bricks on the left. When she had been blindfolded the girl began the exercise as we teach it, that is, she took up at random two objects with both hands at the same time, felt them, and put them in their proper places. Sometimes she picked up two cubes, sometimes two bricks, and at other times a brick in her right hand and a cube in her left. A child has to recognize the form and remember the position assigned to the different objects throughout the exercise. This seemed to me to be a very difficult task for a three-year-old child.

As I watched her, though, I noticed that she not only carried out the exercise with ease, but that she did not need to distinguish the objects by feeling all around them. She took up two objects at once and handled them with a light touch, since she was graceful and refined in her actions. If the brick was in her right hand and the cube in her left, she immediately exchanged them and then only began the laborious task of stroking them with her hand as she had been taught, and which she regarded as her duty. But she had already recognized the objects by simply touching them lightly, that is, she identified them just as soon as she picked them up. Reflecting on this later, I came to realize that the child was functionally ambidextrous. This is very common among three- or four-year-old children, but it later disappears. I then had other children repeat the exercise and learned that they also recognized the objects before touching them all over, and this was often the case even among the younger children. Our educational methods thus provided the children with wonderful experiences in making comparisons and led them on to a surprising facility in forming judgments.

These exercises for the stereognostic sense can be widely extended. They are a great delight to the children since they are not concerned with the perception of a single stimulus, such as that of heat, but rather with the reconstruction of a whole, well-known object. They can stroke toy soldiers, marbles, and especially money. They ultimately gain the ability to distinguish objects that are small and closely related, like bird-seed and rice.

Children are proud of being able to "see" without using their eyes. Holding out their hands, they will shout: "Here are my eyes, I see with my hands, I no longer need eyes!" And I often answer their happy cries by saying: "Well! let's get rid of our eyes! What else can we do?" This causes them to break out in laughter and cheers.

Our little children surpassed our anticipations and really surprised us with their unexpected progress. At times they seemed to be almost mad with joy, and this made us reflect deeply upon them.

Later on the children of their own accord discovered one of the most interesting exercises now carried out in Children's Houses. They systematically began to use over again all the material which lent itself to recognition by touch: the solid insets, the geometric plaques, and the three series of blocks. Children who had already some time before passed on to higher exercises returned to take up the three series of solid insets and, blindfolding their eyes, touched the cylinders and corresponding insets, frequently taking all three of the containers and mixing up the cylinders of the three different series. Or they took up the geometrical plaques and, with their eyes closed, carefully and thoughtfully touched their different edges and felt for the corresponding shape among the frames. Very often the children sat down on their rugs and repeatedly touched the long rods, running their fingers from top to bottom, as if to determine the extent of movements made by their arms. Or they would gather the blocks for the pink tower about them and construct it with their eyes blindfolded.

Muscular exercise, therefore, is a kind of repetition of a child's education, which, through sight, as will be described later, leads to an exact appreciation of different shapes and sizes found in various objects.

Training the Senses of Taste and Smell

It is not easy to make the exercises connected with these senses attractive. I can only say that exercises like those commonly used in psychometry do not seem to me to be suitable and practicable, at least for very small children.

Our second attempt was therefore to organize games for the senses which the children could repeat by themselves. We had a child smell fresh violets and jasmine; or, late in May, we used the roses gathered for the flower vases. We then blindfolded a child, saying to him: "Now we are going to give you something—some flowers." Another child would bring a bunch of violets close to his nose and he would have to recognize them. Then, as a test of the strength of an odor, he was offered a single flower, or a quantity of them.

Then we decided it would be easier to let the environment do much of this educational work. Scents for exercising the sense of smell must first of all to be present; and since these, unlike sights and sounds, are not necessarily at hand, we decided to sprinkle perfumes systematically about with the idea of making them progressively more delicate.

Some sachets decorated with Chinese motifs were hung on the walls as ornaments. Flowers and herbs from the garden and soaps scented with such natural fragrances as almond and lavender were arranged about the children. Only later, after we had laid out little plots of fragrant herbs to attract the children's attention with this green garden as we did with pretty flowers, did we discover that the greatest interest in searching for different scents is to be found in children about three years old. To our astonishment, the children brought us herbs which we had not planted and which we did not know were scented; but when the children insisted that we smell them, we discovered that they actually did possess a delicate fragrance.

A plot of ground so planted that there is a uniformity of color and only slight differences in the shapes of the plants helps to isolate the materials useful for exercising the sense of smell. It thus becomes a center of "research." When a child's attention is directed in an orderly fashion towards the exercise of his various senses, even the sense of smell becomes more "intelligent," and thus also an instrument for the exploration of his environment.

But even still smaller children, by their ability to choose or refuse different types of food, showed us that the sense of smell is a natural assistant to the sense of taste in eating. This aspect of a child's training is connected with his nutritional life, but it is so delicate that it deserves a special treatment. When we recalled the fact that the sense of taste is based upon the ability to identify four simple flavors, we came to the conclusion that a natural time for the training of a child's sense of smell was at his meals.

The children become quite interested in distinguishing different tastes and coming to recognize the four basic flavors. Sweet and salt are both pleasant, but even bitter is tried as an experiment, and sour, especially in various fruits, is distinguished in various degrees.

Once interest has been aroused in tastes and their definite limitations, the world of fragrances is more clearly distinguished in its countless varieties of mixed sensations of taste and smell experienced in eating and drinking, as for example, in milk, fresh or dried bread, soup, fruit, and so forth. And the tactile sensations of the tongue, which arise from contact with sticky, oily, and other types of substances, are distinguished from the sensations of taste and smell through an effort of the mind which is a real exploration of oneself and one's environment.

Five-year-old children were suitable subjects for having their tongues touched with specific solutions of bitter, sour, sweet, and salt. They lent themselves to this research as though it were a game, and they took delight in rinsing out their mouths, without suspecting that they were being subjected to experiments clothed by adults with the august mantle of science. In the meantime the smaller children were seriously engaged in seeking out those fragrances which nature had bestowed upon the tiny plants of the fields.

8. Visual and Auditory Distinctions

Material: Solid Insets and Blocks

Perfecting the Perception of Dimensions by Sight Alone

Various series of materials show differences in dimensions: the first is concerned solely with differences of one dimension, height; the second shows a graduated distinction in two dimensions, area; the third takes up the differences in all three dimensions.

Solid Insets

These consist in four well-varnished blocks of naturally colored hardwood having the same size and shape (22″ long, 2″ high, 3″ wide). Each block holds ten smooth cylindrical insets, which are easily slipped in and out of their individually corresponding holes by means of a knob on their tops.

The container with its different cylinders looks like an ordinary set of weights for a scale.

The dimensions of the cylinders are regularly graduated:

1) In the first container, the cylinders all have the same diameter but different heights. These vary from $\frac{3}{16}″$ to $1\frac{7}{8}″$, with regular increases in height of $\frac{3}{16}″$ in each of the ten cylinders.

2) In the second container the cylinders all have the same height but regularly decreasing diameters. The graduated difference is again $\frac{3}{16}″$, and the diameters of the cylinders vary from $\frac{3}{16}″$ to $1\frac{7}{8}″$.

3) In the third container both the height and diameter are

123

gradually diminished, thus combining the differences of the other two sets.

On principle, a child uses only one set at a time. This means that three children can be engaged in the exercise at once.

The exercise is the same for all three insets. They are placed on a little table and all the pieces are removed and scrambled together, and then an attempt is made to replace them all in their proper places. (The exercise is so basic that three little tables should be prepared for it with recesses for the removable cylinders.) In the exact correspondence between the cylinder and the space of its container is to be found the "control of error."

As a matter of fact, if a child, for example, makes a mistake when using the first set, one of the cylinders will disappear within a hole that is too keep for it and another will stick out because the hole is too shallow. The resulting irregularity, which is both tangible and visible, becomes an absolute control over the mistake made. The consequence of this is that the objects must be carefully put back into their places and their positions must be repeatedly noticed so that all are in their proper places at the same level in the stand.

Still more evident is the mistake made with a set of the second type. The cylinders are all of the same height, but their diameters gradually diminish in size. There are thus instead of longer and shorter cylinders those that are wider and narrower. If a child takes one of the cylinders by its knob and places it in a hole too large for it, the error may pass unnoticed, and he will continue to place cylinders in holes that are too large for them. He can thus think for a time that he is doing well, but in the end there will be a cylinder left over that cannot be fitted into the still empty hole.

The mistake is so obvious that it immediately destroys the child's earlier illusion. His attention is brought sharply to bear upon an obvious problem.

He must take out all the wrongly placed cylinders and put each one of them back in its proper place.

We now come to the third type of insets. Here the cylinders vary in size according to both their dimensions. Not only are the diameters gradually diminished as in the second type, but their heights are also lessened. The result is that each of the cylinders, from the smallest to the largest, has the same shape but different dimensions. These insets provide an exercise analogous to the other two and also a control of error.

The three series of insets, which are at first indistinguishable from each other, reveal their least differences to a child who uses them, and all three create an increasing interest in a child as he learns how to use them. There naturally follows as the result of the repetition of this exercise a sharpening of the eye in making distinctions, a greater keenness in observation, and a greater attentiveness in carrying out a systematic operation; and this in turn stimulates the reasoning power, which notices and corrects its errors. It may almost be said that it lays hold of the child's personality through the senses and affords him a constant and far-reaching exercise.

The Blocks

Three differently appearing sets of blocks repeat the observations made of graduations in one, two, and three dimensions.

These consist in three series of large, brightly-painted pieces of wood. They create three systems which we have called: the system of rods and lengths, the system of prisms, and the system of blocks.

The rods, which are painted red, have identical square cross sections measuring $\frac{3}{4}'' \times \frac{3}{4}''$. They vary in length, however, from $4''$ to $40''$ with graduated differences of $4''$.

The handling of such long, unwieldy objects entails the movement of the child's whole body. He has to go back and forth carrying these rods and place them next to each other according to their length, thus creating an over-all appearance of organ pipes.

The place for carrying out this exercise is on the floor, but before a child begins it, he spreads out a carpet large enough for himself and the material. After he has arranged the rods to look like the pipes of an organ, he separates them, mixes them up, and rearranges them as often as he finds pleasure in doing this.

A similar exercise which consists in arranging a series of dark brown colored prisms is also carried out on a carpet. The prisms are all of an equal length ($7\frac{1}{2}''$) but have graduated cross sections. The largest of these has a base measuring 3¾" and the smallest ⅜". The prisms are arranged next to each other from the largest to the smallest so that they resemble a staircase.

Finally, there is a series of cubes diminishing in size from 3¾" to ⅜". These blocks are of a bright pink color and represent objects differing according to three dimensions, from largest to smallest. The largest cube is first placed on the carpet, then the second largest upon it. This is continued until a kind of tower has been built. When the tower is demolished it is reconstructed.

Effort and Muscular Memory

The children pick up the blocks with one hand. A child three or three-and-a-half years old can only with difficulty grasp a block that is 3¾" square with his hand. Moreover, these blocks, and a prism 7½" long, are heavy for a child. He must therefore make an effort with his little hand, and this stretches and strengthens it. After making repeated use of the brown blocks, a child's hand finally adopts automatically the precise position necessary for covering a space of 3¾, 3⅜, 3, 2⅝, 2¼, 1⅞, 1½, 1⅛, ¾, or ⅜ inches. In other words, a child develops a muscular memory for definite graduations of space. This is repeated by means of the red blocks. Here there is a further means of improvement. A smaller block should rest on the next largest so that it is centered upon it, leaving a border ³⁄₁₆" wide around on all sides. To achieve this a child's hand and arm must carry out the intended movement. The most difficult of the blocks to place in position is the smallest, which is ⅜" on each side. A child's arm has to be quite steady to place this small object on the center of the next largest block, and this is apparent from a child's close attention and obvious efforts in performing the task.

Without doubt it is the sense of sight which most benefits from the exercises with the solid insets and the blocks. Little by little the children begin to make distinctions which they had not previously noticed.

Further, if the three insets are used together and the children make a triangle of them, placing the cylinders from the three different series in the center all mixed together, they provide a more complex exercise of memory and reason. A child must recall the series to which the insets belong and consequently the container which will receive them. This is what comprises the fascination of the exercises. A child earnestly applies his intelligence to the task before him and carries out those naturally pleasing efforts of which he is capable.

It is also the eye that is particularly exercised in recognizing the various sizes of the blocks and, consequently, in discovering chance errors, such as rods out of place, an irregularity in a series of steps, or a tower with a bulge in it due to a large cube being placed between two smaller ones. Such errors strike the eye, which is also attracted by the brilliant colors. Everything is done to make the eye recognize an error and the hand correct it.

Motor activity is something that accompanies these exercises of the eye. Sometimes this consists in the handling of small objects to be removed, such as the cylinders from the solid insets, sometimes in carrying and setting in place large blocks of wood. The exercise of the senses is, therefore, carried out by movements which are directed towards some intelligible goal.

This movement, with the help of observations already made, assists a child in concentrating upon the repetition of an exercise.

A mathematical proportion may be found in the relative differences in the three different series of blocks.

As a matter of fact the ten rods have a relation to another of a series of numbers:

$$1, 2, 3, 4, 5, 6, 7, 8, 9, 10$$

The ten prisms, which all have the same length, vary in their cross sections and correspond to the squares of the numbers:

$$1^2, 2^2, 3^2, 4^2, 5^2, 6^2, 7^2, 8^2, 9^2, 10^2.$$

Finally, the ten cubes with their three different dimensions stand in relationship to the cubes of the numbers:

$$1^3, 2^3, 3^3, 4^3, 5^3, 6^3, 7^3, 8^3, 9^3, 10^3.$$

Actually a child has only a sensible appreciation of these proportions, but his mind is trained on the basic data that prepares the way for mathematics.

A child finds that of all the exercises those with the blocks, where the differences are greatest, are the easiest, and the exercises with the rods, where the differences are least, are the most difficult.

In his elementary classes, when he takes up arithmetic and geometry he will again have an interest in the blocks of his early childhood, and he will restudy them according to their relative proportions with the help of the science of numbers.

Color Materials

After a long series of trials with normal children I have decided upon the following material to assist children in the recognition of colors, that is, in the training of their chromatic sense. (In institutions for defective children, I used, as mentioned above, insets of wood made up into many series of round colored plaques.) The material finally selected consists of tablets around which are wound threads of brightly colored silk. The tablets have at their extremities a double-faced ridge so that the colors will not touch the table and, also, so that they can be handled without touching the colored thread. The colors thus remain intact for a long time.

I have chosen nine colors, each of which has seven different grades of intensity. There are thus sixty-three colored tablets. The colors are as follows: grey (from black to white), red, orange, yellow, green, blue, violet, brown, and pink.

Exercises: Three colors in their brightest shades are picked out, for example, red, blue, and yellow. A double set of these are placed on the table before the child. He is shown one color and invited to look for its match in the mixture. After he had found it, he places it alongside its mate. The tablets are thus set out in columns two by two, being paired according to colors. A gradual increase is then made in the number of colored tablets shown to the child until all nine colors, that is, eighteen tablets are presented to him. Finally, instead of the liveliest colors the dullest are chosen.

The child is then given two or three tablets of the same color but of different intensity, for example the brightest, the darkest, and one in between in the same series. He must arrange them according to their shades until he can finally arrange all seven of them.

Then the various shades of two different colors, for example red and blue, are successively placed before the child all mixed up. He must separate the two series and arrange each according to its intensity. He then goes on to pick out colors that are more alike, for example, blue and violet, yellow and orange, and so forth.

In one of the Children's Houses I have seen the following game carried out with great success and surprising speed. The directress places on a table as many series of graded colors as there are children seated around it, for example, three. The teacher has each one of the children carefully note the color that belongs to him or which he has chosen. She then mixes all the different groups of colors on the table. Each of the children then rapidly selects from the complex all the gradations of his particular color. He stacks these up and then proceeds to align the pieces according to their various intensities and thus creates the appearance of a ribbon with its colors fading away.

In another house I have seen the children take the entire box of sixty-three colors, turn it over on a table, and mix up the tablets for a long time. They then quickly regrouped the colors according to their intensities and thus created a kind of beautifully shaded carpet upon the table.

Children acquire a skill in this with an astounding rapidity. Three-year-old children can put together all the various shades of the colors.

One can test a child's memory for colors by having him look at one color and then advising him to go and choose a similar color from a distant table where all the colors are laid out in order. Children succeed in this exercise and make few errors. It is children of five years who are amused by this final exercise. They take great pleasure in comparing two shades and deciding upon their identity or not.

Sensorial Knowledge of Geometry

Plane Insets and Geometrical Shapes

The first material: flat insets of wood, their history. At the school for defective children I had insets made, modeling them upon those used by my illustrious predecessors. These were made from two flat pieces of wood, one on top of the other, the lower being solid but the upper with different shapes and figures cut into it. Within the resultant hollows the children had to place corresponding pieces of wood. These were equipped with bronze knobs to make them easier to handle.

Seguin made use of a star, a rectangle, a square, a triangle, and a circle. These were painted in different colors so that each shape had its own color. And the hollow spaces for these insets were all on the same wooden board.

In my school for defectives I increased the number of examples and separated the materials to be used for colors from those for shapes. The insets for the colors were all circular whereas those for the different forms were all of the same color (blue). I had a great number of plaques of many graded colors made, and I kept continuously adding to the figures affixed to the same rigid plank that kept them together.

But since then, in my dealing with normal children, after various attempts I have completely excluded flat insets for colors since material of this type does not provide any control of error; a child covers, and thus conceals, the color he is comparing.

Definitive Material. On the other hand, I have kept the flat insets for the discernment of shapes but have modified the material by separating the figures from each other. Each of the objects to be inserted is given its own simple frame.

Each one of the insets in its square, rectangular, circular, triangular, trapezoidal, oval, or other shape is painted a bright blue, whereas the separate square frames for the individual plaques are all of the same size and painted white. The pieces can thus be arranged in different combinations and the number of groupings increased, since it is easy to place one square frame next to nother.

In order to keep the groups together, I have had wooden containers or frames made. These are large enough to hold six squares for a corresponding number of figures, three in each of two separate rows. The blue background of these wooden frames comes into view when the plaques are removed from their individual frames. The outline that is thus revealed is therefore identical in shape and color with the plaques themselves.

For the very first exercises I had a frame built with a rectangular area of the same dimensions (within the molding) as that of the containers for the plaques already described. The dark blue interior was surrounded by a raised border about ⅛″ high and ¾″ wide. On this border there was hinged a frame made up of wooden strips about ¼″ thick crossed in such a way as to fit exactly over the other below it, dividing the latter into six equal squares by one cross, and two longitudinal strips. This open cover swings on a small hinge and is fastened in front with a small pin.

Six individual frames, 4″ square and ¼″ thick, thus fit exactly on the blue background and are held securely in place by the lattice work closed over them. Since this open cover holds the squares firmly in place, the frame may be freely handled as a unit.

This container has the further advantage over the others already described of making it possible to combine various different geometrical figures by changing the individual frames. It also guarantees the immobility of these same pieces.

The border and the inner and outer edges of the frame are painted in white enamel. The pieces to be imbedded within the frame, that is, the flat geometrical figures, are painted blue like the bottom of the frame itself.

I also had four solid squares painted the same blue color made, and by using them I could adapt the frame so that it held one, two, three, four, or five geometrical figures instead of six. The reason for this was that for the first lessons it is much better to set out only two or three contrasting figures, or at least those of a widely diverging shape, such as, for example, a circle and a square, or a circle, a square, and an equilateral triangle.

In this way various combinations can be set out.

I then had a cabinet made with six drawers. This can be of cardboard or wood. It consists essentially of a box, the front part of which can be lowered like the boxes used by lawyers, and six trays, one on top of the other, resting on small side supports. On the first tray were placed the four full plaques and two plaques for a trapezoid and a rhombus. On the second tray was a square and five rectangles of the same height but of diminishing width. On the third there were six circles of decreasing diameter, on the fourth six triangles, on the fifth plaques of polygonal shapes ranging from five to ten sides, and on the sixth various curved figures, such as ellipses, ovals, and a floral design (four crossed arches).

The three series of cards. Added to this material are square white cards measuring about 5½ ″ on each side. On one series of these is glued a geometrical figure of blue paper corresponding to the blue of the insets. They are of the same size and shape as that of all the various geometrical figures of the collection. On the second series of cards is likewise glued the outline, also in blue, of the same geometrical figures. The outline itself has a thickness of ¼ ″. A third series of cards contains the forms drawn in black showing the size and shape of the figures. This concept is found in Seguin.

The material thus consists in the frame, the various plaques, and the three series of cards.

Exercise with the Insets. This consists in giving a child the frame with its different figures, taking out the pieces, spreading them around, mixing them up on the table, and inviting the child to return them to their proper places.

This is a game suitable for children who are still under three years of age. It has a great attraction for a child, but will not hold them as long as the solid insets. I have never seen the exercise repeated more than five or six times in succession.

As a matter of fact, a child devotes a great deal of energy to this exercise. He must recognize the shape of an object and examine it at length. Many children at first only succeed after several attempts in putting the pieces in their proper places. They try, for example, to put a triangle successively into a space for a trapezoid, a rectangle, and so forth. Or, when they take up a rectangle and recognize the place where it should go, they set the long side against the short, and it is only after many attempts that they succeed in putting it exactly in place. After three or four successful attempts a child very easily recognizes the geometrical figures and places the insets where they belong with a confidence that is accompanied by an air of indifference and contempt for an exercise that is too easy.

It is at this time that a child can advance to a methodical

examination of the various shapes, changing the plaques on his table at will and going from contrasted shapes to analogous ones. The exercise then becomes easy for the child since he has become accustomed to recognizing the figures and putting them back in their respective places without trial or effort.

During the first period, which is one of trial and error, a child is presented with figures of contrasting shapes. His recognition of these is greatly helped when his visual perceptions are associated with those of touch. I have a child touch with the index finger of his right hand the outline of these figures as well as the inner edge of the plaques that contain them and which have as a consequence the same shape as the pieces themselves. I take care that this becomes a habit for the child. Practically, this is easy to do since children love to touch things. Some children who cannot as yet recognize a shape by looking at it can do so when they touch it, that is, when they go through the motions necessary to follow its outline. They get worried when they turn a piece around in every direction as they vainly try to put it in its place; but just as soon as they touch the outlines of the piece and of the molding that contains it, they succeed in their endeavors. There can be no doubt that an association of the kinesthetic with the visual sense is of great assistance in the perception of shapes and in the fixing of them in the memory.

Just as in the case of the solid insets, the control over such exercises is absolute. A particular figure cannot be put anywhere except within its own corresponding recessed plaque. A child therefore can carry the exercise out by himself and perfect his perception of various shapes.

Exercises with the Three Series of Cards

First Series. A child is given some cards on which figures have been painted or glued and inset pieces, that is, the central figures inserted into the plaques in the previous exercise. These are all mixed up and the child must lay the cards out in a row on the table (this amuses him greatly) and then place the pieces over them. Here control is exercised by the eye. The child must recognize the shape and set the piece over it exactly so that it conceals the figure on the card. The child's eye here corresponds to the border which has hitherto physically controlled the fitting of the pieces together. Further, the child must develop the habit of touching the outline of the solid figure as a simple exercise (and a child is always willing to carry out such movements). After he has covered the figure on the card he again feels all around the border of the inset as if he were perfecting the matching of the two shapes with his finger.

Second Series. A pile of cards with figures outlined on them by means of blue stripes are given to a child and solid figures corresponding to those on the cards.

Third Series. The child is given cards on which the figures are simply outlined in black and the corresponding pieces as above.

The child is therefore trained to interpret the outlines of the drawn figures with his eye, and his hand is prepared for drawing them through the motions made by his fingers in tracing their outlines.

Exercises For Distinguishing Sounds

Training in the hearing of sounds brings us in a special way to the relationship that exists between a person and a mobile environment, the only kind that can produce sounds and noises. Where everything is at rest there is nothing but absolute silence. Hearing is therefore a sense which can receive impressions only from movements going on about a subject.

Training in hearing must begin with silence as it departs from immobility to go on the perception of sounds and noises caused by movement.

Later we shall explain the manifold, important aspects of silence for our method. It becomes the controlling factor in the voluntary restriction of the movements that give rise to various sounds.

Silence is also a means of procuring collective efforts, since in order to obtain it everything, or everybody, that it embraces must be completely motionless.

There can be no doubt that the attempt to procure silence should create a lively interest among children, as it actually does. They are pleased with its quest and with knowing the means to obtain it.

The sense of hearing also provides us with a clear concept

of the basic principle for the training of the senses. This consists in the ability to hear better.

We hear better, that is, with greater acuteness, when we notice lighter sounds than we did before. The training of the senses therefore leads to an appreciation of the least stimuli, and the smaller the thing is that is perceived, the greater is the capacity of the sense. Training of the senses therefore essentially assists the minimal perception of external stimuli.

For example, as Itard has so well shown, a person who is half deaf can be trained to perceive slighter sounds than those which he would have heard if he had been left to himself, that is, if he had not been trained; and he can gradually be led on to perceive ordinary noises which one with normal hearing can hear without such training.

Basing his work on this principle, Itard, by using a succession of stimuli going from strong to weak, taught many who were half deaf how to hear others when they spoke, and therefore how to speak themselves. He thus cured a great number of deaf people.

Another principle in the training of the senses is that of distinguishing differences among the stimuli.

In order to help others in this regard one must know how to classify the different kinds of sensations and note their graduated differences.

We can first of all make a distinction between sounds and noises, beginning with notable differences and going on to those that are almost imperceptible. We can then proceed to the different qualities of sound, depending upon their origins, whether, for example, they are those of a person who is speaking or of a musical instrument. Finally, we can distinguish the tones of the musical scale.

To sum up and categorize these fundamental distinctions, we shall indicate four classes of sounds: silence, the human voice, noise, and musical tones.

Lessons in silence are separate independent exercises and are a great help in maintaining discipline.

An analysis of the sounds of speech is intimately connected with the learning of the alphabet.

For the studying of noises, we have in our present system some rather simple and elementary material. This consists in boxes of wood (or cardboard). These boxes are made in pairs and are so constructed that a series of them will produce graduated noises. Just as with the other sense materials, the boxes are jumbled together and then paired off according to the noise they produce when struck. Then by judging the differences among the boxes in one series a child attempts to put them in a graduated order.

For the training of the musical sense, we have adopted a series of bells which Anna Maccheroni had made with a great deal of care. Each one of the bells is mounted on a separate stand. They constitute a group of objects which seem to be identical but which, when struck with a little hammer, reproduce the following notes.

Thus the only perceptible difference is one of sound.

The individual bells, which come in a double series, can be moved about. They can therefore be mixed up just as the other objects used in the training of the senses.

The first exercise consists in moving the bells about by their stands and ringing them with a little hammer so that the two bells producing the same sound can be placed next to each other (the half tones are here excluded). Next there is an evaluation of tones according to their order on the musical scale. For this the teacher places a series of bells in the desired order and leaves the other series all mixed up. The exercise again consists in pairing off the bells, that is, it is carried out by ringing one of the bells in the prearranged series and then striking the other bells in order to pick out its mate. Pairing is here thus carried out according to a predetermined order.

When a child's ear has been sufficiently trained to recognize and remember the succession of simple sounds on the musical scale, he can then arrange the bells in order according to the diatonic scale without any external assistance, but simply through the guidance of his own musical ear. And he may even be able to put in the half tones.

As in the case of the other systems, the name of a sensation is given as soon as it has been clearly perceived.

Just as a child learns that a thing is smooth, rough, red, blue, and so forth, so here also he learns the names of the notes as soon as he has learned how to distinguish them with accuracy.

The utmost that a child of six or seven can attain is the identification and naming of an isolated note.

The half tones are added to the whole tones, and in order not to waste a child's energy, they are identifiable by the bell stand. For the half tone this is black instead of white, in other words, the bell stands resemble the keys of a piano. The exercise with these half tones consists in placing them in their proper places with respect to the whole notes.[1]

There is no need of confusing the training of the musical sense with musical education as such.

The exercise in identifying tones can be carried out without entering in any way into the field of music. This is just as true here as in the study of physics, where musical vibrations are investigated.

The exercise of the senses provides a necessary foundation for a musical education. A child who has engaged in such exercises is eminently prepared for listening to music and can therefore make more rapid progress in it.

But it is not necessary to maintain that music itself will continue and strengthen the training of the senses anymore than that the study of painting will continue training in the perception of colors. Nevertheless, a foundation for further development is laid that can be invaluable for further progress.

Silence

In ordinary schools it is always thought that silence is to be obtained by command.

No thought is given to the meaning of the word. There is no realization that there is a need of immobility and, as it were, of a suspension of life for a moment of silence to be realized. Silence consists in the suspension of every movement and is not, as it is generally thought to be in schools, a

[1] In these exercises with the bells the greatest number of repetitions of the same exercise in a single cycle of six and seven has been two hundred.

suspension of the din added to the ordinary noises tolerated in an environment.

In ordinary schools silence means a stoppage of noise, a cessation of a reaction, a negation of disorder and confusion.

Yet, on the other hand, silence can be positively understood as a state transcending the ordinary run of things. It is a momentary check requiring an effort, a straining of the will, which separates and isolates the soul from the ordinary sounds of life and external voices.

This is a silence which we have attained in our schools. It is a profound silence produced in a class of more than forty little children between the ages of three and six. A command would never be able to produce the marvelous union of wills in checking every act in a period of life when movement seems natural and irresistible. And this collective action is attained by the very children who have been accustomed to act on their own account in their quest for inner satisfaction.

But children must be taught silence. I therefore make them go through various exercises in silence, which add greatly to the remarkable ability of our children in discipline themselves.

I attract the attention of the children to myself as I become silent.

I take various positions. I stand or sit silent and motionless. The moving of a finger could produce a noise even if it were imperceptible. I could breathe so as to be heard, but no, everything is absolutely silent. This is not easy. I call a child and invite him to act as I do. He moves one of his feet to a more comfortable position, and this makes a noise. He moves an arm, brushing it imperceptibly against the arm of his chair, and there is a sound. His breathing is not yet as completely silent, peaceful, and unnoticed as my own.

During these maneuvers and my brief but earnest words that interrupt this silence and immobility, the children remain fascinated as they look and listen. Very many become interested in a fact which they have never before observed, namely, that there are so many noises which they do not notice, and that there are different degrees of silence. There is an absolute silence, where nothing, absolutely nothing moves. They look at me in amazement when I stop directly in the center of the room and seem not to be really there.

Then all strive to imitate me and attempt to do the same. I notice that here and there a foot moves almost inadvertently. The attention of the children is drawn to every part of the body in their eager desire to attain immobility. As they proceed in their efforts, there actually is produced a silence different from that which is superficially called silence. It seems that life gradually disappears, that the room little by little becomes empty, as if there were no longer anyone present. Then they begin to hear the tick-tock of the clock upon the wall, and this tick-tock seems gradually to increase in intensity as the silence becomes absolute. From outside in the courtyard, which has seemed silent till now, come different sounds, the chirping of a bird or the walk of a child. The children are fascinated by this silence as by a real conquest which they have made. "See," the directress says, "now everything is quiet as if there were no longer anyone here."

When the children had attained such a degree of silence, I would close and darken the windows, and then say to them: "Now listen to a little voice that calls you by name."

Then from a neighboring room behind the children I would whisper through the open door drawing out the syllables as if I were calling someone across a mountain valley, and this faint voice seemed to reach the hearts of the children and appeal to their souls. Each one as he was called rose up silently, trying not to move his chair, and walked on tip-toe so as not to be heard. Nevertheless, his passage could be noticed in the absolute silence which was never broken because of the continued immobility of all the others. And he would reach the door with a happy face, make a few jumps in the neighboring room, and suppress little bursts of laughter; or he would cling to my dress, or look at his companions who were still anxiously waiting in silence. A call was considered to be a privilege, a gift, a reward, although each one knew that he would be called, beginning with the one who was the quietest in the room. Thus each one strove to earn through perfect waiting a definite call. I have seen a three-year-old girl attempt to stop a sneeze and succeed in doing it! She held her breath in her tiny breast and resisted until she had won out.

Little children are fascinated by games of this sort. Their intent gaze and patient immobility reveal their expectation of some great delight. At first, when I had not yet understood the soul of a child, I thought of showing sweets and little toys to the children, promising to give them to the one who was called. I imagined that gifts were needed to obtain such efforts from children. But very soon I was forced to admit that this was useless.

The children, after making these efforts and experiencing the joys of silence, were like ships sailing into port. They were happy about everything, about having learned something new, about having won a victory. This was their recompense. They forgot the promised sweets and did not bother to take the objects which I had imagined would attract them. I thus gave up these idle incentives and saw to my amazement that when the game was repeated it was carried out with ever increasing perfection, so that three-year-old children remained motionless in the silence during all the time it took to summon more than forty others out of the room. Then I realized that the soul of a child also has its spiritual joys and rewards. After such exercises it seemed that they loved me the more. Certainly they became more obedient, more sweet and gentle. We had become isolated from the world and had passed some minutes together in union with each other. During that time I had longed for, and called, them; and they had in turn heard in the deepest silence that voice which was directly personally to the one judged to be the best of all at the moment of call.

The Lesson in Silence. The following is an example of a highly successful lesson in teaching perfection in silence. One day, as I was going to a Children's House, I met in the courtyard a woman who was carrying her four-month-old daughter in her arms. The child was wrapped up in swaddling bands as was still customary in Rome, where little infants wrapped up tight in this manner are called *pupi* (cocoons). The tiny, tranquil girl seemed to be the incarnation of peace.

I took her into my arms, and she lay there quietly. I moved on with her still in my arms. The children of the house had run out to greet me as they were accustomed to do and flung their arms about my knees with such violence that they almost threw me to the ground. I smiled at them and showed them the "cocoon." They became interested and jumped up and down, looking at me with eyes sparkling with delight, but they did not touch me through respect for the infant in my arms. I thus entered into the room, and the children walked around me. We took our seats. I chose a high chair directly in front of them, and not one of the little stools that I was accustomed to use. In other words, I sat down with a certain amount of solemnity. The children looked at the infant with mixed feelings of tenderness and joy. We had not yet said anything. Then I told them: "I have brought you a little teacher." They looked at me with surprise and laughed. "A little teacher," I continued, "since none of you can be as quiet as she." All the children stiffened at their posts. "But none of you keeps his feet as still as she." They all carefully adjusted their feet to keep them still. I looked at them with a smile: "Yes, but they will never be as quiet as hers. You move your legs a little, and she does not. No one of you can be like her." The children became serious; they almost seemed convinced of the superiority of their little teacher. One of them smiles and seems to indicate with his eyes that this is all due to the swaddling bands. "Moreover, no one can be as silent as she." There is a general silence. "It is impossible to be as silent as she, because ... Hear how gentle is her breathing. Come up on tip-toe." Some of the children rise up and advance very slowly on their toes, stretching out their heads and directing their gaze at the infant. There is a great silence. "No one can breathe as quietly as she." The children gaze in astonishment; they had never before thought that even when they were still they were making noises, and that the silence of little children is more profound than that of those who are larger. They almost tried to stop breathing. I get up. "I am going away quietly, quietly," and I walk away on the tips of my toes without making any noise. "No matter how quietly I go you still hear some noise that I am making. But she, she is going with me and doesn't make a sound; yes, she is leaving and is silent." The children smile, but they are moved. They understand both the truth and the humor of my words. I restore the "cocoon" to her mother through a window.

The little girl leaves behind her a fascination that seems to take possession of their souls. Nothing in nature is sweeter than the silent breathing of the newly born. In comparison with it, Wordsworth's observation on the silent peace of nature fades away: "How calm, how quiet! One single sound, the drip from the suspended oar." And even children feel the poetry of the silence of a tranquil, newborn human life.[1]

---

[1] This silence has become one of the best known characteristics of the Montessori method. It has been adopted in many schools and has succeeded in bringing to them something of the Montessori spirit. It was through her influence that the "silence of immobility" has penetrated even into public manifestations of a political and social order.

9. Generalizations on the Training of the Senses

The method of training the senses of normal children from three to six years of age which I have just explained certainly does not represent everything that can be done in this regard, but it does open up, I believe, a new path for very fruitful psychological investigations.

Up until now experimental psychology has aimed at perfecting instruments for the taking of measurements, that is, for determining different degrees of intensity in stimulants. But there has not been a serious attempt to prepare a systematic method for training the senses of individuals. Yet I believe that psychometry should be more concerned with the development of the individual than of the instrument.

But prescinding here from these matters of purely scientific interest, we may say that the training of the senses is a matter of the greatest importance in education.

As a matter of fact, we have a two-fold aim in education. One is biological and the other social. The biological objective is to assist the natural development of the individual; the social objective consists in preparing the individual for his environment, and this also embraces professional education, which teaches an individual how to make use of his surroundings. The training of the senses is, in fact, of utmost importance on both counts. The development of the senses actually precedes that of the higher intellectual faculties, and in a child between the ages of three and six it constitutes his formative period.

We can therefore assist the development of the senses during this very period by graduating and adapting the stimuli to which a child is exposed just as we should assist him in learning how to speak before his speech is completely developed.

143

The education of early childhood should be based entirely upon this principle: Assist the natural development of the child.

The other aspect of education, namely, that of adapting an individual to his environment, will be more important later on, when the period of intensive development will have passed. The two elements are always interlaced, but the dominance of one over the other depends upon a person's age.

As we know, the period of life extending between the years of three and six is marked by rapid physical growth and the development of the psychic faculties. During these years a child develops his senses, and his attention is therefore directed towards his environment.

He is attracted more by stimuli than by reason. During this period he should therefore be methodically exposed to stimuli that will develop his senses rationally and thus lay the foundation for his mental powers.

Further, through the education of the senses it is possible to discover and correct positive defects which would otherwise pass unnoticed, or would only become apparent after they had become so serious that it would no longer be possible for a child to adapt himself to his surroundings because of his deafness, for example, or his poor sight.

It is therefore a child's physiological education that directly prepares the way for his psychic development by perfecting his sense organs and his habits of projection and association.

But the other aspect of education, that which enables an individual to adapt himself to his environment, is also indirectly affected. At the present day men are greatly concerned with observing their environment, since they must use its riches to their utmost extent.

Art, today, as it was in ancient Greece, is also based upon the observation of truth. The positive sciences advance through observation, and all the discoveries made during the last century and their practical applications, which have done so much to transform the world, have followed along this same road. We should therefore engender this attitude in the oncoming generation, since it is necessary for modern civil life and an indispensable means for continuing the work of human progress.

Some of the results of observations in our own time have

been the discovery of X-rays, radioactivity, and telecommunications. The discovery of radium has led to new concepts of matter itself.

The training of the senses, insofar as it makes a man an observer, not only fulfills the generic function of adapting him to the contemporary mode of civilization, but it also prepares him for the exigencies of life.

I believe that up until now we have not been very practical in our approaches to concrete problems. We start with theories and then go on to carry them out in practice. Education, for example, has always attempted to teach through an intellectual approach and then gone on to action. As a rule when we teach we talk about objects that interest us and try to induce a pupil to carry out some task connected with them. But frequently a student, even after he has understood something, finds it enormously difficult to execute a task he is expected to perform, since his education lacks a factor of prime importance—the perfecting of his sensations.

A few examples can bring this out. We tell a cook to buy some fresh fish. She understands the command and sets about executing it. But if she does not have her nose and eyes trained to recognize freshness in fish she will not be able to carry out the order received.

Such a deficiency is even more evident in the kitchen itself. A cook may be able to read and be perfectly familiar with the measures and times set down in a cookbook. She may know how to make the movements necessary to mold the various dishes and so forth, but when the time comes to test by smell the right moment to begin cooking or to decide by sight or taste when a certain seasoning should be added, her performance will break down if her senses have not been adequately prepared. She will have to attain this ability through long practice, and such practice is no more than a late training of the senses, which in adults is frequently no longer effective.

The same can be said of manual labor and, in general, of all the arts and crafts. Everyone must acquire skills through repeated exercises. And learning of this sort includes a training of the senses that must be taken up at a later age. For example, spinners have to learn how to use their sense of touch to distinguish threads; weavers and embroiderers have to acquire a notable keenness of vision in order to be able to distinguish details in their work, especially differences in colors.

Finally, to learn a craft, especially if it is of an artistic or refined nature, means that one must develop his senses and the movements of his hands, and these movements are assisted by a consequent refinement of the sense of touch.

If training of this sort is undertaken at an age when the formative period is naturally over, it will be difficult and imperfect. The secret of preparing one for a particular skill consists in utilizing that period of life between the ages of three and six, when there is a natural inclination to perfect one's senses and movements.

This same principle is operative not only with respect to manual labor but also with respect to the higher professions involving some form of practical activity.

The medical profession can provide us with an example. A medical student makes a theoretical study of the pulse and goes to the bedside of a patient with the intent of recognizing its various symptoms. But if his fingers cannot identify its throbbing, his desires and studies will be in vain. He lacks the capacity for discriminating among different sense stimuli that is necessary for a doctor. The same may be said of the sound of heart beats which a student may know in theory but which he cannot in practice distinguish with his ear. The same also may be said of tremblings and flutterings to which a hand is insensitive. The less a doctor is responsive to heat stimuli, the more he needs a thermometer.

It is well known that a doctor may be learned and highly intelligent but not very practical, and that he needs much experience to become so. As a matter of fact, this lengthy experience is nothing more than a belated and often ineffective training of the senses. After he has mastered profound theories, a physician finds himself constrained to undertake the unpleasant task of learning how to recognize symptoms of different diseases in order to put these same theories into fruitful practice. He is therefore like a novice as he methodically proceeds through feeling, tapping, and listening to recognize the vibrations, tones, murmurs, and other sounds that can help him to form a diagnosis. From the uncertainty of recognizing and evaluating symptoms arises a deep discouragement in young doctors and doubts about exercising a profession with such great responsibilities. The whole art of medicine is based on sense activity, but schools prepare physicians through a study of the classics. The intellectual training of a doctor proves to be powerless because of his inadequately trained senses.

One day I heard a surgeon deliver a popular lecture to women on how to recognize the early symptoms of rickets in their children. He wanted to persuade them to take their rickety childern to a doctor at an early stage of the disease when it can still be cured. The women got the idea, but were unable to identify the early deformities since they lacked the sense training that would have enabled them to identify slight deviations from normality. The doctor's lecture thus turned out to be fruitless.

If we reflect upon it, we shall see that almost all adulterations of food are made possible because of the sluggishness of the senses of the masses. Industrial fraud is fostered by the lack of a training of the senses among the people, just as the frauds of a swindler are successful because of the simplicity of his victims. We often see buyers relying upon the honesty of sellers or the integrity of a firm when making purchases. This is due to the fact that they lack the ability to make the judgments by themselves, that is, to distinguish with their senses the specific qualities of the materials they are purchasing.

We maintain, in brief, that the intelligence is frequently rendered useless through lack of practice, and that this practice almost always consists in a training of the senses. In practical life everyone needs to be able to acquire exact knowledge from the stimuli furnished by his environment.

But very often it is difficult to train the senses of adults, just as it is difficult to teach them how to become pianists. The training of the senses must begin in the formative period of life if we wish to perfect them later through education and make use of them in any particular human skill. This is why such training should be begun methodically in childhood and then be continued during the time when an individual is preparing himself through education for the practical life he will have to live.

Otherwise, we isolate a man from his surroundings. In fact, when we think that we are completing a person's education by providing him with an intellectual culture, we are actually making him a contemplative hardly fit for the practi-

cal life of men. And then, when we wish to provide an
education for the practical aspects of life, we limit ourselves
to a life of action and neglect the real foundation of a
practical education which would place us in direct contact
with the external world. And just as professional training
almost always prepares a man to make use of his environment, so it must also make up for the appalling lack in his
earlier education. In other words, after he has finished his
formal education, a professional man must train his senses so
that he comes into direct contact with the surrounding world.

Aesthetic and moral education are also closely connected
with the training of the senses. By multiplying sense experiences and developing the ability to evaluate the smallest
differences in various stimuli, one's sensibilities are refined
and one's pleasures increased. Beauty is found in harmony,
not in discord; and harmony implies affinities, but these
require a refinement of the senses if they are to be perceived.
The beautiful harmonies of nature and of art escape those
whose senses are dull. The world is then cramped and cruel.
Our surroundings provide us with inexhaustible sources of
aesthetic pleasure, but men can still move about in the world
as if they had no senses or were like brute beasts looking for
pleasure in strong and sharp sensations since these are the
only ones accessible to them.

Crude pleasures are often the source of vicious habits.
Strong stimuli do not, as a matter of fact, sharpen but rather
dull the senses, which as a consequence need ever stronger
stimuli.

From a psychological point of view, we can see the importance of the training of the senses by looking at the outline of
the reflex arc which summarizes the function of the nervous
system.

The senses are organs for the apprehension of images of
the external world necessary for the mind, just as the hand is
the organ for grasping material needed by the body. But both
hand and senses can be perfected to perform much higher
tasks and thus become ever more worthy servants of the
spirit that retains them in its service.

Any real education of the intellect should also raise the
potentialities of these two faculties, which are capable of
almost indefinite improvement.

10. The Teacher

A teacher who wishes to prepare herself for this special kind of education must therefore keep clearly in mind the following principle: It is not a question of giving a child a knowledge about the qualities of things, such as size, shape, and color, by means of various objects. Nor is it her aim to train a child to use the materials correctly. This would put our material in competition with that of others, for example, that of Froebel; and it would demand the continual active operation of the teacher in providing information and hastening to correct a child's every mistake until he had learned his lesson. In fine, it may be said that our materials are not a new means to be placed in the hands of an "active" teacher to help her with her teaching.

Rather, there is a radical change in method. Activity has hitherto been the special competence of the teacher, but in our system it is left mainly to the child.

The work of education is divided between the teacher and the environment. For the "teaching" teacher there has been substituted a much more complex combination consisting of teacher and many different objects, and both teacher and objects cooperate in a child's education.

The profound difference that exists between our method and the so-called "objective lessons" of the older systems is that the objects are not a help to the teacher.

The objects in our system are, instead, a help to the child himself. He chooses what he wants for his own use, and works with it according to his own needs, tendencies, and special interests. In this way the objects become a means of growth.

The principal agent is the object itself and not the instruction given by the teacher. It is the child who uses the objects; it is the child who is active, and not the teacher.

The teacher nevertheless has many difficult functions to perform. Her cooperation is not at all excluded, but it becomes prudent, delicate, and manifold. She does not have need of words, or energy, or severity; but she must be able to make prudent observations, to assist a child by going up to, or withdrawing from, him, and by speaking or keeping silence in accordance with his needs. She must acquire a moral alertness which has not hitherto been demanded by any other system, and this is revealed in her tranquility, patience, charity, and humility. Not words, but virtues, are her main qualifications.

In brief, the teacher's principal duty in the school may be described as follows: She should explain the use of the material. She is the main connecting link between the material, that is, the objects, and the child. This is a simple, modest duty, and yet it is much more delicate than that found in the older schools, where the material simply helps the children to understand the mind of the teacher, who must pass on her own ideas to a child, who must in turn receive them.

In our schools a teacher does no more than facilitate and explain to a child the very active and prolonged work laid out for him in choosing objects and employing himself with them. It is something like what takes place in a gymnasium where both teacher and apparatus are necessary. An instructor shows his students how to use parallel bars and swings, how to lift weights, and so forth. But it is the students themselves who use these objects and by so doing increase their strength, agility, and everything else that can be developed when muscles are exercised with the various objects available in a gym.

A gym teacher is not a lecturer but a guide. And just as he would never succeed in strengthening a single one of his students through his talks on the theory of gymnastics, so the older types of schools have failed miserably in strengthening a child's character and personality. Our schools, on the contrary, where the teacher restricts herself to giving guidance to children, have furnished them with a gymnasium for mental exercises. They grow stronger, develop a distinctive personality, are well-disciplined, and acquire an inward health that is the direct and brilliant product of the freeing of the mind.

The teacher must undertake a twofold study: she must have a good knowledge of the work she is expected to do and of the function of the material, that is, of the means of a child's development. It is difficult to prepare such a teacher theoretically. She must fashion herself, she must learn how to observe, how to be calm, patient, and humble, how to restrain her own impulses, and how to carry out her eminently practical tasks with the required delicacy. She too has greater need of a gymnasium for her soul than of a book for her intellect.

Nevertheless, she can learn the active aspect of her duties easily and clearly, that is, how she should place a child in contact with the objects to which he reacts. She must be able to choose an object suitable for a particular child and place it before him in such a way that he understands it and takes a keen interest in it.

A teacher must therefore be well acquainted with the material and keep it constantly before her mind. She must acquire a precise knowledge of the techniques that have been experimentally determined for the presentation of the material and for dealing with the child so that he is effectively guided. All this constitutes a major part of the preparation of a teacher. She can study theoretically certain general principles that will be very useful to guide her in practice, but it is only through experience that she will acquire those delicate insights needed for treating different individuals. She should not hold back minds that are more developed by giving them materials beneath their individual capacities and thus bore them; and, on the other hand, she should not present objects to others who cannot as yet appreciate them and thus discourage their first childish enthusiasm.

Knowledge of the Material. To become acquainted with the material, a teacher should not simply look at it, study it in a book, or learn its use through the explanations of another. Rather, she must exercise herself with it for a long time, trying in this way to evaluate through her own experience the difficulties of, or the interests inherent in, each piece of material that can be given to a child, trying to interpret, although imperfectly, the impressions which a child himself can get from it. Moreover, if a teacher has enough patience to repeat an exercise as often as a child, she can measure in herself the energy and endurance possessed by a child of a determined age. For this final purpose, the teacher can grade the materials and thus judge the capacity of a child for a certain kind of activity at a given stage of his development. This will be further discussed in chapters on the order in which the exercises are to be carried out.

Maintenance of Order. The teacher, besides placing the child in contact with the material, also places him in contact with the order that exists in his environment. She imposes upon him a rule that forms the basis for organized external discipline. It is extremely simple, but sufficient to guarantee peaceful work.

It is that every object must have a definite place where it is kept and where it stays when not in use. A child may take a piece of material only from the place where it is exposed for free choice, and when he has finished using it, he must put it back in its place in the same condition that it was when he took it.

This means that no child can give up his work simply when he has satisfied his own desires: he must be willing to continue his work to the end out of respect for the environment and the rules that govern it. A child may never pass on his material to a companion, much less may he take material from another.

In this way, from the very start an end is put to any rivalry. An object that is not set out does not exist for one looking for it. Even if he wants it badly, he can do nothing but be patient and wait till his companion has finished using it and put it back in place.

Prefecting. Finally, the teacher keeps watch so that a child who is absorbed in his work is not disturbed by one of his companions. This office of being the "guardian angel" of minds concentrated on work that will improve them is one of the most solemn duties of the teacher.

Giving Lessons. In her duty of guiding a child in using the material, a teacher must make a distinction between two different periods. In the first she puts the child in contact with the material and initiates him in its use. In the second she intervenes to enlighten a child who has already succeeded in distinguishing differences through his own spontaneous efforts. It is then that she can determine the ideas acquired by a child, if this is necessary, and provide him with words to describe the differences he has perceived.

11. The Technique of the Lessons

The First Period: Initiations

Isolating the Object. When a teacher gives a lesson or wishes to assist a child in using the sense materials, she should be aware of the fact that the child's attention must be isolated from everything but the object of the lesson. She will therefore take care to clear a table of everything else and place on it only the material she wishes to present.

Working Exactly. The assistance which a teacher should give a child in presenting the material to him consists in showing him how to use it. She performs the exercise herself once or twice, removing, for example, the cylinders of the solid insets, then mixing them up, and putting them back in position by a process of trial and error. Or she mixes up the spools of colors that are to be matched and then picks up one at random in the proper way, that is, without touching the silk, and places it alongside its mate, and so on.

Rousing the Attention. Whenever a teacher offers an object to a child, she should not do so coldly but rather display a lively interest in what she is doing and attract the attention of the child to it.

Preventing Errors in Using the Material. If a teacher sees that material is being used in a way that will not attain its goal, that is, in a way that does not benefit the development of a child's intelligence, she should prevent him from continuing. She will do this with the greatest sweetness if the child is calm and good-tempered; but if he shows a tendency to misbehave, she will check him with earnest words, not in a way that can seem to be a punishment for noise and disorder, but rather as an indication of her authority over the child.

Authority, in fact, becomes in such a case a necessary

support for the child who, having lost control of himself momentarily, needs a strong support to which he can cling. just as one who has stumbled needs to grab something to keep from falling. The work of assistance at such a time means extending a strong and friendly hand towards one who is weak.

But when a child is working, he is like one who is perfectly balanced and has the material he needs for exercise: one who is striving to perfect the suppleness of his body has need of a gymnasium.

We must carefully distinguish two kinds of errors a child can make. There is first the error controlled by the material itself and which rises from the fact that the child, though he is perfectly willing to carry out exactly the exercise which he knows well, does not succeed because he is still too immature to carry it out perfectly, either because he does not distinguish with his senses the various stimuli, or because he cannot execute specific movements since his faculties are as yet not well developed. For example, he may make a mistake in putting cylinders into their holes because he does not yet distinguish the differences among them, or, similarly, he places a large cube over a small one in building a tower, and so on.

Such errors are controlled by the materials themselves, since they do not allow a mistake to go unnoticed. They can be corrected only by the further development of the child, by that modification of his powers which will be the result of a long and proper use of the material. Errors such as these may be placed in the same category as those which we recognize when we say that we learn by making mistakes. They are overcome by a good will with the assistance of some external means.

The second type of error is due to a kind of ill will, to negligence on the part of the teacher, as for example when a child drags the whole stand of solid insets around as if it were a cart, or when he builds houses of the spools of colored silk, or walks on the rods laid out in a row, or wraps one of the cloths for teaching how to button about his head like a scarf, and so on. When material is used wrongly so as to create confusion, or for needs that it cannot satisfy, it is not really used at all. The result is a waste of energy and uproar. This prevents a child from being able to concentrate and therefore from being able to grow and develop. This might be compared to a hemorrhage in the body which releases blood that should flow through the heart if one is to remain healthy or even alive. It cannot be said that one learns by making mistakes of this type. The longer one persists in such an error the farther removed he is from the possibility of learning.

It is, then, in such conditions that the teacher's authority intervenes to assist the endangered little soul, offering it now gentle, now energetic help.

Respect for Useful Activity. If, on the other hand, a child uses the material in exact imitation of the way he has learned from his teacher or in some other way which he has discovered for himself but in a manner that shows his intelligence at work, which is in itself something that favors a child's development, the teacher will permit him to continue to repeat the same exercise or make his own experiments as often as he wants without interrupting him in his efforts, either to correct slight errors or to stop his work through fear of his becoming tired.

A Good Finish. But when a child has spontaneously given up an exercise, that is, when that impulse which urged him on to use the material has been exhausted, the teacher, if need be, can, and indeed must, intervene so that the child puts the material back in place and everything is left in perfect order.

Second Period: The Lessons

The second period is that in which the teacher intervenes in order to determine the child's concepts who, after being introduced to the exercises, has already carried many of them out and has succeeded in distinguishing the differences in the sense materials.

The principal intervention consists in teaching a child the exact names of the things which which he is working.

This assists a child to speak correctly, something which is easily learned when one is small.

One of the most delicate tasks for the teacher in our system is to provide a child with the precise terms for the ideas which the material should have fixed in his mind. When she gives him these words, the teacher speaks clearly and correctly, pronouncing each syllable exactly, but without assuming a false manner of speaking, that is, without exaggeration.

The Three-Staged Lesson

I have found that Seguin's method for obtaining an association between an object and its corresponding term in teaching defective children is also very useful for those who are normal. He divided the lesson into three stages, and we have adopted this same practice in our schools.

First Stage: The Association of the Sense Perceptions with Names.

The teacher should first pronounce the necessary nouns and adjectives without adding anything else. She should pronounce the words very distinctly and in a loud voice so that the various sounds that make up a word may be clearly and distinctly heard by the child.

Thus, for example, when she has had a child touch first a smooth card and then sandpaper in the first exercises for the senses, she will say: "It is smooth," "It is rough." She repeats the word many times over with various modulations of her voice but always with clear vowel tones and a distinct pronunciation: "Smooth, smooth, smooth," or "Rough, rough, rough." In the same way, when dealing with sensations of heat, she will say: "It is cold." "It is hot." And later: "It is ice cold," "It is luke warm." "It is scalding."

Then she will begin to use the descriptive terms "hot," "hotter," "less hot," and so forth.

Since the lesson in terminology should consist in establishing an association between a name and its object or with the abstract concept of the name itself, both object and name should strike the child's understanding at the same time, but only the name itself, and not some other word, should be pronounced.

Second Stage: The Recognition of the Object Corresponding to the Name.

A teacher should always test to see if her lesson has attained its end.

The first test consists in finding out if the name has remained associated with the object in the child's memory. She will therefore have to allow the necessary time to lapse between lesson and test. Several moments must therefore pass between them. Then she will ask the child slowly and very distinctly only the noun or adjective that has been taught: "Which one is *smooth?*" "Which one is *rough?*"

The child will point with his finger at the object and the teacher will know if the association has been established.

This second period is the most important of all and comprises the real lesson, the real assistance to the memory and the power of association. When the teacher sees that the child understands her and is interested, she will repeat over and over again the same question: "Which one is *smooth?*" "Which one is *rough?*"

By repeating the question many times over, the teacher repeats the noun or adjective that will finally be remembered; and at every repetition the child, by pointing at the object in answer, repeats the exercise of associating with it the word which he is learning and which he is fixing in his mind. If the teacher, however, notices at the very first that a child is not inclined to pay attention to her and makes mistakes in his answers without attempting to do well, she should, instead of correcting him and insisting upon the exercise, suspend the lesson for the time being and start it again at some later time. Actually, why should she correct him? If the child did not succeed in associating the name with the object the only way for him to succeed would be to experience again the sense stimulus as well as the name, that is, he should repeat the lesson. But when a child has made a mistake, it means that at that particular moment he was not ready for the psychic association that the teacher wanted to establish in him. It will therefore be necessary to choose another time.

Moreover, if, in addition to correcting the child, we were to say to him, for example: "No, you are mistaken; it is this," all of these words of reproof would make much more of an impression upon him than the others such as "smooth," and "rough." They would remain in his mind and hinder his learning of the names. Instead, the silence that follows a mistake leaves the area of the child's consciousness intact, and the next lesson can be effectively superimposed upon the first.

Third Stage: Remembrance of the Name Corresponding to the Object.

The third stage is a rapid verification of the first lesson.

The teacher asks the child: "What is this?" and if the child is ready to do so, he will reply with the proper word: "It is *smooth*." "It is *rough*."

Since a child is often uncertain of the pronunciation of these words, which are often new to him, the teacher can insist that they be repeated once or twice, encouraging the child to pronounce them more clearly, saying: "What is it?" "What?" And if the child shows marked defects in his speech, this is the time to take careful note of them so that corrective exercises in pronunciation may be later given.

Practical Applications—A Guide to the Use of the Material

The Solid Insets

Dimensions. After a child has had long experience in handling the three solid insets and has acquired confidence in their use, the teacher takes all the cylinders of equal height and spreads them out on the table next to each other. Then she takes the two extremes in size and says: "This is the thickest," and "This is the thinnest." She then places them side by side so that the comparison is more effective, and then, taking each one of them by its knob, she places the bottom of one against the bottom of the other to show their differences. Then she again places them upright and close together to show that they are of equal height. In the meantime, she can keep repeating: "Thick, thin." Each time she should continue with the other stages of verification and say: "Give me the *thickest*, the *thinnest*," and finally she should give the language test: "What is this?" In later lessons the teacher removes the largest and smallest cylinders in the set and repeats the lesson with the next largest and smallest that still remain. Finally, she uses all the pieces. She takes one, for example, at random and says: "Give me one that is *thicker* than this, one that is *thinner*."

The teacher proceeds in a similar way with the second set of solid insets. She sets all the pieces upright, and they all have a sufficiently wide base to stay in this position, and says: "This is the *tallest*." "This is the *shortest*." Then, after she has taken them out of the row, she places the end pieces next to each other. She then places their ends together and thus shows that they are equal. From the two extremes she passes on to those in between as in the first exercise.

With the third set of solid insets, the teacher, after she has placed all the pieces in a graduated row, points to the first and says: "This is the *largest*," and then pointing to the last, she says: "This is the *smallest*." Then she placed them next to each other and shows how they differ in height as well as in diameter. The procedure is similar to that of the two preceding exercises. She proceeds in the same way with the graduated systems of prisms, rods, and cubes. The prisms in one system are *thick* and *thin*, and *high* and *low* in another, and are of equal length. The rods are *long* and *short* and of equal thickness. The cubes are *large* and *small* and differ in three dimensions.

Form. After a child has shown that he can identify the shapes of the flat insets with certainty, the teacher begins the lessons in terminology with two opposite shapes, a square and a circle, following the usual method. She will not teach all the names of the geometrical figures, but only some of the principal ones such as the square, circle, rectangle, triangle, and oval, pointing out especially that there are *long* and *narrow* rectangles, and others that are *wide* and *short*, and that squares are equal on all sides and can be *large* or *small*. This can be quite easily shown with the insets. A square piece, for example, in no matter what way it is turned will always enter into the hole, but a rectangle cannot do so if it is placed crosswise. A child readily engages in such an exercise, and for this purpose I place within the frame a square and a series of rectangles with their longer sides equal to the side of the square and the other side gradually decreasing in five successive stages.

The teacher proceeds analogously to demonstrate the differences between an oval, an ellipse, and a circle. A circle, no matter how one turns it, will always enter its socket. An ellipse will not enter its socket if it is turned crosswise, but it will fit equally well rightside up or upside down. An oval on the other hand will not fit in its socket when placed upside down but must be inserted with the wide curve facing the wide hollow in the plaque and the narrow curve towards the narrow. Circles, both large and small, enter their holes turned in any direction. I suggest that the difference between an oval and an ellipse should be taught much later, and not to every child, but only to those who have shown a special interest in shapes either by their frequent choice of the material or their questions. I would prefer that such differences should be recognized spontaneously by the children much later on, for example, in the elementary schools.

A Guide to the Child

The work of the new teacher is that of a guide. She guides the child in his use of the material, in finding the exact word, in facilitating and clarifying all his labors, in preventing him from wasting his energies, and in rooting out chance disturbances.

She thus gives the necessary help for swift and sure progress in intellectual growth.

As a sure guide on the path of life, she neither urges a child onward nor holds him back, being satisfied that she has fulfilled her task when she has guaranteed this precious traveler, the child, that he is on the right road.

If she is to be a safe and sure guide, a teacher needs a great deal of practice. Even after she has understood the fact that the periods of initiation and intrevention are diverse, she is frequently uncertain about a child's maturity for passing from one to the other. If she waits too long to intervene in teaching terminology, a child will go on to make distinctions by himself.

I once found a five-year-old child who could already put together entire words since he knew the alphabet perfectly. He had learned this in fifteen days. He could write on the blackboard, and in his free drawings, by the way he had drawn a house and table, he showed that he was not only an observer but that he had intuitively grasped the notion of perspective. When he exercised his perception of colors, he would mix together all seven shades of the nine colors that we use. He would then rapidly separate the sixty-three spools of differently colored silk threads and group them together according to their separate colors and degrees of intensity, thus covering the whole table with what looked like a shaded colored spread. I made the experiment of showing the child, in the full light of a neighboring window, a colored card, telling him to remember it well so that he could recall it to mind. I then sent him to a table on which were spread all the different shades of colors to get a tablet that seemed to him to be of the same color. He made only very slight errors. He frequently picked out the identical shade but more often one that was next to it. Very rarely did he miss it by two degrees. He therefore possessed an almost prodigious memory for colors and ability to discriminate among them. The little boy, like almost all the rest, was extremely fond of exercising his sense of colors.

When I asked him for the name of a white table, he hesitated for a long time, and only after a number of seconds did he answer with some hesitation: "White." Now a child of such intelligence, even without the special help of a teacher, could have learned the name of this color at home. The teacher told me that she had noticed that the child experienced great difficulty in remembering the names of the colors, and that she had up to the present limited him to sense exercises. She had thought it better not to intervene as yet in the teaching.

Obviously, the education of this child had been a bit confused and he had been left too free with respect to the spontaneous unfolding of his psychic activities. However praiseworthy it may be to provide sense education as a basis for ideas, speech and perceptions must not be neglected. A teacher should avoid what is superfluous, but she should not forget what is necessary.

The presence of what is superfluous and the lack of what is necessary are the two chief errors of a teacher. Her perfection is reached when she can take the middle course between these two extremes.

The end to be obtained is the orderly stabilization of a child's spontaneous activities. Just as no teacher can furnish a student with the agility that is acquired through gymnastic exercises, but the student through his own efforts much reach this perfection by himself, so here, in like manner, a child must perfect his own sense perceptions and must in general further his own education.

We can think of the conduct of a piano teacher. He teaches his pupil how to hold his body, instructs him on the notes, shows him the relation between the printed note, the key to be touched, and the position of his fingers, and then leaves him alone to practice by himself. If the pupil is to become a pianist, he will have to engage in long and patient exercises which will limber up his fingers and afford that automatic coordination of his muscles characteristic of an accomplished musician.

A pianist therefore will have to mold himself, and his success in this will be in proportion to the extent that his natural talent will have induced him to continue his exercises. And yet one never becomes a pianist simply by practice and without the direction of a teacher.

Actually, it might be said that the same thing happens in every kind of education: a man's accomplishments do not depend upon his teachers, but upon what he himself has done.

One of the difficulties that we have encountered in teaching our method to those trained in the older systems is that of preventing them from interfering with a child who is worried about some mistake he has made and is making repeated attempts to correct it. At such a time these teachers are seized with pity and can hardly resist coming to his assistance. When one prevents them from intervening in this way, they have words of compassion for the little fellow; but he very soon shows by his joyous contenance that he has overcome the difficulty.

Normal children repeat such exercises as these many times over, but the number depends upon the individual. Some become tired after five or six repetitions, but others continue for more than twenty times to remove and replace pieces without ever losing their expression of lively interest.

On one occasion, after I had seen a little four-year-old girl perform an exercise sixteen times, I had a hymn sung to her to distract her attention; but unperturbed she continued to remove, mix up, and replace the cylinders in their positions.

An intelligent teacher could carry out very interesting psychological studies with a child and, up to a certain point, measure his resistance to the strength of different distracting stimuli.

Indeed, as long as a child is teaching himself and the material he is using contains its own control over error, the teacher has nothing to do but observe.

One who follows my method teaches little, observes a great deal, but rather directs the psychic activities of the children and their physiological development. This is why I have changed her name from teacher to that of "directress."

At first this caused people to smile. Everyone asked whom the teacher was to direct, since she had no one under her and had to leave her little pupils free. But her direciton is much more important and profound than is commonly thought because she is a teacher who gives direction to intelligent beings. The directresses of Children's Houses must be convinced of two things—that the guidance is the responsibility of the teacher, and that individual exercise is the work of the child. Only after they have fixed this clearly in their minds can they rationally proceed to the application of a method which guides the spontaneous education of a child and imparts essential concepts.

12. Observations on Prejudices

In our method the task of the teacher is much simpler than that of ordinary teachers. She is taught to indicate what is necessary and to avoid what is superfluous. The latter is harmful because it is an obstacle to a child's progress. Her activities are therefore confined within limits.

Ordinary teachers, on the other hand, are preoccupied with many things and tire themselves out with many duties, wheras "only one thing is necessary."

To help teachers free themselves from old concepts and prejudices, I shall here briefly refer to some of the needless difficulties which dissipate their energies and distract their attention.

They are particularly concerned with the extent of the difficulties which a child must overcome and with his need for rest.

One of the obstacles that we have removed from the teacher's path is her prejudice with respect to the ease and difficulty of learning. This cannot be determined by prejudice but only by direct experience after the individual difficulties have been analyzed.

Many people, for example, seem to think that when we are teaching geometrical forms we are teaching geometry, and that this is too difficult for preschool children. Others are of the opinion that if we wish to give them geometrical forms we should use solid instead of plane figures.

I believe that a word is necessary to combat such prejudices. To observe a geometrical form is not to analyze it. And this is where the difficulty begins. When, for example, one speaks to a child of sides and angles and explains to him, possibly by the objective methods used by Froebel, that there are four sides to a square and that it can be constructed with four equal rods, then one actually enters into the field of geometry; and I think that early childhood is too immature for such a step. But the observation of forms cannot be unsuitable to this age. The top of a table at which a child sits to eat his soup is probably a rectangle. The plate which holds his food forms a circle, and we certainly do not believe that a child is too immature to look at a table or plate.

The inset pieces which we present to a child simply call his attention to a form. Moreover, as far as the name is concerned, it is analogous to other words in their vocabulary. Why should we find it premature to teach a child the words for circle, square, and oval, when at home, for example, he repeatedly hears the word "round" (*tondo*) for a plate (*piat-to*)? Do we think that the latter causes an injury to his tender mind? Also, he very often hears people at home speaking of a square table, an oval table, and so forth; and these common words will remain confused in his mind and speech for a long time if he does not receive assistance like that we give in the teaching of forms.

One must take into account the fact that very frequently a child when left to himself makes an effort to understand the speech of adults and the objects that are about him. But teaching, when it comes at the right time and in the right way, anticipates such efforts. The result is that the child is not wearied but refreshed and satisfied in his desires.

A further prejudice is found to exist in the conviction that when a child is left entirely to himself his mind is completely at rest. If that were the case, he would be a stranger to the world. Instead of this we see him making a gradual and spontaneous conquest of ideas and speech. He is like a pilgrim who is constantly seeing new things and who strives to understand the unknown tongue of those about him. He must make great efforts to understand and imitate. The instructions given to little children should be aimed precisely at lessening such efforts and at converting them into the pleasures derived from easier and more extensive victories. We are the guides for these travelers making their entrance into the intellectual world, and we help them to avoid wasting time and strength on useless matters.

The other prejudice we have mentioned is the one which maintains that it is more suitable to give a child solid rather than plane geometrical figures, that he should be given spheres, cubes, prisms, and so forth.

We may prescind from the physiological fact that the vision of solids is more complex than that of planes and restrict ourselves to the area of practical life.

The majority of objects in the external world that confront our eyes are comparable to our plane insets. Doors, panelings, window frames, pictures, and wood or marble table tops are certainly solid objects, but they all have one of their dimensions so greatly reduced that the two more prominent ones give them the appearance of a plane. The result is that the plane surfaces prevail, and we say that such and such a window is rectangular, that such a frame is oval, and that such a table is square.

Solids whose shapes are determined by the surface with the greatest dimensions are actually those which almost always meet our eyes. And it is precisely solids of this sort that are represented by our solid insets.

A child will very frequently recognize in his environment forms thus learned, but he will very seldom recognize geometrical solids.

He will see that the long leg of a table is a prism and that a rotunda is a truncated cone or an elongated cylinder much later than that the top of a table on which he places various objects and which he sees together with them is a rectangle. We do not therefore speak of recognizing a cupboard, much less a house, as a prism or cube since solid geometrical forms almost never exist purely as such in external objects but only in combinations. Prescinding from the enormous difficulty of embracing with the eye the complex shape of a cupboard, a child should recognize its shape as analogous to, and not as identical with, the forms he has already learned.

On the other hand, he will recognize simple geometrical forms in windows, doors, surfaces of solid domestic objects, pictures which adorn walls, walls themselves, floors, tiles of terraces, and so forth. In this way the knowledge which he gains from the flat insets will be for him a kind of magic key for the interpretation of almost all his surroundings, and he will be able to console himself with the illusion that he knows the secrets of the world.

I once took with me for a walk on the Pincio a boy from an elementary school who was studying mechanical drawing and knew how to analyze geometrical planes. When we had reached the high terrace from which one may see the Piazza

The sense of hearing relates us to our environment in a special way. We develop acuity in hearing by learning to recognize the smallest amount of stimuli.

Convent of the Visitation   St. Paul, Minnesota

The perception of musical sounds is aided by use of a series of bells. Here the child is matching identical sounds.

Alcuin Montessori School   Oak Park, Illinois

The moveable alphabet provides an exercise in the analysis of words into their component letter-sounds, the step before being actually able to read. *Alcuin Montessori School   Oak Park, Illinois*

The numerical rods satisfy the child's need for exactness and concreteness and give him a basis for counting and judging relative lengths.

Convent of the Visitation
St. Paul, Minnesota

The exercise with numerals and counters aids in the realization of odd and even numbers and in the counting by twos.

Convent of the Visitation
St. Paul, Minnesota

With the tens and teens board the child learns to associate quantities with the figures 11-99, and gains an understanding of the sequence of numbers.

Convent of the Visitation   St. Paul, Minnesota

The addition strip board provides a reinforcement of the decimal system and gives an opportunity for the repetition of skills already learned in building additional combinations.

Convent of the Visitation   St. Paul, Minnesota

Work with the decimal beads relates quantity to the numerals of the decimal system, establishes an understanding of place value and the powers of ten.

Alcuin Montessori School   Oak Park, Illinois

The trinomial cube gives the child a visual image of algebraic concepts. *Alcuin Montessori School   Oak Park, Illinois*

The practical life activities are naturally interesting exercises for the child. They are a means of achieving hand-eye coordination and of developing poise and independence.

Convent of the Visitation   St. Paul, Minnesota

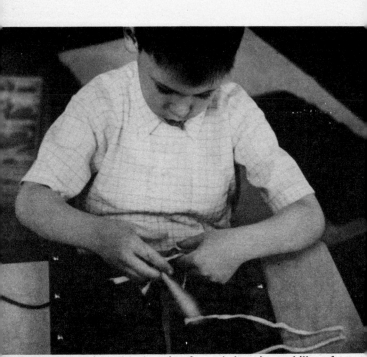

The child working with the tying frame is learning a skill, and his concentration is helping to lengthen his attention span.
Alcuin Montessori School   Oak Park, Illinois

The baric tablets are used for development of the ability to discriminate, in this case through judging weights. The blindfold helps to isolate a single sense.

Convent of the Visitation   St. Paul, Minnesota

As the child repeats the exercise of fitting the knobbed cylinders into their proper places, his ability to observe and make distinctions is sharpened, and his reasoning power is stimulated through noticing and correcting errors. The thumb and fingers that will be used for writing are also being strengthened as he grasps each cylinder by the knob.

Convent of the Visitation   St. Paul, Minnesota

The rods and lengths (above) and the pink tower and brown stairs (below): Work with the various systems of blocks builds "muscular memory," improves the ability to make visual distinction and develops memory and reasoning power. Minds trained on this basic physical data are having the way prepared for mathematics. *Convent of the Visitation   St. Paul, Minnesota*

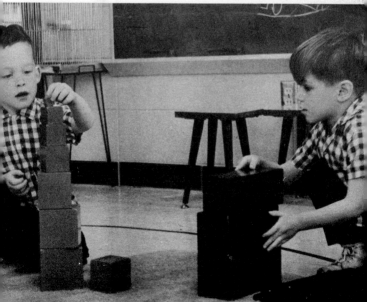

The ability to distinguish colors in their various shadings is cultivated with several series of color tablets. Here a child is matching basic colors. *Convent of the Visitation   St. Paul, Minnesota*

In placing the geometrical figures in their proper settings, or on the matching cards, the child's visual judgment is aided by his sense of touch, and his hand is trained to draw the figures as he outlines them with his hand.

The constructive triangles are used to build geometrical shapes, training the eye to discriminate.

Alcuin Montessori School   Oak Park, Illinois

del Popolo and the wide expanse of the city, I said to him: "See how all of man's works are a great heap of geometrical figures." As a matter of fact rectangles, ellipses, triangles, and semicircles perforate and adorn in a hundred different ways the grey rectangular façades of buildings. Such widespread uniformity seems to prove the limitations of the human intellect. In contrast to this a neighboring plot of grass and flowers displayed superbly the infinite variety of nature's forms.

The boy had never made such an observation. He had studied the sides, angles, and shapes of the geometrical figures that he had drawn without thinking any further and only experiencing the boredom of the dull work he was obliged to do. At first he laughed at the idea of men heaping up geometrical figures, but then he grew interested and gazed out over the city for a long time. I saw his face light up with an expression of deep thought.

To the right of the Ponte Margherita a new building was being constructed, and its framework also consisted of rectangles. "How hard they are working," I said, speaking of the workers. Then we went to the neighboring plot and remained for a little time in silence looking at the plants growing there. "It is beautiful," the boy said, but that "beauty" could have been better referred to the inner workings of his own mind.

Another concern of ordinary teachers is to widen the knowledge of a child through continual appeals to the environment and generalizations. To make one see everything, to make one reflect on everything, is an anxious business, and it unfortunately exhausts a child's energies and cruelly deprives him of everything that could raise his interests. It is the spiritual part of that fatal intervention of an adult who wants to substitute herself for a child and to act for him, and who, in so doing, erects the most serious obstacle to his development. The beauties which a child discovers on his own in the world about him could bring him frequent joy and satisfaction, but instead, because of this teaching by an adult they become a source of tedium and mental inertia.

A teacher should therefore not fear that a child, as so many would like to insinuate, is miserably hampered by the limited material which we have substituted for the great variety of things offered by nature or the larger environment that surrounds a child at home and in school.

If a child has exercised his faculties with the sense material and has increased his ability to distinguish things from each other and has opened up his soul to an ever increasing desire for work, he has certainly become a more perfect and intelligent observer than before, and one who is genuinely interested in what is less will be all the more keenly interested in what is more.

We should expect normal children to spontaneously investigate their external surroundings, or, as I say, "willingly explore their environment." When they are so disposed, children experience a new happiness at every discovery they make. This gives them a feeling of dignity and satisfaction, encourages them to go in search for ever new sensations in their environment, and automaticatly makes them observant.

A teacher should restrict herself to keeping watch with utmost diligence over a child when he begins to generalize his ideas. For example, on one occasion one of our little children, who was four years old, stopped suddenly while running on the terrace and cried out: "Oh, the sky is blue!" And he stood still for a long time gazing at the expanse of the heavens.

One day as I entered one of the Children's Houses, five or six of the little ones came up and stood quietly about me, gently stroking my hands and dress and saying: "It is smooth." "It is velvet." Then many others came up, and all of them with a serious expression on their faces repeated the same words as they touched me. The teacher wanted to interrupt them to free me. I made a sign for her not to move and stood in still and silent admiration of this spontaneous activity of the children. The greatest triumph of our system of education will always be to obtain the spontaneous progress of a child.

Once when a child was following one of our exercises that consist in filling in with colored pencils an outline that has already been drawn, and which, in this instance, was a tree, he picked up a red pencil to color the trunk. The teacher was about to interrupt: "Do you think that trees have red trunks?" I restrained her and let the child color the tree red. This drawing was valuable in that it showed us that the child was not an exact observer of his surroundings. He continued to carry out the exercises in colors. He used to go into the garden with his companions and was always able to notice the color of tree trunks. When the exercise of his senses would reach the point where they would automatically direct his attention to the colors of the world about him, he would experience a wonderful moment when he realized that tree trunks are not red. It would be like that of the boy who noticed as he was running that the sky was blue. One day he actually did pick up a brown pencil to color the trunk and another to color the branches and leaves green. Still later he colored the branches also in brown and used green only for the leaves.

Instances such as these give proof of the intellectual progress made by a child.

We do not create observers merely by saying, "Observe," but by supplying individuals with the means for making observations, and the means is the education of the senses. Once this connection has been established between a child and his environment, his progress is assured. His refined senses enable him to observe his surroundings more effectively and the objects he observes, attracting his attention by their variety, continue this training of his senses.

If, on the other hand, we neglect the education of the senses, knowledge of the properties of physical bodies become simply a part of our general culture, which is strictly limited to things that we have learned and remembered, and this is something sterile. In other words, when a teacher has taught the names of the colors according to the other method, she has given information on determined qualities, but she has not trained one to take an interest in colors. A child will know these colors, but he will also forget them again and again, and his knowledge will at best remain within the limits of his teacher's lessons. When, moreover, a teacher of the old school suggests the generalization of an idea by asking, for example: "What is the color of this flower, of this ribbon?" the attention of the child will probably be poorly directed upon the objects set before him by his teacher.

If we should compare a child with a watch or some other complicated piece of machinery, we might say that the old method can be compared to what is done when we press our thumb against the toothed wheels of a stopped watch to make them go around. Their spinning depends entirely upon the pressure exerted by the thumb. We have a parallel to the effect produced by a teacher's work with a child. Our new system of education, on the other hand, is like a taut spring which provides an intrinsic motion to the whole mechanism. It is a driving force inherent in the watch itself and is not simply that of the person who has wound it. Similarly, a child's spontaneous psychic development continues indefinitely and is in direct dependence on the psychic potentialities of the child himself and not on his teacher's efforts.

The driving force, that is, the spontaneous psychic activity, in our case arises from the education of the senses and is maintained by the intelligence of an observer. Thus, for example, a hunting dog achieves its skill not from the training received from its master but from the particular keenness of its senses. Nevertheless its owner, by taking the dog hunting, sharpens its sense perceptions and provides his dog with pleasure and a passion for hunting. The same may be said of a pianist who at one and the same time perfects his appreciation of music and the nimbleness of his fingers. He takes pleasure in creating new harmonies on the instrument, and this in turn sharpens his senses and increases his dexterity. The perfection that he will ultimately attain will be limited only by his personal powers. On the other hand, a physicist can know all about harmonies, which is a part of his scientific education, but he may not be able to play the simplest piece of music; and his education, however extensive, will be definitely limited by the science of acoustics.

Our goal in the education of a young child should be to help him develop, and not to furnish him with a kind of culture. Therefore, after we have offered a child material suitable for promoting the development of his senses, we should wait for his powers of observation to unfold.

The Touchstone

Children frequently reveal remarkable powers of observation, noticing things which they had not previously noticed before. They also seem to compare present objects with those they remember from past experiences. Their striking judgments show that children have within themselves a kind of touchstone which we do not ourselves possess. They compare external things with their mental fantasms and show a surprising accuracy in judgment. Once a workman came into a classroom in Barcelona carrying in his hand a piece of glass which he was going to put into a window in the room. A five-year-old child said in a loud voice: "You can't use that piece of glass; it's too small." Only when the workman tried to fit the glass into the frame did he notice that it was about one fourth of an inch too short.

Two children of five and six were carrying on the following conversation in a Children's House in Berlin: "Do you think the ceiling is ten feet high?" "No," the other replied, "it is about ten feet, nine inches high." When the height was measured it was found in fact to be somewhat over ten feet.

A little five-year-old girl, seeing a lady coming into the room, said to her: "The color of your dress is just like that of the flower over there." The lady went into the next room, where she found a flower which could not be seen from the room she had first entered, and, comparing the flower with her dress, she found that the two colors were surprisingly alike.

Children have within themselves a touchstone which sets them on a different plane from our own and enables them to do many striking things. The reason for this seems to be that certain periods of life are more suited for certain psychic operations than others. A proof of this may be found in the ability of little children to remember and reproduce the sounds of spoken words.

Nature has placed an extraordinary sensitivity in a child for fixing words and accents and it is precisely during the period of childhood that a person's language is fixed for life. There is no going back: what a child's mind assimilates during the sensitive period remains as a permanent acquisition for his whole life, and it can never be acquired at another stage. Thus there are periods in childhood for gaining sense impressions and fixing habits which, if they are neglected, can never be redeemed.

Once we are aware of this fact, we shall frequently notice slight variations in the activities of children that will illustrate it. A child of three years is able to repeat an exercise such as that of the solid insets forty times in a row, whereas a child of six cannot repeat it more than five or six. A child of six, however, can do things of a higher order than those of which a child of three is capable, or of which he is even aware.

This interesting fact is also found in moral matters. The intensely formative period of early childhood is also that in which there can be established a kind of perfect obedience, the outer manifestation of which has been evaluated as a tendency to imitation. But when one studies this phenomenon, and when the surrounding circumstances are favorable to a child's development, we see that a child has a natural tendency to adapt himself to the other human beings who surround him in a striking way. In this tendency we should strive to find a basis for a love for, and a solidarity with, all mankind. Later on, except in noteworthy instances that must be attributed to supernatural assistance, there will not be found that same kind of obedience, but simply a reasonable adherence or a forced submission.

The same phenomenon may be strikingly noticed in the development of a religious sense. A small child has a tendency which can be best described as a sensitive period of the soul. During this period it has intuitions and spiritual longings which are surprising to anyone who has not observed children able to express the needs of their interior life. It thus seems that little children are exceptionally endowed with spiritual insights and are marvelously called by divine grace. Although it is not possible to give a child the kind of logical religious education which he will later receive after attaining the so-called "use of reason," he can absorb the truths of faith and he will grow as a man because his intelligence has been illuminated by this same faith. The sensitive period thus provides a foundation for the attainment of wonderful qualities which can never, or only with great difficulty, be attained at a later age.

Mental Order

The mind of a little child is certainly not a blank when he begins the education of his senses, but his concepts are all confused. The chaos of his mind has greater need of ordering what it already knows than of gaining more knowledge. He begins to distinguish various traits in objects already known. He distinguishes quantity from quality and separates form from color. He distinguishes dimensions in objects that are long or short, thick or thin, large or small. He separates colors into groups and calls them by their names— white, green, red, blue, yellow, violet, black, orange, brown, and pink. He notices the varying intensities of colors, calling the two extremes light and dark. Finally, he distinguishes tastes from smells, lightness from softness, and sounds from noises.

Just as a child has learned to put everything in its place in its surroundings, he succeeds through the education of his senses in ordering his mental images. This is the first act of ordering in his developing mind, and it is the point of departure since the psychic life develops by avoiding obstacles.

The conquest of the external world through sense impressions will now be easy and orderly. This sense of order that has been acquired early is of utmost importance for later life.

Men who have made a mark in the world through their insights have been educated in this way. Through their observation of the world about them they began to make distinctions and classifications. They invented terms to describe their new discoveries and determined the uses to which they could be put. In the light of their ever increasing knowledge they have advanced and have overcome the darkness of ignorance.

13. Elevation

Silence—Materialized Abstractions

One of the differences between our method of education
and that commonly used in schools for the instruction of
normal children is the way in which we educate a child.

Perhaps "silence" may serve to illustrate this point.

In ordinary schools we find a concept of order even though
it has never really been defined. It is that state in which the
behavior of the students makes it possible for the teacher to
give a lesson.

However, since the class is acting under compulsion, it has
a tendency to drift from this mediocre state of order into a
kind of disorder in which various kinds of movement that are
uncoordinated and without purpose create a noise and rest-
lessness which makes it difficult or even impossible for a
teacher to conduct a class. This is obviously a disruption of
order. In such a case the teacher must make an energetic
appeal for silence, meaning by this the order we have just
described.

Since this mediocre order is something that has already
been attained, and is normal and customary, a simple command suffices to secure it.

In our method, however, the mediocre order (which, however, is of a different kind, since it results from the labors of
the individual children) is a point of departure for rising to a
higher level not yet attained or even known. Silence is therefore a positive conquest which must be attained through
knowledge and experience.

A child's attention is drawn to his slightest movements and
he is taught how to control his acts in every detail in order to
obtain the absolute immobility which leads to silence. This is
something new and striking, and has never before been ap-

preciated. In ordinary schools a request for silence aims at bringing life back to its normal condition.

The silence of immobility, on the other hand, suspends normal life and work, and has no practical aim. All its importance and fascination comes from the fact that by suspending the ordinary routine of life it raises an individual to a higher level. Here there is no question of utility; the only attraction is that of self-conquest.

When little children of three or four ask for silence, or when having been invited to create it, they immediately respond with the keenest interest, they afford us with a meaningful proof of the fact that children have a tendency to raise themselves up and that they enjoy higher pleasures. Many people have been present at one or other of those surprising scenes when a teacher begins to write the word "silence" on the blackboard and have noticed that before she has even finished writing the word a profound silence has pervaded the room, where seconds before forty or fifty little children were intent on their occupations.

The life of movement has been suspended almost instantly. Some child or other read the first letter of the word and understood that the order for silence was coming. Then, suspending his own activities, he began the silence which the others immediately suspected and joined in keeping. Thus silence called for silence without a single word being spoken.

Similar comparisons could be made with respect to all the other operations of the two different types of schools.

In the ordinary school a certain medium level represents what is good. But this "good," which has neither been defined nor studied, is regularly considered to be the level of learning that a child should reach.

In our schools we look upon the medium of "good" as that which an individual spontaneously attains in his work, and we go on from there to raise it to a higher level of perfection.

It should be obvious that a child, if he did not have a natural tendency towards this perfection, could never actually attain it. But if he does have a tendency, and if he does make undoubted progress, we should feel that as educators we have a newly revealed obligation.

The education of the senses may serve to point this up. As is known, many educators regard the training of the senses as a mistake. They do so because they take the average life as an end and thus believe that a training of the senses is a deviation from the natural way of learning.

Objects, as a matter of fact, are seen in their entirety as a unity made up of many individual traits. A rose has color and scent, a marble base weight and shape, and so on. Therefore, the right attitude in teaching would seem to be to take real objects just as they are. This type of reasoning is dependent upon the belief that the medium order of things is the ultimate goal.

But if we consider the medium order not as a fixed end but as a point of departure, we may suspect that little children spontaneously notice much more than these "objective lessons" are accustomed to explain, provided, of course, that the children are left free to observe according to their own instincts and are not weakened by functional inhibitions, that is, by the fear of acting by themselves.

I say that we can suspect this, because even if we have not made a methodical study of a child's spontaneous reactions, we can at least have a theoretical understanding of such a truth. A child has the natural inclination to explore his environment however great it may be, just as he has a similar tendency to listen to speech. Through this driving instinct he comes to know the external world and learns how to speak himself. During the sensible period of his life he comes to observe the objects in his environment and to listen to the sounds of the human voice.

There is thus no need to describe objects for him but simply to refrain from stifling his natural instinct of observation.

If we wish to assist him, we must place ourselves on a higher level. We must give him more than what he could attain by his own unaided efforts.

On this point I would like to be emphatic: we should furnish him with a realistic philosophy.

We may begin with abstractions. Abstract ideas are synthetic concepts of the mind which, independent of actual objects, draw some common qualities from them. These, however, do not exist by themselves but in real things. Weight, for example, is an abstraction since it does not exist by itself but only in heavy objects.

The same can be said of shapes and colors. These words indicate abstractions, which, however, are in themselves synthetic, since they mass together in an abstract manner and in a single idea a quality variously dispersed in an infinite number of real objects. Children who prefer to touch things rather than to look at them seem to have minds less capable of making abstractions. But here a careful distinction must be made. Is it the absence of an object that makes the process of abstraction difficult for a little child or does he lack the mental capacity for grasping that synthesis of many things, which is an abstract idea of quality?

If we succeed in materializing an abstract idea, in presenting it in a form suitable for a child, that is, under the guise of palpable objects, will his mind be capable of appreciating it and having a deep interest in it?

The sense material can certainly be considered from the viewpoint of its being materialized abstractions. It provides a child with color, size, shape, smell, and noise in a distinct, tangible, and orderly graded manner that permits him to analyze and classify these qualities.

When a child finds himself confronted with this material, he applies himself to it with a serious, concentrated effort that seems to draw out the best that is in him. It actually seems as if children then do more than what they could naturally do with their minds. The material opens up to their intellects paths that would otherwise be inaccessible at their tender age.

Through this material children learn how to concentrate, for it contains things designed to absorb the attention of a child.

A Comparison Between the Education of Normal Children and That of Those Who Are Mentally Defective

This system of educating normal children has had its origins in the means elaborated by Itard and Seguin for teaching mentally defective children. Many, aware of this, have objected that it is impossible to employ the same system in the education of normal children. This seems all the more true at the present time when various levels of intelligence even among normal children are being distinguished with an ever increasing exactitude.

I therefore believe that it will be well to point out the

differences which our system so clearly discerns between children who are rich or poor in natural gifts. The two types have different reactions when confronted with the same material, and this provides us with an extremely useful means of comparison.

The basic difference between a normal child and one who is mentally inferior is that when they are placed in front of the same objects the deficient child will not show a spontaneous interest in them. His attention must be continuously aroused; he must be invited to observe and encouraged to act.

Suppose that we are using as our first object one of the series of solid insets. The exercise, as we know, consists in removing the cylinders from their places in the stand, setting them on the table, mixing them up, and then replacing them, each in its own place. With a child who is indifferent and mentally weak, however, we must begin with exercises that afford much more strongly contrasting stimuli. Only after many simpler exercises have been performed can such a child profit by the exercise with the solid insets.

But this is the first object which can be presented to normal children, and little tots from two-and-a-half to three-and-a-half years of age prefer it to all the rest of the sense material. On the other hand, when the solid insets are finally given to those who are retarded, their attention has to be constantly and forcibly attracted and they must be encouraged to observe and compare. And once such a child has succeeded in replacing all the cylinders in the stand, he stops and the game is ended. When a retarded child makes a mistake, he must be corrected or urged to correct himself, and even when he does recognize a mistake he usually remains indifferent.

But a normal child takes a spontaneous and lively interest in the game. He corrects himself and this very act of self-correction intensifies his attention to the differences in size and his desires to make comparisons.

When a normal child is concentrated on his work, he refuses to be interrupted by those who try to help him. He wants to be left alone with his problem. The result is a spontaneous activity that is of far greater value than simply noticing differences in things, which is, of course, of great value in itself. The material thus proves to be a key which puts a child in communication with himself and opens up his soul so that he can act and express himself. Concentration on a voluntary exercise frequently repeated indicates the superiority of a normal child.

Another difference in a normal child is his ability to distinguish between what is essential and what is only secondary.

Part of the technique of training the senses consists in isolating the sense to be exercised. Thus, for example, when we are about to indicate differences in touch, it is well to remove visual impressions from the child. This can be done by darkening the room or covering his eyes with a band. But in other instances silence is required.

All these procedures actually succeed in assisting a normal child to concentrate on a single, isolated stimulus, and they increase his interest in it.

On the contrary, a defective child is easily distracted by these same conditions and led away by them from the very object which should attract his attention. In the dark, he easily falls asleep or misbehaves. He is fascinated by the blindfold rather than by the sense stimulus on which he should fix his mind. The exercise then degenerates into useless game or into outbursts of silly laughter.

Finally, there is a further fact that should be particularly noted, namely, that both defective and normal children have obtained excellent results from what I have called Seguin's "lesson in three stages," which enables a child to associate a word with an acquired idea simply and clearly.

This leads us to reflect on the fact that the differences between more intelligent and less intelligent children become less noticeable when they passively receive instruction from a dominating teacher.

A simple and psychologically perfect lesson, like that of Seguin, succeeds in attaining its goal with both types of children.

This is a clear and eloquent proof that indvidual differences are only revealed and intensified through spontaneous work and unprovoked expression, that is, through the direct manifestation of inner impulses.

The association of a name with sense perception as devised by Seguin not only succeeds in fixing this connection within the mind of a defective child but it also stimulates his perceptive powers. A defective child is helped by this lesson to observe an object better. It now seems to be doubly attached to him, by name and by appearance.

A normal child does not need this help in observing. Rather, his habit of observation has already preceded his need for the lesson in terminology. He receives it with great joy since he has already noted the differences in his sense perceptions. The lesson in terminology, as a consequence, clarifies and completes his own voluntary labors. He has the idea, and he has vitalized it through his own efforts. Now it is baptized, given a name, and consecrated. It is interesting to note a child's great joy when he has associated a word with something which he has learned through his senses.

I remember one day teaching a little girl who was not yet three the names of three colors. I had the children place one of their little tables in front of the window and, seating myself on one of their little chairs, I made the child sit down on another to my right. On the table there were six colored tablets, two of red, two of blue, and two of yellow. First I set one of the tablets in front of the child and asked her to find its mate, and I did this with all three colors arranging each of the two colors in columns. I then passed on to Seguin's three stages. The little girl learned to recognize the respective names and the three colors.

She was so pleased that she looked at me for a long time and then began to dance. As I saw her jumping up and down before me, I said to her with a smile: "Do you know the colors?" And she replied as she danced about: "Yes." Her happiness was boundless. She continued to dance and to turn around to hear me ask the same question so that she could answer it with her enthusiastic "Yes."

A retarded child, on the other hand, is helped by the lesson to understand materials; his attention is insistently directed at the contrasting differences, and he finally becomes interested and begins to work; but the object itself does not possess a sufficiently strong stimulus to arouse his activity.

A Comparison Between Our System of Teaching Normal Children and Experimental Psychology

There is a very interesting parallel, though quite generally neglected, between the research conducted by Itard on the education of deaf-mute and defective children and the attempt made much later through the efforts of the Germans Fechner, Weber, and Wundt to subject psychology to experimentation by means of instruments of measure.

Itard, who lived during the French Revolution, was led by his studies on diseases of the ear to put educational experiments on a positive basis. He looked for means which would systematically stimulate the senses, attract attention, and arouse a person's interest and activity. The objects which he envisaged were, therefore, effectively "stimuli."

Later, Fechner, Weber, and Wundt tried to create an experimental psychology by first testing the sensitivity of normal individuals to minimum stimuli and then striving to determine with mathematical exactitude the time required by various subjects to react to these stimuli. The importance of the objects consisted in the possibility of their being more or less directly a means of measurement. They could be used for esthesiometry, that is, for the measuring of sensibility.

These two independently born programs were also carried on independently. The first, as it became better known, led to the erection of schools for deaf mutes and the mentally deficient. The second developed into institutes of experimental research for the taking of measurements and thus to the creation of a new science.

All of this research, however, since it relied upon instruments that measured sense reactions, came eventually to determine objects that were quite similar and analogous to each other, although in the one case these objects constituted material for the education of the senses whereas in the other they were instruments for measuring sense reactions.

But the aim of each of the two procedures, which are so much alike in the material used, is essentially different.

Esthesiometry attempts to identify the smallest stimulus perceptible to a grown man or to a child of a certain age by pure experimentation.

The importance of such data was that it showed that psychic reactions can be measured mathematically. This embraced the axiomatical concept that the manner of feeling, or better, of perceiving, that is, or recognizing stimuli was an absolute natural quality not dependent upon knowledge or the orderly working of the mind or intellectual achievements.

In other words, it was not dependent on the artificial psychic differences resulting from education.

Anyone can see that one thing is larger or smaller than another and can feel a tiny object that comes in contact with his skin. Individual differences in perception are due to nature, which normally creates its own variations and which, therefore, makes men more or less sensitive, just as it makes them more or less intelligent, more or less dark or fair. Psychological judgments were therefore taken as indicating the natural psychic development of a man. In fact, psychologists later proposed the setting up of standards of various psychic levels according to age and individual differences, whether the persons under consideration were normal, subnormal, and so forth.

The system of Itard, on the other hand, aimed at using strong, contrasting stimuli to attract the attention of children shut out from their environment and incapable of obtaining precise knowledge of it in ordinary ways. He consequently aimed at leading them gradually through repeated exercises to perceive less violent contrasts and ever more refined differences in the separate qualities of the objects presented to them. This was not a simple task given to a subject to determine his mental state, but a modifying action aimed at awakening the intellect and animating its contacts with its external environment, at making precise judgments with respect to qualities, and at establishing a harmony between the intellect and the outer world.

A modifying action that increases one's powers of discrimination is a true and proper function of education.

The Education of the Senses Leads to a Sharpening of the Senses Through Repeated Exercises

There is therefore an education of the senses which is as a rule completely neglected in psychological research, but which is something that must be taken into consideration.

I have, for example, often seen cubes of different sizes placed at different distances to test the mental capacity of children. A child had to recognize the largest and the smallest, and a watch is used to measure the time that elapses between command and response, and errors also are noted.

Such experiments disregard the element of education, and by this I mean the training of the senses.

The children in our schools have as a part of the material used for the training of the senses a series of ten cubes of graduated dimensions. The exercise connected with these cubes, which are all painted a light pink, is to place them on a dark carpet spread on the floor and build a tower from them, placing the largest cube at the bottom and then continuing with the next largest until the smallest is place on last. The child must therefore choose each time the largest cube that remains on the carpet. Two-and-a-half-year-old children like to play this game a great deal. Just as soon as they have built the tower, they knock it down with light blows, admire the pink shapes that have fallen on the dark carpet, and begin again to construct the tower, and they repeat this any number of times.

If one of my children of three or four was confronted with the test described above and a six- or seven-year-old child from the first grade, my child would certainly react more promptly and choose more quickly the largest and the smallest cubes, and he would make no mistakes. The same could be said for tests dealing with colors, touch, and so forth.

This fact strikes at the roots of psychometry and, in general, at all forms of experimental psychology that rely on tests. They pre-suppose intellectual levels for each age, but these can vary in individuals because of their natural endowments.

Our method of education can therefore be taken into account even by the devotees of experimental psychology, who hope to determine through instantaneous responses the level of mental attainment, as if they were taking an absolute measure of the whole by means of a single factor, as is done by measuring height to determine the development of the body at various ages. A systematic training of the senses would disrupt these criteria and would show that they do not provide absolute data with respect to mental growth.

If an attempt is made to use experimental psychology as a practical means to reform methods of teaching, then the mistake in principle becomes all the more clear.

If there is to be a science of education, it must have its origins in active and modifying stimuli and not in stimuli used as measures.

From the very beginning I based my own research on this principle. The practical result of this was that I was able to establish an experimental type of education for normal children and, at the same time, reveal psychological factors that had not as yet been recognized in children.

The introduction of experimental psychology into primary schools with its tests and reactions has not had any practical effect on the schools themselves or upon educational methods. The only effect has been to indicate the possibility of modifying examinations, that is, the tests given to the students. For some time American educators seriously thought of replacing the old type of examination, that is, one which tests what has been learned, with another type that would scientifically reveal individual aptitudes. A child, after he had finished his studies, would thus have to pass the same kind of examination as that given to individuals to determine their capacities for certain types of work.

Itard's study, on the other hand, had an immediate practical effect at the very heart of education itself. It effected the cure of partially deaf children, who through exercise were to strengthen their powers of hearing and at the same time their ability to speak. Success here then led to the education of actual deaf mutes and eventually the retarded.

Schools established in Switzerland, Germany, France, and America spread this work of redeeming these unfortunate children and raised the mental and social level of all the children with whom they came in contact.

And, just as soon as this same orientation was introduced into schools for normal children, the schools were themselves radically modified and the children in them were raised to a higher level. The social concept of the independence and freedom of a child has thus been spread throughout the whole world.

14. Written Language

Should our plan for assisting the natural development of a child be arrested by an artificial attainment due solely to the progress of civilization, that is, by the written language, comprising both reading and writing? This is something that is obviously connected with teaching, and with a kind of teaching that no longer takes into account human nature. This brings us to the point where we must consider the problem of culture in education and the efforts needed to attain it even at the sacrifice of natural impulses. We all know that reading and writing is the first obstacle in school, the first torment experienced by a man who must subject his own nature to the demands of civilization.

Educators who have reflected on this problem have come to the conclusion that it would be well to delay as long as possible taking up such a painful task, and they believe that a child of eight is barely suited for such a difficult enterprise. As a general rule, a study of the alphabet and writing is begun at the age of six, and any earlier introduction to letters and the written word is considered almost as a sin. Written language is in fact regarded as a kind of second "teaching," or no use except to one who is somewhat older. It is a language which permits us to express our thoughts that have already been logically organized and to obtain from books the ideas of a vast number of individuals who live far off or who are long since dead. As long as a child is incapable of using the written language because of his immaturity, he can be spared the hard labor of learning it.

But we believe that a solution can be reached by a more profound study of this problem. First of all we should take into account the countless errors in the means used to teach writing. This would take too long to discuss here, but a single example, that of the method used by Seguin to teach the

185

retarded how to read, can illustrate our point. Another problem for investigation would be to consider the nature of writing itself, analyzing its various components and seeking to separate these into independent exercises which could be employed at different ages and thus be distributed according to the natural powers of a child. This is the criterion which we have used, and which will be described in the following pages.

The Old Methods of Teaching Reading and Writing

Criticism of Seguin's Method of Teaching Writing

In his work on education Seguin does not give any reasoned methods on teaching how to write. Here is what he has to say on the subject:

> In order to make a child go on from drawing as such to writing, which is its most immediate application, a teacher needs simply ot describe the letter "D," as a section of a circle with its two extremities posed against a verticle line, an an "A" as two slanting lines that meet at the top and are crossed by a horizontal line and so forth.
>
> It is therefore no longer a question of knowing how a child will learn to write; he draws, and therefore he will write. After this it is not necessary to say that he must draw the letters according to the laws of contrast or analogy, putting, for example, "O" near "I," "E" near "P," "T" near "L," and so forth.

According to Seguin, therefore, it is not necessary to teach a child how to write; a child who can draw will write. But writing for him consists in tracing printed capital letters, nor does he explain further whether or not a person of low intelligence will write in other characters. Instead, he gives a lengthy description of how to teach drawing, which is supposed to prepare an individual to write and includes writing; but teaching a child how to draw is a difficult matter in itself and has been described by both Itard and Seguin.

Chapter XL—*Drawing*. In drawing, the first important

concept to be acquired is that of the flat surface destined to receive it, and the second is that of the lines traced on the surface.

These two concepts embrace all writing, all drawing, all (linear creations).

The two are correlative. Their mutual relationships beget the idea, the capacity to produce lines in this sense, since they deserve such a name only when they follow a reasoned and methodical course. An aimless mark is not a line; it is a product of chance and has no meaning.

A rational mark, on the contrary has a name since it follows a direction; and since all writing and design is nothing more than a composite of lines running in different directions, it is necessary before taking up writing in the proper sense of the word to insist upon these concepts of line and plane. A normal child acquires these instinctively but they must be explained in a precise and sensible manner in all their applications to the mentally retarded. Through methodical drawing they will come into rational contact with all the parts of a plane and through imitation will produce first simple lines and later those that are complicated.

They are taught in successive stages: 1) to trace different kinds of lines; 2) to draw them in different directions and in different positions with respect to the flat surface; 3) to join these lines so that they form graduated figures of increased complexity. They must therefore first be taught how to distinguish straight lines from curved, vertical lines from horizontal, and the infinite variety of slanting lines, and, finally, the principal points of union of two or more lines to form a figure.

This rational analysis of drawing, which will give rise to writing, is so essential in all its parts that a child who was able to draw materially many letters before he was entrusted to me has taken six days to draw a perpendicular and a horizontal line, and fifteen days to reproduce a curved and a slanting line. Most of my pupils are unable to imitate the movements of my hand on paper before they are able to draw a line in a definite direction.

The more imitative and the intelligent produce a mark diametrically opposed to the one I show them, and all confuse the point of union between two lines, even the easiest to understand, such as top, bottom, and middle. It is true that the thorough knowledge which I have given them of the plane, lines, and configurations prepares them to grasp the relationship which must be established between the plane and the different lines which they must use to cover its surface; but the deficiencies of my pupils makes it necessary that the progression from the vertical to the horizontal, to the oblique, and to the curve must be determined by taking into account the difficulty which their dull intelligences and unsteady hands have in understanding and executing their tasks. It is not simply a question of making them carry out a difficult operation, since I prepared myself to make them overcome a series of difficulties. I therefore have asked myself if some things were harder to do than others. This then has been what has guided me in these matters.

The vertical is a line which the eye and hand follow directly by raising and lowering themselves. A horizontal line is not natural either to the eye or to the hand, which glide down and follow a curve like that of the horizon which gives the line its name.

A slanting line implies concepts that are comparatively more complex, and curves demand a consistency in their different relationships with respect to the plane and are so variable and difficult to grasp that it would be a waste of time to begin the study of lines with them. The simplest line is therefore one that is vertical, and I shall now describe how I have been able to make the children grasp its idea.

The first principle of geometry is the following: Only one straight line can be drawn from one point to another. Starting with this axiom, which only the hand can demonstrate, I fixed two points on the blackboard and joined them with a vertical line. The children tried to do the same between dots which I had made on their papers, but some drew the line down to the right of the lower dot and others to the left, without taking into account those whose hands wandered all over the page in every direction. In order to put a stop to these deviations, which are often much more in the intellect and sight than in the hand, I thought it well to restrict the usual surface of the plane by drawing two vertical lines, one to the right and one to the left of the dots which a child was to join with a line parallel to, and between, the other two, which served, I might say, as barriers. If these two lines were not enough, I fastened two rulers vertically on the paper, which effectively kept the hand from wandering; but such material controls are not useful for long. They first stop using the rulers and turn to using the parallel lines. A mentally retarded child will soon be able to draw a line between them. Then one of the guiding vertical lines is removed and there is left only one, sometimes the one on the right, sometimes the one on the left, to preclude any deviations. Finally, even this line is suppressed and then the dots, beginning with the one at the top which indicates the point of departure for the hand and line. In this way a child learns to draw a vertical line by himself without any assistance and without any points of comparison.

The same method is used, the same difficulties encountered, and the same means of direction are employed for straight horizontal lines. If by chance they are begun quite well, one must expect that a child will curve them slightly as he moves from the center towards the extremities as nature impels him for the reasons already given. If dots placed at intervals are not sufficient to keep his hand up, it is forced to go straight by parallel lines drawn on the paper or by rulers.

Finally, a child is made to draw a horizontal line while resting a square against a vertical line that forms a right angle with it. He will thus begin to understand the meaning of a vertical and of a horizontal line and will be able to surmise the relationship of these two primary concepts for drawing figures.

From the order in which lines are generated it would seem that the study of slanting lines should immediately follow those that are vertical and horizontal, but this is not the case. A slanting line, which shares its inclination with the vertcial and its direction with the horizontal and is naturally like the other two in that it is straight, because of its relationships both with the plane and with other lines presents an idea that is too complicated to be grasped without further preparation.

Seguin continues for several pages to speak in this way of

lines slanting in all directions which he had his pupils draw between two other parallel lines. He then goes on to the four curves which he had drawn to the right and left of a vertical line and above and below another that was horizontal. He concludes as follows:

> In this way the problems which I was investigating were solved, for vertical, horizontal, slanting, and four curved lines which join together to make up a circle contain in principle all possible lines, all writing.
>
> When we had arrived at this point, Itard and I stopped for a long time. Since the lines were known, it seemed proper to have a child draw some of the regular figures beginning, of course, with the simplest. Itard had had some experience in this and he advised me to begin with a square. I followed this advice for three months without being able to make myself understood.

After a long series of experiments and reflection on the origins of geometric figures, Seguin discovered that the easiest figure to draw was the triangle.

> When three lines meet in this way, they always form a triangle, whereas four lines can meet in a hundred different directions without preserving their parallelism, and they thus form an imperfect square.
>
> From these experiments and observations, which have been confirmed by many others which it would be useless to narrate, I have deduced the first principles of writing and drawing for the mentally retarded. Their application is too simple for me to dwell longer upon it.

This then was the procedure used by my predecessors to teach the mentally deficient how to write. In order to teach them how to read, Itard proceeded as follows. He hung wooden geometrical figures from nails on a wall. These were triangles, squares, circles, and so forth. Then he drew exact copies of them on the wall. After this, when he had removed the figures, he had them replaced on their respective nails by the Savage of Averyron, who was guided simply by the drawings. It was from these drawings that Itard himself then got the idea of flat insets. Finally, he had capital letters made and used them as he had earlier done with geometrical figures, that is, he drew letters on the wall and placed nails in such a way that a child could hang the wooden letters over the drawings. Later on Seguin used a horizontal plane instead of the wall, drawing the letters on the bottom of a box and having his pupils cover them with the movable letters.

Twenty years later Seguin had not changed this procedure. Criticism of the method used by Itard and Seguin in teaching reading and writing seems to me to be superfluous. It contains two fundamental errors which make it inferior to the means used for teaching normal children. The first of these is that the writing is taught with printed capitals. The second is that geometry is used to prepare the pupils for writing, but today this is only presented to students in secondary schools. Seguin has actually confused different ideas in a surprising way. He passes immediately from a psychological observation of a child and his relationship with his environment to a study of the origins of lines and figures and their connection with a flat surface.

He maintains that a child will easily draw a vertical line but that when he attempts to draw a horizontal line it will very soon start to curve because "nature commands it," and this command of nature is explained by the fact that a man sees the horizon as a curved line.

Seguin furnishes us with a valuable lesson on the need of special training for a man to observe and to think logically. Observation should be absolutely objective, that is, it should be free from preconceptions. In this particular case, Seguin's preconception was that geometrical drawings should prepare one for writing, and this hindered him from discovering the truly natural foundation for the art. Further, he believed that the deviation in a line, and the inaccuracy with which it is drawn by a child, is due to a child's mind and eye rather than to his hand. He therefore wore himself out in explaining for weeks and months the directions of lines and in guiding the vision of mentally defectives.

Seguin seems to have thought that it is a good method to start at the top, with geometry, with a child's intelligence, and with certain abstract relationships. These are all that one needs to take into account.

But is not this a common mistake?

A great deal of time and intellectual effort are wasted in

the world because what is false seems great and what it true seems slight.

Seguin's method for teaching one how to write illustrates the tortuous ways we follow in teaching because of our tendency to complicate matters. It resembles the tendency that we have to put a high value only on complicated things. Seguin furnishes us with an example of this since he taught geometry in order to teach writing and forced a child's mind to attempt to understand geometrical abstractions to free him from the much simpler effort required to draw a printed "D." But further, will not a child have to make an effort to forget printed, in order to learn cursive letters? And would it not be simpler to begin with the latter?

Did not many believe that it was first necessary to teach a child how to make strokes in order to teach him how to write? This used to be a deep-seated conviction. It seemed natural that, in order to write the letters of the alphabet, all of which are rounded, it was necessary to begin with straight lines and with strokes furnished with a line at a sharp angle. Can we really wonder then at the fact that the beginner experienced great difficulty in getting rid of harsh angularity in forming the beautiful curves of the letter "O," or how much effort was required on our part and his to get him to make strokes and write with sharp angles?

Let us rid ourselves for the time being of such prejudices and move along a simpler path. We may be able to spare men of the future the painful efforts now required for learning how to write.

Must one begin with strokes? The logical answer is "No." These require too much of an effort on the part of the child to make them. If he is to begin with the stroke, it should be the easiest thing to execute.

But, if we note carefully, a straight stroke is the most difficult to make. Only an accomplished writer can fill out a page with regular strokes, whereas a person who is only moderately proficient can cover a page with presentable writing. In fact, the straight line is unique in that it follows the shortest distance between two points. Every variation from this means that a line is not straight. The countless variations are therefore easier to make than the single stroke which is the standard of perfection. If one is ordered to draw a straight line on the blackboard without any other consideration, he will trace a long line beginning now from one side of the board and now from another, and almost anyone can do this. But if one is ordered to draw a line in a particular direction starting from a predetermined point, he will be much less likely to succeed and will fall into many more irregularities, or errors.

Almost all the lines will be horizontal because the individuals will move in carrying out the command.

If we now order the same persons to draw short lines within fixed limits, they will commit still more errors, since they can no longer move in one direction as they draw the line. Next we can order them to hold the writing instrument in a particular way and not as each one chooses.

In this way we come to the first act of writing which we think children should perform. This consists in preserving the parallelism between separate strokes. But his is hard and trying since the children do not understand its meaning.

I noticed in the notebooks of defective children whom I visited in France, and Voisin also mentions this same phenomenon, that the pages of strokes, although they start off well, end up as rows of "C's." This means that a defective child, whose attention is less resistant than that of a normal child, gradually loses his first impulse to imitate, and little by little substitutes a natural movement for the one imposed. The straight lines are thus slowly changed into curves that more and more resemble a "C." This phenomenon does not occur in the notebooks of normal children since they persist in their efforts to the end of the page and, as often happens, thus conceal the error in their teaching. But let us observe the spontaneous drawing of normal children when, for example, they are drawing lines on the sand of a garden path with a fallen branch. We shall never see them draw short, straight lines, but long curved ones variously interlaced. Seguin observed the same phenomenon when he had them draw horizontal lines which soon curved and which he attributed to an imitation of the line of the horizon.

The efforts which we thought were necessary to learn how to write are completely artificial since they are connected not with writing but with the methods used in teaching it.

My first experiments with defective children. For the moment let us abandon all dogmatism with respect to this matter. Let us disregard the cultural background. Let us give up our interest in the question as to how man first learned to write and how writing itself developed. Let us renounce the conviction which usage has established that writing must begin with small strokes and imagine that our minds are stripped bare like the truth which we want to discover.

Let us observe an individual as he is writing and seek to analyze the acts which he performs while writing.

This would be to carry out a psycho-physiological study of writing; it would mean examining the writer and not the writing, the subject not the object. It was always by beginning with the object, by examining writing, that a method was built up. A method starting from an investigation of the individual instead of writing would be completely original and far different from any other method that has preceded it.

If I had thought of giving a name to this new method of writing when I undertook experiments with normal children before knowing its results, I would have called it a psychological method because of its source of inspiration. But experience has furnished me with another name for it: "the method of spontaneous writing."

During the time when I was teaching defective children I happened to notice the following. A eleven-year-old retarded girl, who had normal strength and mobility of hand, could not learn how to sew or even to take the first step, that of pushing a needle in and out, over and under the cloth, thus leaving a few stitches in it.

Then I set the girl to work at Froebel's weaving exercise. This consists in threading a strip of paper transversely through other vertical strips fixed at top and bottom. I was struck by the analogy between the two types of work and watched the girl with keen interest. When she had mastered Froebel's weaving, I put her back sewing and saw with pleasure that she succeeded in stitching.

I realized that the necessary movement of the hand for sewing had been prepared without sewing, and that before teaching it is first necessary to find the way to teach. This is particularly true when it is a question of gaining facility in movements. These could be carried out almost automatically through repeated exercises even apart from the work for which they were directly intended. In this way one could set himself to a task and be already capable of carrying it out without ever having directly put his hand to it, and he could complete it almost perfectly at the first attempt.

I thought that one might be prepared to write in this way. The idea interested me greatly, and I marveled at its simplicity. I was surprised that I had not thought of this procedure before observing the girl who was unable to sew.

Actually, since the children had already been taught to touch the outlines of the geometrical figures of the plane insets, they only had to touch with their fingers the shapes of the letters of the alphabet as well.

I had a splendid alphabet in cursive script made with the letters three inches high and the strokes of the letters in proportion. The letters themselves were made of wood about $8/16$ of an inch thick. All were enameled, the consonants in blue and the vowels in red, except at the bottom where there was a very elegant brass sheath affixed with small brads. Corresponding to this alphabet, of which there was only one copy, were numerous cards on which were painted the letters of the alphabet of the same size and color as the movable letters and grouped according to ther contrasts and similarities in shape.

Corresponding to every letter of the alphabet was a hand-painted water-color which reproduced the shape and color of the cursive letter, and near it, but much smaller, the same letter in a small printed character. On the card, moreover, were painted objects whose first name began with the letter in question, for example, for "*m*" there was *mano* (hand) and *martello* (hammer), for "*g*," *gatto* (cat), and so forth. These pictures served to fix the sound of a letter in the memory. The pictures certainly did not represent a new idea, but they completed a whole which had not previously existed.

The interesting part of my experiment was that, after the movable letter had been placed over the corresponding letter drawn on the cards, I had the children trace the letters repeatedly as if they were writing them. These exercises were then carried out simply on the letters drawn on the cards. In this way the children succeeded in mastering the movements necessary for reproducing the shapes of the letters without actually writing them. I was then struck by an idea that had never before entered my mind, namely, that two different kinds of movement are used in writing. Besides the motion for reproducing the shape of the letter, there is also that of handling the writing instrument. As a matter of fact, when defective children became expert in tracing all the letters of the alphabet according to their shapes, they were still unable to hold a pen in their hands. Holding and manipulating a rod with confidence corresponds to a specially acquired muscular mechanism that is independent of the actual movements involved in writing. It is however common to all the various movements needed to trace the different letters of the alphabet. It must therefore be a distinct mechanism which exists along with the memory of how to draw the individual letters. This muscular mechanism for controlling the writing instrument had therefore to be prepared. To do this I added two other exercises to the one already described. The children had to touch the letter not simply with the index finger of the right hand as at first, but with two fingers, the index and the middle finger. They then had to follow the letter with a small wooden rod held like a pen in writing.

In general I had them complete the same movements now with, and now without, the instrument in their hand.

It should be noted that a child must follow the visible image of the drawn letter with his finger. It is true that his finger has already become accustomed to touching the outlines of geometric figures, but this exercise does not always succeed in achieving its goal. Even we ourselves, when we are retouching a drawing, for example, cannot follow exactly the line even though we see how it should be retraced. Strictly speaking, the drawing should have some special quality capable of attracting the point of our pencil as a magnet attracts iron, or the pencil should have a mechanical guide on the paper so that it can follow exactly the lines that are sensible only to the eye. Retarded children, therefore, did not always follow the drawing closely either with their finger or with a stylus. The teaching material did not offer any real control over the work done but only the uncertain control of a child's eye, who could see if his finger was following the shape of the letter or not. I thought that it would be a good plan to prepare hollowed out letters so that the movements of writing might be carried out more exactly and that their execution might be guaranteed or at least directed. I planned having the letters made in such a way that they would be represented by a groove which could be traced with a wooden rod, but since the project would have been too expensive, I did not put it into execution.

I spoke at length on this method to teachers in my lectures at the Teachers' College for Defectives. In the second year of the course, I passed out notes on this method. I still have about a hundred copies of these as documents of the past.

Here are words which were publicly spoken twenty-five years ago and which remain in the hands of more than two hundred elementary teachers without anyone of them, as Professor Ferreri has noted in an article,[1] getting a single profitable idea from them:[2]

At this point a card is shown to the child with the vowels painted on it in red. He can see the irregular figures drawn in color and then takes wooden vowels also painted in red and places them over the drawings on the card. He must then trace the wooden vowels as he would in writing and name them. The vowels are arranged according to their similarity in shape:

o, e, a,   i, u

Then the child is told, for example, "Find me an *o!*" "Put it in its place." Then, "What is this letter?" Here it will be seen that many children make mistakes because they simply look at the letter and guess without touching it. Interesting observations can be made which reveal individual types, visual and motor.

The child is then made to touch the letter drawn on the card, first with his index finger alone, then with the index and middle finger, and finally with a little wooden rod held like a pen. The letter should be touched as if it were being written.

The consonants are drawn in blue and placed on cards according to their similarities in shape. Corresponding letters made of wood and painted blue are also provided so that they can be placed on the cards as was done with the

[1] G. Ferreri, "On the Teaching of Writing: the System of Dr. Maria Montessori," *Bulletin of The Roman Association for the Medico-Pedagogic Care of Abnormal Children and Poor Defectives*, I.4 (Rome, Oct., 1907).

[2] "Summary of the Lectures of Teaching" by Dr. Montessori in 1900. Roman Lithograph Company, Via Frattina 62, p. 46: "Simultaneous Reading and Writing."

vowels. Along with the alphabet there is a series of other cards where, next to the consonants like those made of wood, are painted one or two figures of objects whose names begin with the letter drawn on the card. In front of the cursive letter is also painted in the same color a small letter in print.

The teacher names the consonants phonetically, points to a letter and then to the corresponding cards, and finally pronounces the names of the objects painted on them, dwelling particularly on the first letter, for example, *m* ... *mela* (apple) "Give me the consonant *m*, put it in its place, touch it," and so forth. As this is going on, defects in a child's language may be noted.

Touching the letters as if they were being written initiates the muscular training that prepares for writing. One of our children of the "motor" type, taught by this method, reproduced with surprising regularity all the letters in writing about ¼ of an inch high before she could recognize them. This little girl is also very successful in manual work.

A child who looks at, recognizes, and touches the letters as if he were writing is prepared at one and the same time for reading and writing.

Touching the letters and looking at them at the same time fixes their images more quickly because of the cooperation of the senses. Later the two will be separated: seeing will be employed in reading and touching in writing. According to their different types, some learn how to read first and others how to write.

I therefore began my system of reading and writing along its basic line many years ago. One day I noticed to my great surprise the ease with which a retarded child, after he had taken a piece of chalk, traced in a good and steady hand all the letters of the alphabet, writing them for the first time; and he did this much more quickly than one would have imagined. As is expressly stated in my lecture notes, some children used to write beautifully with a pen all the letters before they were able to recognize any of them. I noticed the same in normal children, and, as I said at the time: The muscular sense is the most highly developed in childhood. Writing is therefore very easy for children. It is not so with reading, which demands an extensive period of instruction and requires a higher intellectual development, since it involves interpreting the signs and modulating the voice in order to understand the meaning of a word; and all this requires purely mental work. Writing on the other hand, as is indicated below, means that a child translates sounds materially into signs. The process involves motion, which is always present and easy for him. Writing develops easily and spontaneously in a little child in the same way as speech, which is also a motor translation of sounds that have been heard. Reading on the other hand, forms a part of an abstract intellectual culture. It interprets ideas represented by graphic symbols and is acquired only later.

First Experiments with Normal Children. My first experiments with normal children were begun in the first half of November, 1907.

From January 6th in the first Children's House in San Lorenzo and from March 7th, in the second house, the dates of their foundations, until the end of July, when there was a month of vacation, I had simply given the children exercises in practical living and in training the senses. I had done so because, like all the rest, I was a victim of the prejudice that the teaching of reading and writing should be put off as long as possible and should not be introduced before a child was at least six. But during the months which had elapsed, the children seemed to be asking for some conclusions to the exercises which had already developed their intellects to a surprising degree. They could dress and undress and wash themselves. They knew how to sweep the floor, dust the furniture, set the rooms in order, open and close boxes, turn keys in locks, replace objects in cupboards in their proper order, and water the flowers. They were able to observe and knew how to recognize objects merely by touching them. A number of the children had come and asked us frankly to teach them how to read and write. After we refused some of the children came to school able to draw *o*'s on the blackboard and presented this fact to us as a kind of challenge. Then a good many of their mothers came and asked us as a favor to teach their children how to write, "because," they said, "here they learn so easily that, if you taught them how to read and write, they would learn quickly and would be spared the great burdens of elementary school." The confidence of these women that their children could learn to read and write from us without weariness struck me forcibly. Remembering the results I had obtained in the schools for defective children, I decided during the August holidays to make a similar attempt when school opened up again in September. But then I thought it would be better to take up teaching where it had been left off and to begin reading and writing only in October, when the elementary schools opened. This would have the further advantage of beginning to teach the same matter at the same time as they.

In September, therefore, I began looking around for someone who could make the material, but I could find no one willing to do so. A professor advised me to have my orders carried out at Milan, and this led to a great loss of time. I wanted a splendid wood and metal alphabet made like the one I had used with the defectives. But later I would have been content with painted letters like those used for signs in shop windows, but I could find none. No one wanted to make them out of metal. I was on the point of getting letters hollowed out of wood so that the grooves could be touched with a rod from a training school, but the work proved to be too difficult and was never completed.

In this way the whole of October passed. The children in the first grade had already filled pages with strokes and mine were still waiting. Then the teachers and I decided to cut out very large letters of the alphabet from pieces of paper. One of the teachers roughly colored one side of these in blue. So that the children might be able to touch the letters, I thought of cutting them out of sandpaper and gluing them on to smooth paper. This furnished us with objects very much like those used in the first exercises of the sense of touch.

Only after I had made these different objects, did I notice how far superior they were to the alphabet I had used with the defectives and which I had vainly sought to obtain for two months. If I had been rich I would have forever used this elegant but sterile alphabet of the past. We desire the old because we fail to understand the new, and we always look for past grandeur without recognizing in lowly simplicity the new stirrings of a germ that must develop.

I thus learned that a paper alphabet could be easily multiplied. This meant that many children could use them at once not only for recognizing letters but also for composing words. I also learned that a sandpaper alphabet furnished the desired guide for touching the letters so that they were no longer simply seen but felt. The motions required for writing could thus be taught under exact control.

The two teachers and I, full of enthusiasm that evening after school, cut up a great number of letters of the alphabet from simple writing paper, glued sandpaper letters to smooth pieces of paper, and colored the others blue. We then spread them out to dry on the tables so that we might find them ready in the morning. While we were thus working, a very clear picture of our method in all its entirety took shape in my mind. It was so simple that it made me smile to think that I had not thought of it earlier. The history of our subsequent efforts has been most interesting.

One day when one of the teachers was sick, one of my pupils, Miss Anna Fedeli, a teacher of education in one of the normal schools, went to take her place. When I went in the evening to see Miss Fedeli, she showed me two modifications she had made in the alphabet. One of these consisted in placing at the bottom of each letter a small transverse strip of white paper so that the child might recognize the right side of the letter, which otherwise was often turned around in all directions. The second consisted in making a cardboard box with separate compartments for each group of letters. Previously these had been kept all mixed up. I still have that box made out of an old broken container which she had found in the porter's lodge and had stitched together with white thread. As she showed me the box, Miss Fedeli was almost apologetic for her poor work, but I was enthusiastic. I immediately realized that letters placed in such a box would be a valuable assistance in teaching. It offered a child's eye the possibility of comparing all the letters and picking out the one that had been designated.

This, then, was the origin of my method of teaching how to write and of the materials employed, which I shall now describe.

Here it should be sufficient to note that less than a month and a half later, that is, at the time of the Christmas holidays in the following December, when the children in the elementary schools were laboriously trying to forget the strokes and angles which they had learned with so much trouble so that they could draw the curves of an *o* and of the other vowels, two of my own little pupils, who were only four years old, were writing neatly without erasures or smudges; and their writing was later judged to be comparable to that of children in the third grade.

15. The Mechanism of Writing

Writing is a complex act which needs to be analyzed. One part of it has reference to motor mechanisms and the other represents a real and proper effort of the intellect.

I have distinguished first of all two principal groups of movements. One is concerned with managing the instrument of writing, and the other with the drawing of the different shapes of the separate letters of the alphabet. Taken together these two groups of movements constitute the motor mechanism of writing. A machine could be substituted to carry on this work, and in such a case we would have a mechanism of another type which would have to be developed. An example of this might be found in typewriters. The fact that a man can use a machine for writing enables us to understand how two things, that is, the actual mechanics of writing and the higher function of the intellect which uses written language for expression can be distinguished and separated from each other.

An accurate analysis can be made of physiological mechanisms, for if we notice how one writes and observe the various components of the activity, we cannot only distinguish them but also separate them from each other.

Let us begin then to study the two groups of movements.

Let us first take up the one that is involved in manipulating the writing instrument, that is, in holding a pen or pencil. This is grasped by the first three fingers of the hand and is moved up and down with that consistent uniformity which we are accustomed to call "the style of writing." Even though we all use the same alphabet, the motions we make are so individual that each one has his own particular style of writing, and there are thus as many forms of writing as there are men.

It is impossible to forge a person's handwriting. The infinitesimal differences that exist between different hands are unfathomable in their origins, but it is certain that they were "sensibly" fixed in each of us when our own particular mechanism was established, and this prevents us from ever changing it greatly. Writing becomes a mark of recognition and is one of the clearest and most indelible that we have. In the same way are fixed the accents of our voice, our pronunciation of our native language, and all those various movements which form a part of our way of acting and which are destined to survive even after many of our physical characteristics have undergone a slow but continuous transformation.

It is in childhood that the motor mechanisms are fixed. Through practice a child elaborates and fixes these traits of his personality, following the guidance of an individual, invisible law. During childhood the motor mechanisms are in their sensitive stage and are prompt to obey the secret orders of nature.

In every effort involving motion, a child therefore experiences the joyous satisfaction of responding to a vital need.

It is necessary to find out at what age the mechanisms for writing are ready to be fixed. They will then be fixed naturally and without effort; and they will also be a source of pleasure and provide an increase of vital energy.

This is certainly not the age in which they try in ordinary schools to excite the motor mechanism of writing. To ask the little hand, which is now adult in that its motions are already fixed, to turn back on the way of its development is to make a tortured effort at reform. The hand of a child of six or seven has already lost its precious period of sensitivity to movement. This delicate little hand has left behind that blessed period in which its movements were coordinated. It is therefore condemned to make unnatural and painful efforts to acquire new modes of operation.

We must therefore go back and find the still uncoordinated but pliable hand of an infant. It is that of a child of four who strives to touch everything about him in his irresistible and unconscious attempt to stabilize his various movements.

An Analysis of the Movements of a Hand that is Writing

In order to help one learn how to write, we must first

analyze the various movements required, and we must strive to develop these separately in a way that is independent of actual writing. In this way we will be able to make different ages, each one with its own potentialities, cooperate in erecting this difficult and complex mechanism.

We shall find the psychological moment and the external means best suited for a remote preparation of the mechanism for writing in the exercises of the senses which accompany the fine movements of the hand and which are so attractive to a child that he is led to repeat them over and over again.

The hand that writes should be able to hold in its fingers an instrument for writing, a pen or pencil, and be able to guide it lightly so as to make definite marks.

This requires not only the work of three fingers to hold the writing instrument but also the cooperation of the whole hand, which must lightly pass over the flat surface upon which one is writing.

Actually, the first difficulty of ordinary students is not so much that of holding a pen in hand as that of keeping the hand light and not pressing down too heavily upon it. An inexperienced student will make a piece of chalk screech on the blackboard and a pen on paper, and he will often break both chalk and pen. He grasps the writing instrument convulsively and drags it over the object on which he is writing. His efforts consist in struggling with the unsupportable weight of his own feeble little hand.

Further, an uncoordinated hand cannot execute signs as precise as those of the letters of the alphabet. This can only be done by a hand which is already capable of guiding itself steadily. A necessary condition for writing is to have what is called a "firm hand," that is, a hand under the control of the will.

Long exercises patiently repeated are necessary to attain this. If a hand is too clumsy to write, it must acquire the necessary delicacy, and this will be its greatest obstacle to progress in the art.

But in our system little children acquire a hand which is practiced and ready to write.

They are unconsciously preparing themselves for writing when in the course of the sense exercises they move the hand in various directions, constantly repeating the same actions though with different immediate ends in view. Let us consider some of the exercises already completed by our children.

The three fingers which handle the instrument. Three-year-old children remove the cylinders from the solid insets by grasping the knob, which is about the same size as a pen or pencil, with their three fingers. The three fingers thus carry out an exercise that coordinates the motor organs needed for writing a countless number of times.

A light hand. We may observe a child of three-and-a-half as he dips the tips of his fingers into tepid water and with his eyes blindfolded devotes his energies toward a single effort, that of moving his lightly poised hand so that the fingers barely glide over the surface of a smooth or rough plane.

This effort to move the hand lightly is accompanied by a sharpening of the sense of touch in those fingers which someday must write. In this way the most precious instrument of the human will is constantly perfected.

A firm hand. There is something that precedes the hand's ability to draw a figure; it is the capability of moving it for some specific goal, of being able to guide it in a precise fashion. This ability is a generic property of the hand, since it has reference to the ability to coordinate one's movements or not.

We may recall the exercise with the flat insets, which consists in carefully touching the outlines of the various geometrical plaques and their corresponding frames, using as a guide the wooden edge which helps to keep the inexperienced hand within the prescribed limits. In the meantime the eye becomes accustomed to seeing and recognizing the form which the hand is touching.

This is a remote and indirect preparation of the hand so that it will be able to write, but it is not an immediate preparation for writing. These two preparations should not be confused with each other.

Direct Preparation for Writing

An Analysis of Its Various Factors

We must now analyze the various factors of writing, making use of matters already discussed as illustrations. Writing contains a complex set of difficulties which can be separated from each other and which can be overcome one by one through different exercises, and also at different times or periods of life. The exercise relative to each factor, however, must be kept independent from writing itself. As a matter of fact, if writing is a result of various factors, the individual factors, when they are isolated from each other are no longer writing. We can find an analogy for this in chemistry. Water, when it is broken down into hydrogen and oxygen, is no longer water, but something else, two gases, each with its own properties, and each able to exist by itself. Thus, when we speak of an analysis of factors, we mean separating out the constituent elements of writing into interesting exercises which can by themselves provide motives of activity for children. This is quite different from an analysis which aims at breaking up a whole into parts simply as parts and is therefore devoid of interest (strokes, curves, and so forth). Instead of this, our analysis of the factors makes each one of them live in an independent exercise. It separates the various factors, but it looks for elements in this separation that exist by themselves and which can be used in exercises having a rational end in view.

First factor: handling the writing instrument: drawing. I have taken advantage of the instinct which children have for filling out figures drawn in outline with colored pencils. This is a primitive kind of drawing, or better, an act that precedes drawing. To make this work more interesting, I have provided means so that the children themselves can draw the outlines of the figures to be filled in. These outlines guarantee the preservation of an aesthetic order in the drawings and a child can choose the one he prefers. For this purpose I have prepared special material, iron insets, which will be described later. These enable a child to draw the outline of geometric figures. These in turn have given rise to a kind of decorative design which we have called "the art of the insets," but this should not be considered to be in any way a direct preparation for writing.

Second factor: the drawing of alphabetic symbols. For the other group of movements, that is, for the drawing of written symbols, I offer a child material consisting of smooth cards on which are glued the letters of the alphabet in sandpaper. They trace these as if they were writing. In this way the movements on hand and arm are fixed so that they are able to reproduce a sign which the eye has the opportunity of fixing at the same time from a distance. A letter is thus memorized in a twofold manner, by sight and by touch.

Summing up, we may say that the two mechanical factors of writing are resolved into two independent exercises, that is, drawing, which gives the hand the ability to handle the writing instrument, and touching the letters of the alphabet, which serves to establish a motor memory along with a visual memory of the letters.

A description of the material for directing both drawing and writing at the same time: desks, metal insets, outlined figures, and colored pencils.

I have had two identical stands made with slightly sloping tops and supported on four short wooden legs. At the lower edge of the sloping top is fixed a transverse bar which prevents objects from sliding off. Each desk has exactly four square plaques for insets. Each of these are made of iron painted brown. In the center of each of these plaques, which are four inches square, is the inset, also of metal painted in blue and furnished at the center with a bronze knob.

Exercises. When the two stands are placed next to each other they look somewhat like a single stand containing eight figures. They may be set on a ledge, a teacher's table, a cupboard, or even on the edge of a child's table itself. This is an elegant object and it attracts a child's attention. He can choose one or other figure and take the plaque along with the inset. These are very much like the flat insets already described, except that here a child has at his disposal free pieces that are thin but very heavy. He first takes the outer frame, places it on a white sheet of paper and with a colored pencil outlines the empty figure in the center of the plaque. Then he removes the plaque and has a geometrical shape on the paper.

This is the first time that a child reproduces a geometrical figure by drawing. Up until now he has only placed the flat insets over the first, second, and third series of cards.

Next, on the figure which he has himself drawn, the child placed the inset, just as he did with the plane insets on the cards of the first series. He outlines it with pencil of a different color, then takes it away, and then has the figure doubly outlined on the paper in two colors.

After this the child with a colored pencil of his own choosing, which he holds like a pen for writing, fills in the outlined figure.

He is taught not to go outside the outlined figure.

The exercise of filling in one single figure makes a child repeat movements that would be sufficient to fill ten pages with strokes; and he does this without becoming weary, for he is freely coordinating the necessary muscular activities and is delighted to see a large, brilliantly colored figure coming to being under his very eyes.

At first children fill many sheets of paper with these squares, triangles, ovals, and trapezoids in red, orange, green, purple, blue and pink.

When we examine a series of figures drawn by the same child, we can notice a twofold progress. First, the lines cross less and less over the outline, so that eventually they are all contained perfectly within it, and the filling in is steady and uniform all about the edge as well as in the center. Second, the strokes used in filling the space, which were at first short and confused, are drawn parallel to each other and are increasingly lengthened to the point where the figures are at times filled in with a perfectly regular series of strokes running from boundary to boundary. When this happens, we may be sure that a child has mastered the pen, that is, he has stablized the muscular activity needed for handling an instrument of writing. From an examination of such drawings one can therefore draw a safe conclusion with respect to the child's ability to hold a pen in his hand.

The outlined drawings already mentioned are also used to vary the exercises by combining them into different geometrical figures and various decorative motifs. Flowers and landscapes are also colored. These drawings perfect a child's skill in that they oblige him to draw lines of different lengths and make him ever more skillful and sure in the use of his hands.

Now, if we were to count the lines drawn by a child in filling up the figures, and if these were translated into strokes for writing, they would fill up scores of notebooks. Our children as a consequence write with a confidence which could be compared with that reached in the third grade by ordinary methods.

When our children take a pen in their hands for the first time, they are able to handle it almost like a writer.

I do not believe that any means could be found more efficacious in gaining such a victory in less time and which could afford so much amusement to a child. In contrast to this, the old method which I used of having retarded children touch the outlines of letters drawn on cards with a rod is quite poor and fruitless.

Even when the children know how to write, I always have them continue with these exercises. They contribute to their continued progress since the drawing can be varied and complicated in all kinds of ways, and the children, by constantly practicing what is essentially the same exercise see that they are accumulating a gallery of different pictures of increasing merit of which they are naturally proud. Consequently, I do not simply promote, but perfect writing, but the same so-called "preparatory exercises." In the present case, for example, the pen will be held more and more securely, not because of repeated exercises in writing, but because of the filling in of the outlines. My children thus perfect themselves in writing without writing.

Material for touching the letters: Letters of the alphabet in sandpaper. Large cards with letters grouped according to a similarity of form. The material consists in a copy of each letter of the alphabet cut out of fine sandpaper and fastened to a card of proportionate size. The card is covered with smooth green paper, whereas the sandpaper is light grey; or the card is replaced by polished white wood, and the sandpaper is then black. The reason for this is that the colors help to make the shape of the letter stand out more distinctly from its background.

Similar mounts, but much larger made of cardboard or wood, carry various groups of letters exactly corresponding to the letters on the small cards, but they are combined in groups according to their likeness or contrast in form.

The letters should be beautifully drawn and with the proper shading. They are written vertically if this is the style employed at the time in the elementary schools. The character of this material is determined by the style of writing in common use. We do not aim at making a reform in the manner of writing. This would be completely foreign to our goal. We only wish to facilitate writing, no matter what kind it may be.

Exercises. One begins at once with the teaching of the

letters of the alphabet, starting with the vowels and then taking up the consonants. These are pronounced according to their sound and not their name. A sound is immediately united with a word, and the syllables are pronounced according to the well-known phonetic method. The teaching proceeds according to the three stages already described:

I. *Sensations of sight and touch associated with the sounds of the alphabet.* The teacher gives the child two green cards or two white tablets, depending upon the teaching material at her disposal, on which are the letters *i* and *o*. She says: "This is *i*." "This is *o*." And she continues in a similar manner with the rest of the letters. She makes the child touch the letter at once, saying: "Touch," and without further explanation, she shows the child how to trace the letter, and, if it is necessary, she actually guides the index finger of the child's right hand over the sandpaper as if he were writing.

A child learns immediately, and his fingers, already expert in tactile exercises, is guided by the light resistance of the fine sandpaper over the exact path of the letter. He is then able to repeat by himself indefinitely the necessary movements to produce the letters of the alphabet without fear of making mistakes as he follows the shapes of the letters. If his finger wanders, the smooth paper beneath the sandpaper warns him at once of his error.

Children between the ages of four and five, just as soon as they have acquired skill in touching the letters, like very much to repeat the exercise with their eyes closed. The sandpaper enables them to follow the form without seeing it, and it can be said that the perception of the letters by direct tactile-muscular sensations is of a great assistance in overcoming the difficulties of writing.

If, on the other hand, the exercise is given to a child who is too old, to one, for example, who is six years old, he will be more interested in seeing the letter which represents a sound and is used in words, and the attraction of touch will not be sufficient to interest him in the exercises of movement. He will write less easily and less perfectly, since he has already lost the joy in movement which belongs to an earlier age.

A small child, on the other hand, does not move his hand around an exclusively visible shape. He is not interested in this but in the feeling of touch which makes his hand carry out the movement, which will then be fixed in his muscular memory.

When a teacher has a child see and touch the letters of the alphabet, three sensations come into play simultaneously: sight, touch, and kinesthetic (muscular) sensation. This is why the image of the graphic symbol is fixed in the mind much more quickly than when it is acquired through sight in the ordinary methods.

It should be noted, moreover, that the muscular memory is the most tenacious in a small child and is also the readiest. Sometimes even he does not recognize a letter when he sees it but he does when he touches it.

These images are associated at the same time with the hearing of the sounds of the alphabet.

II. *Perception: a child should be able to compare and recognize the shapes when he hears a sound corresponding to them.* The teacher asks a child, for example: "Give me *o!* Give me *i!*" If a child cannot recognize the signs when he looks at them she invites him to touch them, but if also in this instance he does not recognize them, the lesson is terminated and will be taken up again some other day. I have already noted the necessity of not pointing out an error to a child and of not insisting upon a lesson when the child does not respond to it at once.

III. *Speech: a child should know how to pronounce the sounds corresponding to the letters of the alphabet.* After the letters have been left upon the table for a few moments, the child is asked: "What is this," and he should reply: "*o*," "*i*."

In teaching the consonants, the directress pronounces only the sound, and as soon as she has pronounced it, she joins it to a word and pronounces one or more syllables changing the vowels, always emphasizing the sound of the consonant. In the end she repeats this sound alone for example: "*m, m, m, ma, me, mi, m, m.*" When the child repeats the sound, he will repeat it both isolated by itself and accompanied by a vowel.

It is not necessary to teach all the vowels before passing on to the consonants; and as soon as one consonant is learned, it is immediately used with words. Further variations in the method are left to the the judgment of the teacher.

I have not found it practical to follow any special rule in teaching the consonants. Very often a child's curiosity about a graphic symbol leads to a teaching of the consonant he desires. The sound of a name may arouse the interest of a child in knowing the consonants necessary to form it. And this desire of a child is a more efficacious means for deciding the order to be followed than any kind of reasoning.

When the child pronounces the sounds of the consonants he experiences an obvious pleasure. This series of sounds so varied and so well known, which come to life in the presence of an enigmatic symbol like a letter of the alphabet, are a novelty for him. There is a mystery about it that arouses in him an intense interest. One day when I was on a terrace and the children were playing freely around me, and I had by my side a little boy two-and-a-half years old who had been momentarily left there by his mother. I had placed entire alphabets all mixed up on several chairs, and I was sorting them into their respective boxes. When I finished the work, I placed the boxes on some stools. The little boy kept looking at me. He came up and took a letter in his hand. It was an *f*. At that moment some boys were running in a line, and seeing the letter, they all together pronounced the corresponding sound and passed on. The child paid no attention. He replaced the *f* and took an *r*. The boys, as they ran by again, looked, smiled, and began to shout "*r, r, r, r! r, r, r!*" Little by little the child began to understand that each letter that he took corresponded to a different sound. This amused him so much that I decided to see how long he would engage in the game without becoming weary and I waited for a good three-quarters of an hour! The boys had taken an interest in the game and stopped in groups, pronouncing the sounds together and laughing at the child's amazement. Finally the child who had taken up most frequently the letter *f* and lifted it on high when he always obtained from his audience the same sound, took it again, showed it to me, and said himself: "*f, f, f.*" He had learned that sound in the midst of the great confusion of sounds he had heard. He had been impressed by the long letter which, when it had been seen by the children running in a file, had caused them to shout.

It is not necessary to emphasize the fact that the separate pronunciation of the sounds of the alphabet reveal a child's proficiency in speech. Defects, which are almost all connected with an imperfect development of speech itself, are obvious and a teacher can easily take note of them one by one. A norm for individual instruction can be found in the state of development of a child's speech.

When there is a question of correcting speech, it is well to follow the physiological rules of its development and graduate the difficulties. But when a child's speech is already sufficiently developed and he pronounces all the sounds, it makes no difference whether we have him pronounce one rather than another when we are teaching written language and the reading of symbols.

A great many of the defects which remain permanently in an adult are due to functional errors in the development of speech during the time of childhood. If, instead of correcting the speech of adolescents, we substituted guidance in its development in childhood, we would accomplish a most useful preventive work. Many defects of pronunciation are dialectical, which are almost impossible to correct later on; but it would be very easy to avoid these if a special program were conducted to perfect the speech of children.

We may prescind here from real defects of speech due to anatomical and physiological anomalies or pathological changes in the function of the nervous system and limit ourselves to those defects due to the persistence of a faulty pronunciation in childhood and to the imitation of false pronunciations. Among these should be included such defects as lisping and dialectical variations, which can affect the pronunciation of every consonant. There is no more practical and methodical means of correcting speech than this exercise in pronunciation necessary for learning the written language by my method.

But a question of this importance deserves a separate chapter.

All the mechanics for writing are now ready. Turning now directly to the method for teaching writing, we may notice that it is already contained in the two stages just described. When a child has been given these exercises, he can learn and fix the muscular mechanism necessary for holding the pen and for making graphic symbols. When he has been exercised at length in these methods, he should be ready to write all the letters of the alphabet and simple syllables without ever having taken pen or chalk in his hand to write.

Reading and writing fused at the very beginning. Moreover, with this method, the teaching of reading is begun simultaneously with that of writing. When a letter is given to a child and its sound pronounced, the child fixes an image of it in his mind with the help of his visual and his tactile-muscular senses. And he definitely associates the sound with the relative symbol, that is, he becomes acquainted with written language. When he sees and recognizes, he reads; when he touches, he writes. That is, he begins to become acquainted with two acts which in the course of time develop, separate, and thus constitute the two different processes of reading and writing. The simultaneity of the teaching, or better, the fusion of these two initial actions, thus present a child with a new form of language, without determining which of the two constituent acts should prevail.

We should not worry as to whether a child in the course of his development learns first to read or to write, or which of the two will be the easier for him. We must learn this from experience without any preconceptions, waiting for the individual differences that will make one prevail over the other. This allows us to make a very interesting study in individual psychology and to continue the practical direction of our method which is based on the free expansion of an individual. But in the meantime it is certain that if our method is applied at the normal age, that is, before the age of five, a little child will write before he reads, whereas a child who is already too far developed (five or six years old) will read first, experiencing difficulties in adjusting his clumsy mechanisms.

Intelligence Freed from Mechanisms

Reading and writing are quite distinct from a knowledge of the letters of the alphabet. They really come into existence when a word rather than a graphic symbol becomes a fixed element. Even in the spoken language the beginning is marked by the appearance of words with a definite meaning and not by sounds which can represent vowels and syllables. When the intellect expresses itself with its highest means, it uses the mechanisms which nature or education have put at its service for the composition of words.

A child can find an intense intellectual interest in being

able to represent a word by putting together the symbolic symbols of the letters of the alphabet.

It is much more fascinating at the beginning to create words from letters of the alphabet than to read them, and it is also much easier than writing them since writing involves the additional labor of mechanisms that are not yet fixed.

As a preparatory exercise, therefore, we offer a child an alphabet which will be described below, and he begins to compose words by choosing letters of the alphabet and placing them next to each other. His manual labor consists solely in taking known forms from a box and spreading them out on a carpet. A word is built up letter by letter corresponding to its component sounds. Moreover, since the letters are movable, it is easy to correct mistakes by changing them around. This entails a studied analysis of a word and is an excellent means of improving a child's spelling.

This is study in the true sense of the word; it entails an exercise of the intellect freed from mechanical activities and is not held down by the need to imitate letters in writing. The intellectual energy employed in this new interest can therefore be expended without weariness on a surprising amount of work.

Material. This consists essentially of letters of the alphabet. The letters are identical in size and shape with those made of sandpaper, but they are here cut out of colored cardboard or leather.

The letters are loose, that is, they are not glued upon cardboard or anything else. Each letter, as a consequence, is an object that can be handled.

At the bottom of each compartment in the box for holding them is a letter so fixed that it cannot be removed. There is thus no wasted effort in putting the letters back properly into their respective compartments: the letter at the bottom serves as a guide.

The letters are distributed in two boxes, each containing all the vowels. The vowels are cut out of red cardboard and the consonants of blue. The letters have a strip of white cardboard fixed transversely low on their backs to indicate the proper position of the letter and the level at which it should be placed with respect to the others. The strip corresponds to a line on which the letters would be written.

Composition of Words

Just as soon as a child recognizes some of the vowels and consonants, one of the large boxes containing all the vowels and half of the consonants with the white strip on their backs is placed before him. Some of them he knows already, but others not. Words can be composed with this material by placing one letter of the alphabet after another on a table in such a way that they correspond to the successive sounds that make up a spoken word. The letters themselves are taken from the compartments in the large box in which they are kept. To initiate a child into this exercise, the teacher gives a practical demonstration. She pronounces, for example, the word *mano* (hand), and then analyzes the sounds pronouncing them separately: *m*, taking the letter *m*; *a*, taking an *a* and placing it next to the *m*, and following this with an *n* and *o*. She picks up the letters one by one and pronounces their respective sounds, and thus composes a word. She now has on the table four letters in succession: *m-a-n-o*.

Sometimes a child, when he has understood the procedure sets about finishing the word by himself instead of waiting for the mistress to do so. After a few lessons almost all begin to compose words on their tables. They ask for words to put together, and this gives rise to a kind of dictation.

The composition of words caused some real surprises. Children showed a great interest in the spoken language which they already possessed and sought to analyze it. They were seen walking by themselves and murmuring something or other. One kept saying: "To make *zaira*, you must have *z-a-i-r-a*," and he kept pronouncing the sounds of the letters without using the material. He was therefore not aiming at composing the word, but simply at analyzing the sounds that made it up. He seemed to be making a kind of discovery: The words we pronounce are made up of sounds. This type of activity can be aroused in all children at about the age of four. I remember a man asking his son if he had been good on his reutrn from school. The child replied. "*buono, b-u-o-n-o*" (good). Thus, instead of answering the question, he had begun to analyze the word.

The letters corresponding to the various sounds of the alphabet are clearly seen in the box in which they are kept. The vowels are distinguished from the consonants by their different color, and each letter has its own compartment. The exercise is so fascinating that children begin to compose words long before they know all the letters of the alphabet. On one occasion a little girl asked her teacher: "Which one is the letter *t*?" The teacher who wanted to follow a certain order in presenting the alphabet, had not yet shown her the letter *t*, one of the last letters. But the girl then said: "I want to make 'Teresa,' but I do not know which is the *t*." The teaching of new letters was thus often encouraged by a child's ambition, who went faster than his teacher.

Once interest has been aroused, that is, when the children grasp the principle that each sound of the spoken language can be represented by a symbol, they advance on their own. This certainly facilitates the learning of the written word. A teacher finds that her own position is changed. She no longer instructs but simply tends to a child's needs. Indeed, many children are convinced that they have learned to write by themselves.

Older children will not perhaps have the same keen interests in analyzing words or the same delight in seeing them translated into letters placed in a row.

This can only be explained by the fact that a child of four is still in a formative period of language. He is living in a sensitive period of his own psychic development. All the marvelous phenomena that we witness in this area will only be understood if we admit that such a child is passing through a creative period of intense vital activity and is building up the language he must use as a man.

At five years this sensitivity is already on the decline since the creative period is coming to an end.

Another great source of surprise was that the children composed entire words as soon as they heard them spoken clearly and without needing to have the sounds repeated. This was also the case with long words or words which they did not understand, even those in a foreign language. The children mentally transposed these words after hearing them only once. Just as soon as they were pronounced they were translated into letters on their table.

It is very interesting to watch a child at this work. He stands alert, looking at the box, his lips moving slightly. Then he takes the necessary letters one by one without making mistakes in spelling if the words are phonetic. The movement of his lips is due to the fact that he is repeating to himself over and over again the sounds of the word which he must translate into symbols.

Many people came to observe these lessons, especially inspectors of schools who know the difficulties of dictation in elementary schools, where a teacher must repeat a word many times over so that it is not forgotten. But in our schools four-year-old children remember it perfectly, although they must carry out a task that could easily distract their attention and exhaust their energies for finishing the work. They have to look for the letters of the alphabet in the box with their eyes, take those that are needed with their hands, and continue to do this until they have finished the word.

During the first period of this wonderful experiment an inspector of schools came to visit us and wanted to dictate a word which he thought was very difficult. He pronounced the word clearly, stressing the last two letters, which sound very much alike: "Darmstadt." The child to whom he gave this word composed it as he had heard it pronounced. Another time an official of the Ministry of Public Instruction dictated "Sangiaccato di Novibazar" to a four-and-a-half-year-old child. Taking up the letters, he spelled the word out on his table.

Worth recalling was the experience of the Chief Inspector of the Schools of Rome, who wanted to personally test the children in this regard. He simply dictated his own name, *Di Donato*, to one of the children. The little boy began to compose it, but since he had not heard all the sounds clearly, he made a mistake spelling out *d-i-t-o*. The inspector corrected him by saying *dido*. The child was not in the least disturbed; he took the *t* which he had used in composing the word and without replacing it in the box set it to one side on the table. He filled in the blank space with the required *d* and continued to spell *d-i-d-o-n-a*. . . . Then he took the letter *t* which he had set aside, placed it beside the other letters and added an *o: didonato*, all in one word. The entire word had therefore been carved, as it were, in his mind. He knew in the very beginning that he needed a *t* for the final syllable. He was so certain of this fact that the inspector's correction had not disturbed him. The latter was really amazed: "This *t*," he said, "makes me believe that we shall soon see a miracle effected in the history of education."

It was not simply a single child but rather many who showed this same surprising ability. They obviously had a special sensitivity for words and were ravenous in their desire to master the written language.

A child evidently composed these words with the movable alphabet, not because he remembered them with the help of his ordinary memory, but because he had "carved" and "absorbed" them into his mind. It was from this image which he had, as it were, before his eyes that he copied the word. However long or strange the word might be, it was so reflected that the child could reproduce it. We should also note that this exercise was absolutely fascinating to the children who repeated it without becoming tired since it was a vital exercise.

The children who composed words in this manner did not know how to read or write. They were not, indeed, interested in written words. They acted, or rather reacted, to a stimulus that instead of provoking an inferior reflex produced a response corresponding to a creative sensitivity.

The explosion of writing. The entire method for learning a written language consists in these three stages: The necessary psycho-physiological activities are separately mastered and these are then combined for writing and reading. The muscular movements needed to execute the alphabet in writing and thoses required for holding and handling the writing instruments are trained separately. The composition of the words is also translated into a psychic mechanism that associates audio with visual images. A time comes when a child, without thinking of it, completely fills in the geometrical figures with straight, regular lines, touches the letters with his eyes shut, reproduces their shapes, moving his finger in the air, and is driven on by a psychic impulse which makes him compose words and repeat to himself: "to make *zaira*, you must have *z-a-i-r-a*."

Now it is true that such a child has never written, but he has potentially carried out all the acts necessary for writing. One who can compose a word when it is dictated and instantly embrace in his thought the complete structure of a word, keeping it and its corresponding symbols in his memory, should also be able to write since he knows how to produce the movements necessary for producing the letters with his eyes closed and can handle almost unconsciously the writing instrument.

Such preparatory actions provide a child with a mechanism that can give an impulse that should lead to an unexpected explosion of writing. And this was from the very beginning the marvelous reaction of the normal children in one of the first Children's Houses of San Lorenzo in Rome.

One day in December when the sun was shining brightly we climbed up to the terrace with the children. Some ran around playing freely, but others stayed near me. I was sitting near a chimney and I said to a five-year-old boy as I offered him a piece of chalk: "Draw this chimney." He obediently sat down on the floor and drew on the pavement in a recognizable fashion the chimney. I then praised him highly as I usually do with my little ones.

The boy looked at me, smiled, stood for a moment as if he would explode with joy and then shouted: "I write! I write!" And then bending down he wrote *mano* (hand) on the tiles, then with great enthusiasm he wrote *camino* (chimney) and then *tetto* (roof). As he was writing he continued to cry out loud: "I am writing! I know how to write!" All the other children noticed his shouts and made a large circle about him as they looked on in astonishment. Two or three of them excitedly addressed me: "Chalk, I can write too!" And as a matter of fact they set about writing different words: *mamma, mano, gino, camino, ada*.

Not one of them had ever before even taken chalk or any other writing instrument into his hand. This was the first time that they had written, and they traced out whole words, just as when they spoke for the first time they spoke a whole word.

But if the first word spoken by a child gives ineffable joy to his mother, who has chosen that first word, *mamma*, almost as her own name and as a kind of reward for her motherhood, so the first word written by my little ones fills them with an unspeakable happiness. They see spring into being from themselves a skill which seems to them to be a gift of nature, for they cannot connect what they are doing with the preparatory acts which led up to this particular action.

They thus imagine that one fine day they will know how to write as if they attained this by simply growing up. And it is so in reality. A child that begins to speak has also prepared unconsciously the psycho-muscular mechanisms which will lead him to pronounce a word. A child does practically the same in writing; but direct assistance and the material preparation of the motions required for writing, which are much simpler and coarser than those needed to articulate, bring it about that a written language develops considerably more rapidly and perfectly. And since the preparation is not partial but complete, that is, a child can perform all the movements necessary for writing, written speech does not develop gradually but explosively, that is, a child can write any word he is given.

Thus it was that we shared in the moving experience of the first developments of writing among our children. During those first days we were deeply touched; we felt as if we were living in a dream or had assisted at some miraculous events.

A child who wrote a word for the first time was filled with a great joy. I immediately compared him with a hen that has laid an egg. Indeed no one could escape the noisy demonstration of a child. He would keep calling all to see what he had done; and if someone did not move, he seized him by his smock and forced him to come. Everyone had to come and stand around the written word to admire the prodigy and to unite their shouts of wonder with those of the fortunate author. As a rule this first word was written on the floor, and a child would get down on his knees to be closer to his work and to contemplate it more closely.

After the first word, a child would continue to write everywhere, for the most part on the blackboard, with a kind of frenzy. I have seen children crowding around a blackboard so that they could write on it. Behind them was another row of children standing on chairs writing higher up on the board, and still others were writing on its back. Children who could not get near the board ran aimlessly about in their disappointment or upset the chairs on which their companions were standing as they tried to find a little space. In the end those who lost out bent down and wrote on the floor or ran to the window shutters and doors and filled them with writing.

During those days the floor was almost completely covered with a tapestry of writing. The same thing happened at home, and some mothers to save the floors and even the bread, on the crusts of which they found written words, gave their children paper and pencil. One of the children one day brought a kind of notebook completely filled with writing. His mother told us that the child had written all day and all evening and had fallen asleep in bed with paper and pencil in hand.

Such impulsive work, which I was unable to check during the first days, made me think of nature's wisdom in gradually perfecting speech, and it does this at the same time that a child is gradually getting ideas. If nature acted as imprudently as I had and allowed a rich and orderly stock of material for the senses and a wealth of ideas for the mind to develop, and thus fully prepared a child to speak so that she might say to one who is still mute: "Go and speak," we would witness a sudden mad outburst of speech, and a child would begin to speak and would continue to do so without pause or restraint until his lungs and vocal cords became wearied and exhausted with pronouncing strange and difficult words.

However, I believe that there exists a mean between these two extremes. We should provoke written language more gradually and bring it less impetuously into existence. We should encourage it as a spontaneous action carried out from the very first in a nearly perfect fashion.

Manner of Applying the Method. Later experience has led to a calmer procedure. This has been due to the fact that children see their companions writing. This encourages them to imitate the others in writing as soon as they can. When a child writes his first word, he does not as yet have at his command the whole alphabet. Since this limits the combinations he can make, the number of words which he can write is also restricted. He never loses the great joy of the first written word, but this no longer comes as a tremendous surprise since he sees similar phenomena occurring all the time and knows that sooner or later it must also happen to him. This secures a calm, orderly environment, and one that is still wonderful because of the surprises it contains.

Whenever I paid a visit to the Children's Houses, I would find something new, even if I had been there the day before. Once, for example, I saw two very little children writing quietly, although they were thrilled with pride and joy. The day before they had not yet written. The teacher told me that one of these had begun to write at eleven o'clock on the previous morning and the other at three in the afternoon.

This phenomenon is now regarded with that indifference which is the product of custom and is readily recognized as a natural form of a child's development.

A teacher must decide if it is proper to encourage a child to write or not, when he, after having passed through the three preparatory stages, has not as yet done so of his own accord. This is to prevent a child who has been slow to write breaking out into a frenzy of work which cannot be curbed because of his knowledge of the whole alphabet.

Signs which will enable the teacher to determine the readiness of a child for spontaneous writing are the following: lines drawn straight and parallel in filling in geometrical figures, recognition of the letters of the alphabet in sandpaper with eyes closed, and sureness and ease in composing words. However, even after a child has been judged ready for the spontaneous explosion of writing, it is well to wait a week before encouraging him to write.

Only after a child has begun to write on his own should a teacher intervene to guide his progress in writing.

The first help she gives is to rule the blackboard so that the child has lines that will help him keep his writing in the right size and position.

The second is to urge a hesitant child to keep touching the sandpaper letters without ever directly correcting his writing exercises. This means that a child will not perfect himself by repeated writing but by repeating the acts that prepare for writing. I remember a little beginner who, in order to give his letter a beautiful shape on the ruled blackboard, went back to the sandpaper cards, touched two or three times all those he had to use for the words he was writing, and then wrote. If a letter did not seem to him to be good enough, he erased it, touched again the same letter on the card, and then went and wrote it.

Our children, even those who have already been writing for a year, always continue with the three preparatory exercises, which, just as they have provoked the written language, so also they later perfect it. Our children thus learn how to write and perfect themselves in writing without writing. Actual writing is an external manifestation of an inner impulse.

It is a pleasure that comes from carrying out a higher activity and not simply an exercise.

There is also a definite educational advantage in preparing oneself for a certain activity and in perfecting one's actions before going ahead. Too much correction of errors committed encourages one to attempt things for which he is not really ready and makes one indifferent to the commission of error. My method of teaching writing, on the other hand, contains a valuable educational principle. It teaches a child the wisdom of avoiding errors, the dignity of foresight as a guide to perfection, and that humility which keeps one constantly united with the sources of goodness, from which alone one obtains and preserves mastery over oneself. It also frees him from the illusion that once one has succeeded in doing something it is quite enough simply to continue on the road that has been taken.

Since all the children, those who are just beginning the three exercises and those who have already been writing for many months, are constantly repeating the same actions, they are united and fraternize on an apparently equal level. Here there are no castes made up of beginners and proficients. All may be seen filling up figures with colored pencils, tracing the sandpaper letters with their fingers, composing words with the movable letters. Younger children will go up to those who are older for help and they all imagine that they are doing the same thing. Here is one who is preparing, and here is one who is perfecting himself; but all are on the same road. Thus, just as there is an equality among men which runs more deeply than any social differences that makes them brothers, so here all, both aspirants and those who are perfect, have recourse to the same exercises, since they are making the same spiritual journey.

Writing is learned in a very short time since it is taught only to children who show a desire for it. They indicate this by the voluntary attention they pay to the lessons which the teacher is giving to the older children and to the exercises in which these are engaged. Some learn to write without ever receiving lessons but simply by having observed those given to others.

In general all children four-years-old and over are keenly interested in writing. Some of our children, however, have begun to write at three-and-a-half. They show their enthusiasm particularly in the way they trace the sandpaper letters. During the first period of my experiments, when the children saw the letters of the alphabet for the first time, I one day asked the directress, Miss Bettini, to carry the various types of cards which she had made out onto the terrace, where the children were playing. As soon as the children saw them, they gathered about their teacher and me with their hands stretched out and started to touch the letters with their fingers. Finally some of the larger children succeeded in snatching some of the cards from our hands and handled them as if they owned them, but the crowd of little children got in their way. I remember the joyous enthusiasm of those who had got possession of the cards. They clasped them in their hands, lifted them up on high like standards, and began to march around followed by all the other children who clapped their hands and uttered shouts of joy.

The procession passed in front of us, and all, both large and small, laughed loudly, while the children's mothers attracted by the noise watched the scene leaning out of the windows.

The average period that elapses from the first attempt to perform the preparatory exercises to the first written word is for four-year-old children a month and a half, for five-year-old children it is much shorter, about a month; but one of our children learned to write with all the letters of the alphabet in twenty days. Four-year-old children after two and a half months write some words under dictation and are able to pass on to writing with pen and ink in notebooks. In general our children are proficient after three months, and those who have been writing for six months may be compared with children in the third grade.

After all, writing is one of the easiest and most pleasant achievements for children.

If adults could learn as easily as six-year-old children, illiteracy could be abolished in a month. But two obstacles would perhaps prevent such a brilliant success. For one thing, adults do not have that enthusiasm which is produced in children by their psychic sensitivities, and which is present only during that natural constructive period when language is learned. Moreover, an adult's hand is now too stiff to easily acquire those delicate movements necessary for writing.

But I know that when the procedure we used in the

education of children was applied to adults (to recruits and soldiers of the United States Army), the struggle against illiteracy was made considerably easier.

I later learned that in former times in Rome adults were taught how to improve their penmanship by tracing very large, well-formed letters and not by copying a model as is done today.

Tracing letters and composing words phonetically with a movable alphabet, therefore, facilitates the efforts of anyone learning how to write. But it is certainly true that an adult needs many months to learn what a child can learn in a single month if he has been indirectly prepared for it.

We have said enough about the time needed for learning how to write. As far as the actual writing is concerned, our children from the very moment that they begin to write, write well; and one is surprised at the shape of the letters, rounded and sure, closely resembling the sandpaper models. The beauty of their writing is almost never attained by a pupil in the elementary schools who has not had special training in calligraphy. I have studied calligraphy extensively, and I know how difficult it is to persuade twelve- and thirteen-year-old boys in the secondary schools to write whole words without lifting the pen except for the letter *o*, and how hard they find it is to make the different letters with a single stroke and at the same time keep the lines of the letters parallel.

Our children, on the other hand, of their own accord write whole words with a single stroke and with wonderful deftness, keeping the lines perfectly parallel and an equal distance between the individual letters. On observing this more than one distinguished visitor has exclaimed: "If I had not seen it, I would never have believed it."

Calligraphy, as a matter of fact, is a kind of supereducation needed to correct already fixed defects. It is a long, tedious, and superfluous task. A child, while looking at a model, must carry out the motions needed to reproduce it, and yet he lacks the coordination that should exist between his sight and the required movements.

Further, calligraphy is taught at an age when defects are already fixed and the psychological period when the muscular memory is particularly active is passed. There is no need to

mention the basic error in teaching calligraphy in the same
way that writing is taught, by making strokes and so on.

We, instead, prepare a child indirectly not only for writing
but also for calligraphy according to its two basic principles—
beauty of form (by touching beautiful letters) and vigorous
execution (by exercises in filling in figures).

16. Reading

Experience has taught me to make a clear distinction between reading and writing, and it has shown me that the two acts need not be absolutely contemporaneous. Our experience, however, has been that writing precedes reading, although this is contrary to what is commonly held. I do not call it reading when a child attempts to verify a word he has written, that is, when he retranslates the symbols into sounds since he already knows the word, having repeated it many times to himself as he was writing.

By reading I mean the interpretation of an idea by means of graphic symbols.

A child who has not heard a word spoken but who recognizes it when he sees it put together on a table in movable letters and knows what it means, that it is the name of a child, a city, an object, and so forth, really reads.

The reason for this is that what is read in writing corresponds to what is heard in speech and is a means of understanding others.

A child does not read until he receives ideas from the written word.

We can say that writing, as we have described it, is an act in which the psycho-motor mechanisms prevail. In reading, however, we are engaged in purely intellectual work; but it should be evident that our method for teaching writing prepares the way for reading so that the difficulties are almost unnoticeable. Actually, writing prepares a child for interpreting mechanically the combined sounds of the letters which compose the word which he sees written. In other words, a child can read the sounds of the words. One can notice the fact that when a child composes words from a movable alphabet or when he writes, he has time to think of the symbols which he must pick out or draw. Writing a word takes a much longer time than reading it.

When a child who can write is confronted with a word which he has to read and interpret, he is silent for some time and usually reads the component sounds as slowly as if he were writing them. The sense of the word, on the other hand, is grasped when it is pronounced rapidly and with the necessary intonation. Now, in order to inflect it properly, a child must recognize the word, that is, the idea which it represents. A higher intellectual activity must therefore be brought into play.

Accordingly, I proceed in the following way for practice in reading and what I am going to describe is a substitute for the old spelling book. I prepare pieces of ordinary writing paper upon each of which is written in cursive script one-fourth of an inch high a well-known word that has been frequently pronounced by the children and represents objects that are either present or well-known, for example, *mamma*. If a word refers to a present object, I place it under the child's eye to assist him in interpreting the writing. Here I may note that most of these objects are toys. The Children's Houses possess not only a miniature kitchen, kitchen utensils, balls, and dolls, as I have already had occasion to note, but also cupboards, couches, and beds, that is, all the necessary furniture for a doll's house. There are also cottages, trees, flocks of sheep, papier-mâché animals, celluloid ducks and geese that will float on water, boats with sailors, soldiers, wind-up trains, country estates, stables, cattle in spacious enclosures, and so forth. For one house in Rome an artist gave me beautiful porcelain fruit.[1]

If writing serves to correct, or rather, to direct and perfect the mechanism of speech in the child, reading assists in the development of ideas and language. In brief, writing helps a child physiologically and reading helps him socially.

The first step in reading, as I have already noted, is one of terminology, that is, reading the names of known objects.

I do not begin with easy or hard words, since a child can already read a word as a composite of sounds. I permit him

---

[1] The first Children's Houses had numerous toys, but much less emphasis is placed now on them since experience has shown that children do not look for them.

to slowly translate the written word into sounds and, if the interpretation is exact, I simply say: "More quickly." The child reads it the second time more quickly but often still without understanding it. I repeat: "More quickly, more quickly." He reads ever more quickly, repeating the same group of sounds, and finally guesses its meaning. Then his face lights up with recognition and he beams with that satisfaction which is so frequently seen among our children. This is all that there is to the exercise of reading. It is a very rapid one and presents very little difficulty to a child who has already been prepared by writing.

Truly, all the troubles of the spelling book are buried together with the strokes used in learning how to write!

When a child has read a card he places it against the object whose name it bears and the exercise is finished. After the children had been trained in this way, more for the sake of making them understand the exercise expected of them, than for giving them practice in reading, I thought of the following game to make the various exercises of reading, which must be frequently repeated, more pleasant and reading itself easier and clearer.

Game for reading words. I spread out on a large table a good number of different attractive toys. For each one there is a card with its name written on it. I fold the cards, roll them up, and toss them about in a box, and have the children who can read draw them out by lot. The children must carry the cards to their places, unfold them very slowly, and read them to themselves without letting their neighbors see them, so that what is on a card remains an absolute secret. They then go up to the table with the cards in their hands. A child must pronounce in a loud voice the name of a toy and give the teacher his card to be verified. The card thus becomes a kind of money for getting the toy whose name it bears. If a child pronounces the word clearly and points out the object with the finger, and the teacher can check whether he is right or not with the card, he can take the toy and do what he wants with it for as long as he likes.

When this stage of the game has been finished, the teacher calls the first child and then all the others in the order in which they took the toys and makes them draw lots for another card which each one must read at once. This carries the name of one of his companions who cannot as yet read and, therefore, does not have a toy. Then, politely, as an act of courtesy, the child must offer the toy to his young companion. The toy should be presented in a kindly and graceful manner and be accompanied with a bow. In this way any idea of caste is removed and the feeling that one should give something to others who have no real right to it out of a spirit of kindness is inculcated as well as the feeling that all should share equally in pleasures whether they have earned them or not.

The game of reading went marvelously well. One can imagine the happiness these poor children experienced in the illusion that they owned such beautiful toys and that they could play with them for a long time.

But I was greatly surprised to see that the children, after they had learned how to understand the written cards, refused to take the toys and waste their time in playing and making those friendly gestures to their little companions. Instead, with a kind of insatiable desire they preferred to take out the cards one after the other and read them all. I watched them, trying to fathom the riddle of their minds. After I had thought about this for some time, the thought struck me that through some human instinct children would rather acquire knowledge than be engaged in senseless play, and I reflected on the grandeur of the human mind.

I therefore put away the toys and set about making hundreds of written cards containing the names of children, objects, cities, colors, and qualities which they had come to know through the exercises of the senses. We placed them in several boxes and let the children fish as they pleased. I expected that they would at least pass at random from one box to another, but this was not the case. Each child finished emptying the box which he had before him, and only after he had done this did he go on to another in his insatiable desire for reading. One day I went out on the terrace and discovered that the children had carried out their little tables and chairs and set them up for school in the open air. Some of the children were playing in the sun, others were seated in a circle around tables covered with letters and cards of sandpaper. On one side of the terrace, in the shade of a dormer window, the teacher was seated holding in her hand a very long narrow box full of cards. Its whole length was occupied by little hands fishing in it. The children were opening, reading, and refolding the cards. "I would never have believed," the teacher told me, "that they had been here for more than an hour and were still not satisfied." I made the experiment of bringing out balls and dolls, but to no effect. These vanities had lost their attractiveness to the joy of knowing.

When I saw this surprising result, I was already thinking of trying to get them to read print, and I suggested to the teacher that she write the same word in both script and print on some cards. But the children forestalled me. In the classroom there was a calendar with many words in printed characters, some of which were Gothic. In their craze for reading, some of the children set about looking at this calendar, and to my unspeakable surprise they read both the Roman and the Gothic print.

Thus we had nothing more to do than to give them a book, and they actually read the words in it. At first in the Children's Houses I would give only a book which contained pictures of various objects with their names printed underneath.

The children's mothers immediately took advanage of their progress. We actually discovered in the pockets of some of them pieces of paper roughly written with the prices of spaghetti, bread, salt, and so on. The children were shopping for their parents with the help of the notes. Their parents, moreover, told us that the children no longer ran through the streets because they stopped to read signs in the shops.

A child of four-and-a-half, who had been educated in this same way in a private home, once acted as follows. His father, a deputy in the parliament received a great deal of mail. He knew that his little son two months before had begun exercises which speeded up the process of learning how to read and write in a child at a very early age, but he had not paid much attention to this or put much faith in it. One day as he was reading and his son was playing near him a servant entered the room and placed on the table a large number of letters that had just arrived. The child went over to the table and began to go through the letters and read the addresses in a loud voice. The man could hardly trust his senses.

It may be asked what is the average time needed for a child to learn how to read. Experience has shown us that, beginning from the moment when a child writes, it takes an average of about fifteen days to pass from this lower form of activity, writing, to the higher one of reading. Accuracy in reading, however, is almost always attained more slowly than that in writing. In most cases a child will write very well but read only fairly so.

Not all children reach the same standard of achievement at the same age. Since none of them are ever encouraged, much less forced, to do something that they do not care to do, it happens that some children, since they have never asked for help in learning, have been left in peace and can neither read nor write.

If followers of the old method of teaching, which tyrannizes a child's will and stifles his spontaneity, do not think it necessary to force a child to learn how to write before he is six, much less do I believe he should.

Nevertheless, I would not be able to decide without further experience whether or not it would be best in every instance to encourage a child as soon as he has attained a full command of the spoken language to take up writing.

At any rate, almost all normal children who have been trained according to our methods begin to write at four, and at five they can read and write at least as well as children who have finished the first grade. This means that they would be in a position to enter second grade with the seven-year-old children usually found there.

The Exercise with Classified Cards

The simple reading game described above was taken up again, modified, and then fixed for learning how to read non-phonetic languages such as English. The essential exercise, which can also be applied in principle to phonetic languages, consists in preparing a series of objects and a corresponding number of cards on which are written the names of the objects. After a child has read a card he places it near its corresponding object. When used with phonetic languages, the exercise aims at arousing an interest in written words. When a child recognizes the name of a present object, he is as pleased as if he had discovered a secret; and he enjoys placing the card near the object and thus satisfying and rounding out this intimate activity.

By now his inner drive has been aroused, interest enkindled, and a connection between the source of life and the mastering of externals established.

Something similar must be done when one begins to teach non-phonetic languages. In the teaching of English, for example, we first made a search for a group of phonetic words. As is well known, there are always words of this type even in non-phonetic languages. From these we chose all those that could be built up from some twenty different sounds. We know from experience that this is about all the isolated sounds that can be clearly distinguished by children between the ages of four and five.

In striving to fix this definite number of words, we had only to worry about the difficulties already mentioned, since the length of a word and the complexity of its sounds do not constitute a difficulty for a child. In a matter of this sort, the basic requirement is simply to have something that will interest a child. It is enough that a word should be phonetic and represents known and present objects. When this happens, and a child's interest is aroused in the written word, one can go on to successive difficulties, preparing groups of words according to their spelling. In brief, it is first necessary to aim at rousing a keen interest in reading, for this prepares the way for overcoming the various difficulties connected with spelling. Pains must then be taken to group the objects and the words corresponding to them so that there can be a fixed series of successive exercises. The only thing really necessary is a proper classification of the words so that a child's interest is aroused in the difficulties, which are illustrated by the way in which the words are grouped. This creates in children a pure interest in reading words just as it is found in phonetic languages.

This procedure was developed in England for the teaching of English. It was necessary to build a small chest which contained in different drawers groups of words chosen according to different difficulties in spelling and groups of objects corresponding to them as a kind of means of classification. A child can take a drawer by himself from the cupboard, remove the objects, attach his card to each one, and then after he has finished the exercise return the drawer to the cupboard. He can then take another drawer and so on, coming to know in this way different difficulties-in spelling and pronunciation.

Reversal of the exercise. The practical advantages derived from such exercises suggested a further use of them. This consists in reversing the purpose of the above exercise. Objects that are educationally important are assembled and marked by cards giving their respective names. Whereas in the first exercise the objects were known and the difficulties of learning were connected with words, here a child starts with a sufficient knowledge of the words to teach him the names of the objects which are grouped together for some educational purpose. In a developed form, this exercise has been extended to teaching the names of various materials used in our schools, for example, those of goods, fastenings, polygons, and so forth. Finally, it has been applied to models of plants and animals. Scientific terms indicating their relative classifications are written on separate cards, and these must then be placed on the objects when they are recognized.

These last exercises, however, lead us down a different road from that which is of present interest, namely, learning how to read. They rather resemble the practice of botanists and gardeners who give the Latin names of various plants on tags which they attach to them.

Commands: The Reading of Sentences

As soon as some visitors to the first Children's Houses in San Lorenzo saw that the children were reading printed characters, they sent them a number of beautifully illustrated books as a present. These formed the first nucleus of our library. As I turned over the pages of these books with their simple stories, I realized that the children would not be able to understand them. The teachers, however, were quite pleased and wished to show me how useful they were. They had a number of the children read from the books, and they told them that their reading was much more fluent and correct than that of children who had finished the second grade. But I was skeptical, and made two tests. I first had the teachers tell the children some of the stories contained in the books and note how many of the children were really interested. After a few words the children's attention would wander and the teacher had to call the distracted ones to order.

Thus little by little the class began to become restless, and each one of the children returned to his own customary occupation without listening further.

Obviously, the children who seemed to take pleasure in reading the books were not enjoying their meaning but rather enjoying their ability to translate graphic symbols into the sounds of a word they recognized. Actually, they read the books with much less persistence than they did the cards since they met many unknown words in them.

My second test consisted in having a child read a book without explaining it to him as the teacher had done, interrupting him with such questions as: "Have you understood?" "What have you read?" "The child went to a carriage, did he not?" "Read carefully." "See," and so forth.

I gave a book to the child, placed myself next to him, and asked him with the simple seriousness that I would a friend: "Did you understand what you read?" The child would reply: "No," but the expression on his face seemed to ask a reason for my question. In fact, the idea that reading consists in taking in a series of words from which one can draw the complex thought of another was something which the children would later experience and which would be for them a new source of surprise and delight.

A book is concerned with the language of thought and not with the mechanics of expression. This is why a book cannot be understood by a child before he has mastered logical language. There can be the same difference between being able to read individual words and knowing the sense of the book as that which exists between being able to pronounce a word and making a speech.

I therefore put off the reading of books and waited for further developments.

One day while we were talking, four children got up together with a happy expression on their faces and wrote on the blackboard sentences such as these: "How glad I am that the garden is in bloom." This greatly surprised and moved us. They had on their own account reached a stage where they could compose sentences, just as they had written their first words by themselves. The same forces had been at work, and the result had been the same: Rational spoken language one day led to an explosion of writing.

I understood that the time had come for the children to go

on to the writing of sentences, and I had recourse to the same means, that is, to writing on the blackboard.

"Do you like me?" I wrote so that all could see. The children read the words slowly in a loud voice. They were silent for a moment as if reflecting and then shouted at the tops of their voices: "Yes, yes!" I continued to write: "Then keep quiet and be still." They read it almost as if they were shouting, but as soon as they had finished reading, a deep silence came over the room, only broken by the sound of chairs being adjusted as the children sat down.

We thus began to communicate with each other through written language; and this proved to be most interesting to the children. They gradually discovered the wonderful property of writing, that it transmits thought. When I began to write, they trembled in their eagerness to know what I had in mind and to understand it without my pronouncing a single word.

Written language does not indeed need speech. Its whole grandeur is only understood when it is completely isolated from the spoken word.

One day in 1909, when the first edition of this book was on the press, we succeeded in bringing our little ones in the Children's Houses the full pleasure of reading with the following game.

I wrote on some pieces of paper long sentence describing actions which the children would have to complete, for example: "Close the shutters of the windows and go and open the main door. Then wait for a moment and put the things back as they were at first." "Politely ask eight of your companions to leave their places and stand two by two in a row in the middle of the room. Then make them walk back and forth very quietly on the tips of their toes without making any noise." "Please ask three of your oldest companions who sing well to come to the middle of the room. Line them up in a row and sing with them any pretty song you please," and so on.

I would hardly have finished writing when the children would snatch the cards from my hand to read them. As they placed them on their tables to dry, they read them with great attention in the deepest silence. I asked them: "Do you understand?" And they would reply: "Yes, yes!" "Then do what they say," and I marveled as I saw them quickly pick

out something to do and do it at once. A new kind of life
and activity then spread throughout the room. One child
closed and opened the shutters. Another made his companions run. Another went to write on the blackboard, and still
another went to take objects from the cupboard. Surprise and
curiosity provoked a general silence, and their actions were
carried out amidst the most intense excitement. It seemed as
if a magic force had gone out of me, stimulating them to a
hitherto unknown activity. And this magic was the written
word, the greatest triumph of civilization.

The children appreciated its importance so much that
when they were leaving they came up to me in gratitude and
affection and said: "Thanks! Thanks for the lesson!"

They had taken a great step. They had leapt from the
mechanics to the spirit of reading.

Today this game, which is the children's favorite, is played
as follows. A deep silence is first established; then a box
containing folded strips of paper on which are written long
sentences describing various actions is brought out.

All the children who can read come up and draw out a
card. They read it to themselves until they are sure that they
have really understood it and then, giving the open card to
the teacher, go on to carry out the action. Since many of
these require the help of other companions who do not know
how to read and many others require the use or moving
about of different objects, a general stir is created which is
carried on in a marvelously ordered fashion. The deep silence
of the room is only interrupted by the soft shuffle of little
feet lightly running about their task or by voices singing as
commanded. The whole provides a startling revelation of
perfect spontaneous discipline.

Experience has shown us that composition should precede
the rational reading of sentences just as writing precedes the
reading of words. Further, reading that communicates ideas
should be mental rather than vocal.

As a matter of fact, reading in a loud voice implies the use
of two mechanisms of language, the articulate and the graphic, and this makes the work more complex. Everyone knows
that an adult who has to read a passage in public prepares
himself for the task by first reading it silently to himself so
that he can understand it. And, as we also know, reading
aloud is one of the most difficult intellectual activities. Chil-

dren, therefore, who are beginning to read so as to get the thought should do this mentally. When written language leaps to rational thought, it should be kept separate from speech. The written word can transmit thoughts from a distance and do this even when the senses and muscular mechanisms are at rest. It is a spiritualized language that puts men all over the world in communication with each other.

* * *

The logical consequence of the success of the Children's Houses is that the whole scheme of elementary education should be changed.

A reform in the primary grades that would lead to a continuation of our method is too large a question to be treated here. But this much can be said: The first and second grades could be completely eliminated if our system of early education was universally adapted.[1]

Tomorrow's elementary schools would then receive children like our own. These already know how to take care of themselves. They can dress and undress and wash themselves. They know the rules of good manners and are well-disciplined and yet they are, as I believe it can be said, free precisely because they have been so trained. Further, they not only speak perfectly and without errors in pronunciation, but they can also use language for practical ends and have begun to use it in their reasoning processes.

The fact that these children speak with a good pronunciation and write beautifully, and that their movements are full of grace, indicates that they belong to a race that is advancing in refinement.

Children such as these give bright hopes for the future. They are patient and intelligent observers of their surroundings and make free use of their powers of reasoning.

Elementary schools worthy of receiving such children and of guiding them further along the path of life and civilization

---

[1] Elementary schools following the Montessori method have been developed in places where there are Children's Houses. The kind of education given there has been discussed in various books I have written and especially in my two volumes entitled *The Advanced Montessori Method.*

should be founded, and these should embody the same educational principles that guarantee the freedom and spontaneous development of a child as are found in the Children's Houses, for it is these principles that determine his personality.

17. Speech

Written language, which comprises both dictation and reading, contains articulate language in all its complexity.

Written language can, therefore, be considered from two points of view:

a) It is a new language of great social importance which is added to man's natural spoken language. This is the educational value that is usually attributed to a written language, and this is also why it is taught in school without any regard for its connections with speech. It is simply regarded as a necessary means for putting man in contact with his social environment.

b) It may be used to improve speech. This is a new factor which I wish to insist upon and which gives a physiological importance to the written language.

Moreover, just as speech is a natural function of man and a means of social progress, so writing may be considered in itself, in its formation as a whole new series of mechanisms within the neural system, or as a means that may be employed for social ends.

Finally, there is the question of the development of writing independent of the functions which it is destined to complete later.

I believe that writing entails numerous difficulties at the beginning, not simply because it has hitherto been taught irrationally, but because we have tried to make it carry out, even though it has been recently acquired, the lofty function of teaching the written language that has been fixed and perfected through the efforts of centuries.

We may consider the irrational character of the method. We have in the past analyzed the written signs rather than the physiological acts needed to produce them. And we have done this without considering the fact that the visual representations of the signs have no inherent connection with the motions required for their execution, as, for example, the auditory images of a word have with the motor mechanisms for reproducing it in speech. It is moreover, always difficult to excite a motor action unless there has been some preparation for it. An idea cannot act directly upon the motor nerves, and much less can it do this when the idea itself is incomplete and does not arouse a feeling which moves the will.

Thus, for example, an analysis of writing in terms of strokes and curves has led to a child's being presented with meaningless signs. He is not interested in them and their sight cannot provoke a spontaneous motor impulse within him. Such actions require an effort of the will, and in a child this soon degenerates into weariness, boredom, and pain. Added to this effort of the will is the need of synchronizing the muscular movements entailed in guiding the instrument used for writing.

The sense of discouragement consequent to such efforts causes a child to produce imperfect and erroneous letters. These must be corrected by his teachers, and this depresses him still more because he is constantly being reminded of the mistakes he is making in forming the letters. Thus while a child is being urged on to greater efforts, his mental energies are being lowered rather than raised by his teacher.

Although so many mistakes have been made in teaching a child how to write, writing itself, so painfully learned, is immediately used for social ends.

We should remember that in nature the spoken language is gradually formed and is already established in words when the higher psychic centers use these words in what Kussmaul calls the *dictorium*, that is the gramatical and syntactical formation of a language required for the expression of complex ideas.

After all, the mechanics of oral expression must antecede the higher mental activities which make use of them.

There are, consequently, two periods in the development of language: There is a lower stage which prepares the nervous tracks and the central mechanisms which must put the sensory tracks in relation with the motor mechanisms, and there is a higher stage determined by the higher psychic

activities which are exteriorized by the performed mechanisms of language.

Thus, for example, in the scheme of spoken language given
by Kussmaul, the most important fact to be noted is that a
kind of reflex cerebral arc is established during the early
formative period of speech which represents the pure
mechanics of speech. This can be illustrated in the following
diagram.

Let E stand for the ear and T the motor organs of speech
as represented by the tongue, A the auditory center of
speech, and M the motor center. The channels AE and MT
are peripheral, the former being centripetal and the latter
centrifugal. The channel MA is the intercentral channel of
association.

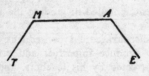

The center A, which contains the auditory images of
words, may be again subdivided into three, as in the following diagram where SO represents sounds, SY syllables, and W
words.

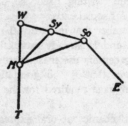

That partial centers for sounds and syllables can actually
be formed seems to be confirmed by certain pathological
speech defects. In some forms of centro-sensory dysphasia,
those afflicted can pronounce only sounds or, at best, sounds
and syllables.

Small children are at first particularly sensitive to simple spoken sounds such as those used by their mothers when they caress them or attract their attention. This is particularly true of the sound *s*. Later they become sensible to syllables which their mothers use for the same end, when they say, for example: *ba, ba, punf, tuf*!

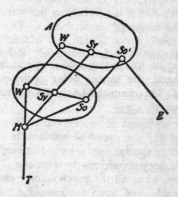

Finally, it is the simple word, for the most part disyllabic, that attracts a child's attention. The same subdivision can be made also in the motor centers. A child at the beginning utters simple or double sounds, such as, for example, *bl, gl, ch*, expressions which his mother greets with joy. He then begins to produce sounds that are definitely syllabic: *da, ba*, and finally, disyllabic words, which are for the most part labial, *mamma, baba*.

We say that spoken language has its beginning in a child when the word he pronounces represents an idea: when, for example, seeing his mother he recognizes her and says *mamma*, or when seeing a dog he says *tete*, or when he wishes to eat he says *papa* (pap, or food).

We thus hold that language has begun when it is linked up with perception, even though speech itself, in its psychomotor mechanism, is still quite rudimentary.

In other words, language is considered to be initiated when, over and above the reflex arc, where the mechanical formation of the language is still unconscious, a recognition of the word takes place; that is, it is perceived and associated with the object which it represents.

Later, language gradually perfects itself on this level, as

the hearing detects more perfectly the component sounds of words and the psycho-motor channels become better suited for articulation.

This is the first stage of spoken language; it has its own beginning and its own development dealing, through perceptions, to a perfecting of the primordial mechanism of language itself. And it is precisely at this stage that the so-called "articulated language" is established. This will later be the means through which a man will express his thoughts, and which an adult will find extremely difficult to perfect or correct once it has become fixed. In fact, it can happen that a high degree of culture can be accompanied by an imperfectly articulated language which hinders an aesthetic expression of one's thoughts.

The development of speech takes place between the ages of two and five, the age of perceptions, in which the attention of a child is spontaneously turned towards external objects and his memory is particularly tenacious. This is also the age of mobility, when all the psycho-motor channels are becoming permeable, and when the muscular mechanisms become fixed. At this period of life, because of the mysterious bond that links the auditory and motor channels of spoken language, it seems that auditory perceptions have the power to excite the complicated movements of articulate speech, which develop instinctively under the influence of each stimuli. It is a well-known fact that it is only during this age that one can acquire all those characteristic modulations of a language which he would seek in vain to acquire later. A person's mother tongue is the only one that is pronounced well, because it is fixed in childhood. An adult who learns how to speak a new language must carry into it the imperfections characteristic of the speech of a foreigner. Only children who in the age of infancy, that is, below seven years simultaneously learn several languages can perceive and reproduce all the characteristic modulations of accent and pronunciation of the different languages.

So also defects acquired in childhood, dialectical variations for example, or the results of bad habit, becomes ineradicable in the adult.

That which develops later, the higher language, the *dictorium*, no longer has its origin in the mechanics of speech but in intellectual growth, which makes use of these mechanics.[1] Just as spoken language develops through the exercise of its mechanisms and is enriched by perceptions, so the *dictorium* develops with the mind and is enriched by intellecutal culture.

Going back again to our diagram of speech, we can see that above the arc defining the lower language, there is established the *dictorium*, D, from which now come the motor impulses for words which have been formed as spoken language able to express the thoughts of an intelligent man.

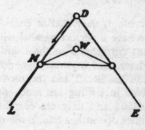

On the basis of preconception, it has hitherto been thought that written language alone should enter into the development of the *dictorium*. It was regarded as the only suitable means for acquiring culture and allowing for grammatical and syntactical analyses. Since the spoken word flies away, it was thought that intellectual culture could only advance with the help of stable objective language which could be analyzed, like that of writing.

We admit that writing is a precious and even indispensable means of education because it fixes the ideas of men and enables them to be analyzed and to be put down permanently in books from which they can always be extracted. But why do we not recognize the fact that writing is also useful for the more humble task of fixing the words which represent perceptions and of analyzing them into their component sounds?

Because of our prejudices with regard to teaching, we are

[1] Here we might compare this with a typewriter which has nothing to do with the thought of the one who uses it for communicating his own ideas.

unable to separate the idea of written language from that of the function which till now we have exclusively attributed to it. And yet it seems to us that by teaching language in this way to children who are still in an age when they are learning how to move about and how to assimilate simple perceptions, we are committing a grave psychological and educational mistake.

But let us rid ourselves of this prejudice and consider written language in itself, reconstructing its psycho-physiological mechanism. It is much simpler than the psycho-psysiological mechanism of speech, and can be taught much more simply.

Writing is surprisingly easy. Let us consider writing that is dictated. Here we have a perfect parallel with speech, since a motor action must correspond to the heard word. It is true that we do not have that mysterious heriditary relationship that exists between the heard and the spoken word, but the movements involved in writing are much simpler than those required for speaking and they are carried out by muscles more distinct in their operations than those of the vocal cords and of the tongue. They are all external, and we can directly influence them through preparatory movements.

This is taken care of in my system, which directly prepares the movements of the hand that is going to write. The psycho-motor impulse of a heard word finds the motor channels already established and explodes into the act of writing.

The real difficulty lies in the interpretation of the graphic signs, but we must remember that we are dealing with children passing through a period of perceptions, when sensations, memory, and primitive associations are all in a natural stage of expansion. Further, our children have already been prepared by the various sense exercises and by the methodical building up of ideas and psychic associations, to appreciate written signs. A child who recognizes a triangle, and calls it a triangle, can recognize the letter *s* and call it by its sound of "s." There is certainly nothing unusual about this. Let us rid ourselves of our prejudices and appeal to experience, which shows that children go on to recognize written symbols presented as objects without great effort and with obvious signs of pleasure.

With this as a preface, let us consider the relationships that exist between the mechanisms of the two languages.

A child of three or four has already, according to our diagram, begun to speak. But he is passing through that period in which the mechanism of spoken language is being perfected. During this same time he is mastering the contents of language along with his wealth of new perceptions.

A child may perhaps not have heard perfectly all the component sounds of the words he pronounces; and even if he has heard them perfectly, it may be that they were badly pronounced and he thus makes mistakes because of what he has heard. It would be to a child's advantage if he could exercise the motor channels of speech and accurately fix the movements required for perfect speech before he has acquired erroneous habits and reached an age when it is no longer easy to change his motor mechanisms and his defects become incorrigible.

If a child is to attain this end, he must know how to analyze words. This is why, just as when we strive to perfect their language, we first train our children in composition and then pass on to the study of grammar, and why when we attempt to perfect their style we first teach them to write grammatically and then pass on to an analysis of style, so here when we aim at perfecting their speech, they must first be able to speak before we can analyze what they are saying. It is therefore only after a child has begun to speak that it is time for him to analyze his words and perfect them.

And yet, just as grammar and style cannot be studied simply in speech but need the help of writing, which enables one to see the passage to be analyzed, so it is with words.

No real analysis can be made of something that is passing us by.

It is necessary to materialize and stabilize language. And we do this through the written word, that is, through a word represented by graphic signs.

The third factor in writing which I take up in my method is the composition of words. This requires an analysis of words by means of objects, that is, by means of the letters of the alphabet. A child hears a word, that is, he knows its meaning, and he then breaks it down into simple sounds and syllables so that he can translate it into a word which he composes with the movable alphabet.

When a child is learning how to speak he can hear the component sounds of a word imperfectly, but this does not happen when he is learning the graphic signs corresponding to the individual sounds of a word. He is given a sandpaper letter, which he can see and touch and its corresponding name. This not only fixes the sound which he has heard clearly in the child's mind, but his hearing of the sound is associated with two other perceptions, the sight and feel of the written sign. These additional sensations strengthen the audial images of the word.

The following diagrams represent the procedure already explained.

Let us consider separately each of the three stages used in teaching the alphabet.

First stage. A teacher shows a letter of the alphabet and says: "This is *a, a, a.*" The visual image of the letter is thus associated with the audial image and deposited within the nerve centers. Later, when giving the sounds of consonants, she immediately unites these with a vowel to form a syllable. Here also a visual image is associated and fixed with the corresponding audial image, for example, *ma, ma, ma.*

The teacher then turning to the child says: "Touch *a,* touch *ma.*" The child touches the *a,* or the *m* and *a,* tracing them as if he were writing. In this way he fixes within his memory the image of the movement carried out by his hand in touching the letters. This new motor image remains associated with his visual and auditory images of the same letters. There is thus established a triple association between the auditory centers of the spoken word and the visual and motor centers of the written language.

Second stage. The teacher repeats many times over: "Which is *A?*" "Point out the *a.*" "Touch the *a.*" Or she asks: "Which is the *m?*" "Which is *ma?*" And in this second stage, by repeating the same exercises over and over again, she reinforces the inner associations that have already been established during the first stage. This is an exercise in association.

Third stage. The teacher, pointing to the letters or to a group of syllables, asks the child: "What is this?" The child answers: "*a,*" or "*m,*" or "*ma.*" The visual image of the written sound is associated with the motor center of the spoken language. In other words, pronunciation is determined by the sight of the letters as well as by hearing.

The association that is established is represented by the two triangles AC VC MCW and AC VC MCS, which have a common base in the association between the two sense centers, that is, between the auditory center of the spoken word and the visual center of the written word, while their apices

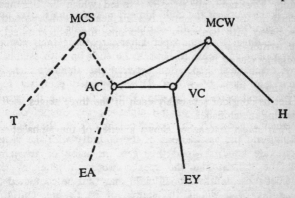

The reflex arc referring to speech is indicated in dotted lines.

EA = Ear
AC = Auditory Center of the Spoken Word
MCS = Motor Center of the Spoken Word
T = Tongue, Organs of Speech
MCW = Motor Center of Written Language
H = Hand
EY = Eye
VC = Visual Center of Written Word

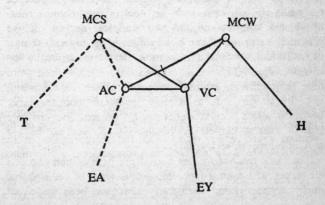

correspond respectively to the two motor centers, one of speech (MCS), and the other of writing (MCW).

As is well known, in our method a lesson is only an explanation of an exercise. By far the most important element is the work of the child himself in repeating it over and over again. When a child continues for a long time to trace with his finger the sandpaper letters, recalling their sounds and pronouncing them to himself, he ends up with establishing a mechanical association between the alphabet and the component parts of words. These repeated exercises represent a real period of growth. During this time the visual images of the letters of the alphabet, the images of the movements necessary to reproduce them with the hand in writing, and the associations of the auditory with the visual images are fixed. A child thus gets the habit of analyzing both the written and the spoken word. A letter of the alphabet presented to a small child may thus be compared to the spring of a watch, the source of its ticking, and this interests him far more than a jack-in-the-box. He becomes at times absorbed in it (periods of concentration). The work of association described above goes on for a period of six or more months, that is, from about the age of three-and-a-half to four years, a time when a child's words are still pliable and easy to analyze since it immediately follows the period in which the child first began to speak.

It is only later, when a child is some months over four, that he masters his analytic mechanisms and uses them in the interesting task of composing words. Then, like a peacock spreading its tail, he reveals his control over these mechanisms and connects up the two analyses. Because of the preceding exercises he can clearly discern the separate sounds of individual words and reorganize almost mechanically the corresponding letters of the alphabet. An alphabetized word now represents an external projection of the spoken word, and the teacher can, as it were, penetrate into the inner labyrinth where a child elaborates his speech. She can help him to express himself orally and visually so that he can perfect his speech and writing.

The same mechanism lies also at the base of non-phonetic languages. The sounds represented by a letter of the alphabet or by a phonogram, when they have once been associated with the symbol, may be more accurately analyzed and employed in the composition of words.

The exercise in composition lasts even longer than the exercise used to establish the mechanism that links speaking and writing together. As a rule, when a child has learned how to spell correctly, he suddenly starts to write. He can then reproduce almost all the words found in phonetic languages and a considerable number of those found in non-phonetic languages.

This association between the two languages, spoken and written, is of the utmost importance. Writing becomes a second form of language and is associated with speech through frequently repeated exercises.

On the other hand, the traditional method for teaching a child how to write treats writing as something independent of speech. Various difficulties of sounds and syllables are studied as if the whole language had to be constructed anew. The fact that the language is already formed, that a child has used it since he was two years old, and that all the difficulties to be found in one's native tongue have been determined by an act of nature is completely forgotten.

Let us consider the advantages of the method we have described. The letters of the alphabet act on the spoken language, exciting almost mechanically an analysis of the spoken word.

It is the spoken word that is thrown into relief by the analysis of its component sounds.

Once this association of signs with sounds has been established, a child can reconstruct with the alphabet all the words he can call to mind and all those he hears pronounced.

Then, after a simple association has been made between signs and sounds, the whole of spoken language can be put down in graphic symbols, and this immediately leads to writing.

Actually, the letters of the alphabet are few in number. In English there are only twenty-six, and these twenty-six letters make up all the words which are found in even the largest dictionaries.

All words are thus composed of one or more of these sounds. If these are connected with the twenty-six letters which they represent, all speech can be represented graphically, and children, taking letters corresponding to the sounds, can compose all the words of a phonetic language and very many of those that are not phonetic.

A word, whether it is long or short, demands the same effort. The supposed difficulties created by syllables, as commonly taught, are ultimately a matter of translating sounds into signs, that is, of recognizing symbols. To compose a simple word like *pipa* (pipe), and to compose a more difficult one like *strada* (street), is basically the same since the two words already exist in a child's native tongue. This is explained by the fact that a child has succeeded in recognizing the separate sounds that make up the words and has analyzed them. If a child has succeeded in recognizing the sounds contained in the syllables *stra* and hears them separately *s-t-r-a*, he will be able to write the word.

There is accordingly only one real difficulty, only one thing to do. This is to make an interior, mental analysis of the sounds. Just as our method teaches a child's hand how to form the letters of the alphabet, so here it also cancels out all those imagined difficulties which are introduced into teaching through the supposed necessity of overcoming a series of increasing difficulties. It is usually thought, for example, that it is easier for a child to write *i*, *e*, and *o*, than the other letters. But a child who has exercised his hand in a general manner and has employed it in all his various sense exercises, and especially in tracing the letters and making numerous geometrical drawings, of which we shall speak later, has no difficulty with individual letters, or even with combinations of them in composing words that interest him and which he wants to fix in his mind with the help of writing. All of a sudden he comes to write, and he writes at once whole sentences and not simply isolated words.

Defects of Speech Due to a Lack of Education

Defects and imperfections in speech are in part due to organic causes such as malformations or pathological defects of the nervous system, but they are also in part connected with functional defects acquired at the time when one is learning to speak. These consist in mispronunciations of the component sounds of a spoken word. Such errors are picked up by a child when he hears a word pronounced imperfectly, that is, when he hears someone speak poorly. Dialectical

variations enter into this category of defects, but there are
also bad habits which cause a child to retain the natural
defects of infant speech. Or, again, a child may imitate the
defective speech of the individuals who were near him in his
infancy.

The normal defects of a child's speech are due to the fact
that his complicated organs of speech do not as yet function
well and cannot as a consequence reproduce the sound which
was the sensory stimulus of this innate movement. The movements necessary for the articulation of the spoken word are
gradually coordinated. But before this is attained, a child will
often speak imperfectly. These defects in speech, which are
grouped together under the term *blaesitas* (defective
speech), are mainly due to the fact that the child cannot
direct the movements of his tongue. They include such faults
as *sigmatism*, the imperfect pronounciation of *s*; *rhotocism*,
the imperfect pronounciation of *r*; *lambdacism*, the imperfect
pronunciation of *l*; and *gammacism*, the imperfect pronunciation of *g*.

Some of the errors that a child makes in pronouncing
vowels, like those connected with the pronunciation of consonants, are due to the fact that he reproduces perfectly the
sounds which he has actually heard imperfectly.

In the first case, it is a question of a functional defect in
the peripheral motor organ and, consequently, of the nerve
tracks, and the cause is to be found within the indvidual; but
in the second case the fault is due to the auditory stimulus
and the cause is to be found in the environment.

Such defects often persist in youths and adults, although to
a less marked degree. They produce a definitely faulty language and errors in spelling such as those found in written
dialects.

There is a great charm in human speech, and one who
does not speak perfectly obviously lacks something that is
highly esteemed. Any form of education that has a regard for
aesthetics must aim at perfecting the spoken language. Although the Greeks transmitted to the Roman the art of oral
delivery, this was not taken up by the Humanists, who were
more concerned with the aesthetics of the environment and
the restoration of works of art than the perfecting of man
himself.

Today we are just beginning to correct through educational methods serious defects in speech, such as stammering; but there has not as yet penetrated into our schools the notion of a universal system of verbal exercises that would perfect a child's speech and his aesthetic sense.

Some teachers of deaf-mutes and some intelligent promoters of correct speech are attempting today, but with little enough success, to introduce into elementary schools means for the correction of various kinds of *blaesitas*, which statistical studies have shown to be common among students. The exercises given to the children consist essentially in silence, which calms and rests the organs of speech, in repeating individual vowels and consonants, and in practice breathing. This is not the place to describe in detail the methods employed in these exercises. They are long and tedious and do not fit in with regular instruction in a school. But all the exercises used for the correction of speech find a place in my method:

a) The exercises of silence prepare the nerve tracks of speech so that they will receive new stimuli perfectly.

b) The different stages in the lessons include the clear and distinct pronunciation by the teacher of a few words (and particularly of the names which she wishes to associate with the concrete idea). In this way clear and perfect auditory stimuli are initiated, and these stimuli are repeated by the teacher when the child has conceived an idea of the object represented by the word (recognition of an object) when its name is pronounced. And, finally, a child is urged to repeat aloud a single word, pronouncing each of its separate sounds.

c) The exercises in writing analyze the sounds of a word and cause them to be repeated separately in several ways. Thus, when a child learns the individial letters of the alphabet, and when he is composing or writing words, he repeats their sounds, which he translates one by one into composed or written speech.

I believe that the concept coming to the fore today of correcting defects of speech in primary schools will disappear and that there will be substituted for it the more rational plan of avoiding them by caring for the development of language in Children's Houses, that is, at the very age when speech is being fixed in children.

The procedure that I have described above has been

confirmed so frequently in countless schools that I am able to draw the following conclusions:

The most favorable age for the development of written language is that of childhood, about the age of four, when the natural processes connected with the development of speech are fully activated, that is, during the sensitive period (see *The secret of Childhood*), when speech naturally develops and becomes fixed. A child's sensitiveness to his own development arouses his enthusiasm for learning the alphabet and urges him on to make a phonetic analysis of words into their component sounds. Later, when the child is six or seven years old, the creative period will have passed, and he will no longer have the same natural interest in analyzing either the spoken or the written word. This is why little children as a rule make better and more rapid progress than those who are older. Instead of becoming bored and weary like the older children, they carry on a constant activity that seems to strengthen them.

Further studies have not only confirmed this surprising fact, which is of particular importance for child psychology, but they have also indicated interesting modifications that should be made in its use.

The conclusion of this long analysis is that written language, in its mechanical aspects, can be directly associated with spoken language and be practically derived from it as another mode of expression. This is especially true during the period when speech is naturally being fixed, that is, during the sensitive period. Written language then becomes an exterior means to guide and perfect the spoken language and to purify it from all its errors and defects. Thus writing helps in teaching speech.

The *dictorium*, which expresses thought and is a product of the intellect, thus finds at its disposal two mutually integrated mechanisms—the spoken and the written word.

The experience described above finally resulted in the children's reading long sentences containing an order to perform some action. It was therefore easy to pass on to the reading of books as soon as the children were old enough to understand them, that is, when they were from five to six years of age.

Afterwards, however, they made great progress. These later experiences even surpassed that amazing miracle of children of four years of age suddenly possessing the ability to write. The progress of the children became even more precocious, the methods more quick and sure in their effects, and the interest of the children even more intense than before.

If one were to state suddenly that children under two could recognize more than twenty letters of the alphabet and knew five or six hundred words, and that at the age of three they began to study grammar and to read, he would hardly be believed. Such a miracle would arouse the same interest and attention which it did more than forty years ago when the learned world first heard about the children of San Lorenzo.

A new book should certainly be written to describe these later achievements; we only want to mention them here. Our attention was drawn to still younger children, that is, from the time of birth to the age of three. It is precisely during this period that speech naturally develops, making its first appearance when a child is about two years old. Speech follows certain rules in its development and its later acquisition comes in what might be called a "grammatical" order. This was first observed and recorded by Stern and later by others interested in psychological research.

A child begins to know nouns, that is, the names of objects, then words that refer to these nouns (adjectives), then prepositions (relating to the relative position of objects), and finally conjunctions (which show how the objects ae connected). Briefly, when a child first begins to speak, he represents things in his environment. It is a curious fact, however, that a child, a few months before reaching the age of two, starts to spout out an abundance of words. He uses verbs, the correct forms of nouns and adjectives with their prefixes and suffixes, and finally he distinguishes the various forms, making the use of past, present, and future and the different persons!

Afterwards, at the age of two, he makes use of proper syntax, puts together sentences, and connects them together.

A real grammatical analysis of language can be made on the basis of such observations. As a matter of fact, if a person did not speak grammatically, he would not be able to express his thoughts at all.

It is worth noting that the only language that anyone, whether he be educated or not, possesses perfectly as far as the sounds and grammatical constructions are concerned, is the so-called "mother tongue." A child, therefore, not only aquires a spoken language, but he acquires it in a special way. His way of speaking becomes a personal characteristic as it is also a characteristic of his race. It becomes impressed upon the individual man.

When we studied and contemplated this marvelous creative phenomenon, we recognized the fact that a child has a mental form different from our own and we called it "the absorbent mind."

The natural growth of language in a child suggests the idea that we should proceed according to a grammatical scheme if we wish to further this development through education. And just as the mechanisms of writing have helped us to integrate it with speech in the first stage of our experiments, so here also language written grammatically, by means of objects, games, and written words, can help a higher spoken language, the language of the *dictorium*, which consists in the expressing of ideas.

The success of this second attempt far surpassed the first. Although the methods that we used initially are still regarded as fundamental, this difference should be noted: the words of spoken language are no longer important merely because they can be reproduced in writing; they are also important for their grammatical meaning. The union between words thus not only helps to translate what one wishes to say into writing, but it leads at once to the discovery of meaningful sentences which are gradually constructed along grammatical lines.

This second period of our experiments has had a much more important and surprising history than the first.

One of the practical aspects of this new development has been the almost complete revolution in learning how to write a non-phonetic language. Here a child's intuition, stimulated by his creative powers, comes into play. Thus, just as we witnessed the phenomena of children in the first grade intuitively reading words written in printed and even Gothic characters without having received any formal instruction in them, so here we find children intuitively reading non-phonetic words of their own native tongues by simply using objects and taking part in attractive games. Their interest and efforts in this regard are somewhat analogous to those which have driven philologists on to the interpretation of undeciphered inscriptions on ancient monuments.

The passionate interest of children in reading may be explained by the other conquests and discoveries they unconsciously made during the first years of their life.

We may now give a few practical illustrations of a grammatical ordering of words.

Nouns taken by themselves do not represent a natural language since we never say simply "chair," or "flower," but at least "the chair," "the flower," and so forth. An article is regularly used with the noun. In the same way a noun is often modified by an adjective so that it may be distinguished from other objects of the same species. We say, for example, "the red flower," "the yellow flower," "the round table," "the large table," and so forth. And adjectives have a very distinct meaning for our children, who, in their sense exercises, become acquainted with qualities through their senses, learning the distinguishing terms such as "thick," "thin," "small," "great," "dark blue," "light blue," and so forth. It is obvious that a child at this period is engaging in mental work that will make him aware of what he has unconsciously acquired and encourage him to amplify and fix it. This natural tendency has been well illustrated by our own efforts; and Mario M. Montessori, during the course of some twenty years of observation, has given us such a picture of a child's intellectual capacities that his work may be described as a real educational monument.

There can be no doubt of the fact that a child absorbs an enormous number of impressions from his environment and that external help given to this natural instinct kindles within him a lively enthusiasm. In this way education can be a real help to the natural development of the mind.

Although, as we have already said, it is impossible to give here the details of this colossal work, which would require several volumes to be of practical use, it should be well to note that written language leads not only to a knowledge of grammar and syntax at an apparently precocious age, but that this language, which so delights a child, can also become the vehicle for a general education.

A teacher must busy herself with finding more and more new names to satisfy the insatiable demands of her young charges. This craving which is manifested in their writing is certainly natural. Between the ages of three and five a child's vocabulary grows spontaneously from three hundred to three thousand or more words. This is a fact that has been ascertained by psychologists, who, however, have limited themselves to observing, counting, and noting down this growth without pointing out the way to assist its natural development.

Our methods have demonstrated still another fact and have shown again that they can furnish us with psychological insights. They have revealed the fact that children are even interested in foreign words and that they remember them in a surprising way during all the time required to reproduce them with a movable alphabet. This indicates that children tend to accumulate words during the sensitive period (between three and five) even when they do not understand them.

In fact, all words will be new to a child until he understands them, and this understanding of them is precisely the conscious act that leads to clarifying, determining, and preserving them.

If there is a tendency to accumulate words that is distinct from the comprehension of their meaning, we may logically ask: Why should so many different, disconnected words be given to a child by a teacher who simply draws them out of her memory? And why, instead, should not this period of a child's life be utilized for putting order into the words he hears and for learning some scientific terms? This work, which has been full of surprises, has also been undertaken methodically by Mario M. Montessori. Instead of using boxes of words of all sorts chosen by chance, we use terms referring to special classes of things, such as, for example, the five classes of vertebrates, animals according to their species, leaves, flowers, roots, and so forth. In such cases pictures are necessary to give meaning to the new words. But in addition to the pictures, living things are also used, and the chidren are taught to follow their own curiosity, and so on.

The success of these measures has been so great that it is possible to elaborate a kind of scientific training adapted to the intellectual level of the children, and the results have been surprising. This type of instruction has had to be expanded considerably beyond the limits fixed at the beginning. The surprising result has been that the children like to make and recall the classifications. This confirms the suspicion that it is natural to group words together and that words should be ordered in the mind according to their meaning. There are thus two extremes in all these exercises. One, grammar is interior. It determines the order in which words should be arranged for the expression of thought and, therefore, for the construction of language. The other is the need for an order according to which external impressions can be classified.

This experiment has gone far beyond our expectations, and today children learn, using language as their guide, a great deal of exact knowledge about biology, geography, and astronomy. And this knowledge is like seed sown in a fertile field. In the mind of a child the seed grows naturally thanks to the promptings of nature which invite a child to acquire a knowledge of the world.

Anyone who considers these pure manifestations of natural development from a psychological point of view will be surprised to discover that five-year-old children have a wide acquaintance with the exterior world and recognize the products of civilization and their names in an almost mysterious fashion. For example, they recognize different makes of cars which their mothers cannot distinguish.

Astounded by such facts as these, Stern concludes: "For thousands of years the child has passed like an unknown being through the midst of mankind, and yet he possesses mental instincts which make us recognize him as a connecting link in the chain of civilization."

18. Teaching How to Count and an Introduction to Arithmetic

The first material used for counting is the series of ten rods already used in the education of the senses for teaching lengths. The rods are graduated in length from 1 to 10. The shortest is four inches long, the second eight, and so on, until the tenth is reached, which is forty inches long. But when the rods are used for counting, they are not all the same color as they were when they were used to make the eye judge graduated lengths. Here, instead, the different four-inch sections are alternately colored red and blue and can thus be counted on each rod. If the first rod represents 1, the others represent successively 2, 3, 4, 5, 6, 7, 8, 9, 10. The advantage of this material is that it represents united together, although distinct and countable, the units comprising each of the represented numbers. The rod of 5, for example, is all one piece representing the number 5, but the five units are distinguishable by the different colors on it. This overcomes a very great difficulty, that of adding one unit after another in a sum total. If small objects of any shape whatever are used for counting, as for example, small cubes of the same size, why does the teacher when she sets down the first one say "1," and when she sets down the second, "2," and so on? A small child tends to say 1 for each new object that is added. He thus says: "1, 1, 1, 1, 1," instead of "1, 2, 3, 4, 5."

The fact that a group is enlarged through the addition of a new unit and that this increasing whole must be considered constitutes the chief obstacle for children of three-and-a-half to four in learning how to count. The grouping together of units which are really separate in themselves into a whole is a mental process beyond a child's capacity. In fact, many small children count by reciting from memory the natural order of the numbers, but they are confused when confronted

with quantities corresponding to these numbers. Counting his
fingers, his hands, and his feet is something more concrete for
a child, since he can always find the same objects invariably
united in a definite quantity. He knows that he has two hands
and two feet.

Rarely, however, can he count with certainty the fingers of
one hand, and when he does succeed in doing this, there is
always the difficulty of knowing why, if the hand has five
fingers, he should say of this same object: "1, 2, 3, 4, 5."
This confusion, which presents no problem to a more mature
mind, is an obstacle to counting at an early period of life.
The extreme exactness and concreteness of a child's mind
needs clear and precise help. When numerical rods are given
to children, we see that even the smallest take a lively
interest in counting.

The rods correspond to numbers and gradually increase in
length unit by unit. They therefore provide not only an
absolute but also a relative concept of numbers. Their proportions have already been studied in the sense exercises.
Here they are judged mathematically, and this provides an
initiation to arithmetic. These numbers which may be handled and compared lend themselves immediately to various
combinations and contrasts. By placing the rod of one unit
next to the rod of two units, there is produced, for example,
a length equal to that of three units. By joining rods of three
and two units the length of a rod of five units is reached.

The most interesting exercise, however, consists in placing
the rods next to each other according to their successive
lengths, just as the whole series was arranged during the
sense exercises. The result of this is that when they are
arranged like the pipes of an organ their red and blue colors
match and form beautiful transverse stripes. By then placing
the shortest rod, which contains one unit, at the top of the
one containing nine, and the second rod over the eighth, and
the third over the seventh, and the fourth over the sixth, a
child builds up lengths that are all equal to the longest rod
with ten units in it. What is this moving and joining of
quantities if it is not the beginning of arithmetical operations?
At the same time it is a pleasant game to move objects about
in this manner, and the intellect, instead of striving to con-
ceive groups of separate unities as sums representing a number, devotes its fresh energies to the higher exercise of

determining and adding together quantities. Once the obstacle has been removed, all a child's mental energies are brought into play and his progress in learning advances as far as his age permits. When a child has begun to read and write, he finds it quite easy to learn the figures which stand for numbers. We give the children cards bearing the numbers in sandpaper at the same time that we give them the letters of the alphabet. By tracing the figures with their fingers, they learn how to write them and they also learn their names. When a card is learned it is placed on the rod of the corresponding quantity. The union of written figures with quantities constitutes an exercise like that of placing a card with a name on it upon the object which it represents. When this exercise is successfully completed, it forms the basis for a lengthy task which a child can continue by himself. The sums of the rods can be written so that they correspond to the numbers. Five-year-old children at times completely fill notebooks with their little sums.

Although the rods are the principal help given to a child so that he can begin arithmetic, two other objects are also used. One of these leads to the counting of separate units and gives a child a concept of numerical groups, and at the same time it fixes before his eyes the succession of the following signs: 0, 1, 2, 3, 4, 5, 6, 7, 8, 9. This material, which we have called the tray of spindles, has compartments, each marked with one of the ten figures placed in sequence. A child groups within these compartments corresponding numbers of separate objects, and thus forms units. Here these objects are represented by long sticks that look like spindles.

The other material, which we have mentioned above, consists in a group of cards in a box containing different objects (colored markers). The cards, which have the numbers from one to ten written on them separately, are shuffled and a child must first place them in a row, showing in this way that he has understood the order of the numbers and that he recognizes the figures representing the numbers. Under each number he then places a corresponding quantity of colored markers, arranging them two by two, that is, one pair under the other. In this way the difference between odd and even numbers is automatically brought out. This is all the material that we have deemed to be necessary for laying the foundations of counting and arithmetical operations.

What follows is a more detailed description that can be of practical assistance to teachers.

The rods are placed next to each other according to their lengths. The child who is performing the exercise must then count the red and blue sections, beginning with side A.

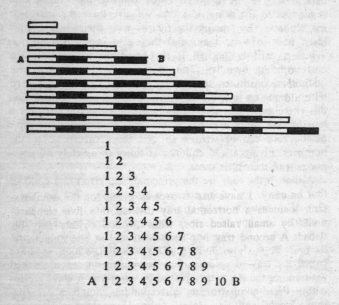

```
              1
              1 2
              1 2 3
              1 2 3 4
              1 2 3 4 5
              1 2 3 4 5 6
              1 2 3 4 5 6 7
              1 2 3 4 5 6 7 8
              1 2 3 4 5 6 7 8 9
          A 1 2 3 4 5 6 7 8 9 10 B
```

He then names the single rods from the shortest to the longest, according to the total number of sections which each contains, touching the rods on side B, where they form a series of steps. This gives the same numbering as found in the sections of the longest piece: 1, 2, 3, 4, 5, 6, 7, 8, 9, 10. The child thus verifies the fact that each side of the triangle corresponds to the number ten, and he repeats the exercise many times over on his own account because he finds it interesting.

The exercise of the senses in recognizing longer and shorter pieces is now combined with that of counting. The pieces are laid on the floor or mixed up on a table. The teacher then picks out one and instead of simply having the child look at it, she has him count its sections, for example, five. She then tells the child: "Give me the next longest one." The child picks it out by sight and the teacher has him verify it by putting the two lengths together and counting their sections. Such exercises can be repeated many times over, and through them a child learns to assign a particular name to each one of the pieces in the stairs. He now calls them "the piece of one," "the piece of two," "the piece of three," "the piece of four," and so forth. And finally, for the sake of brevity, he may finish with calling them as he handles them: "the one," "the two," "the three," "the four," and so forth.

Numbers represented by graphic symbols. At this point, if the child knows how to write, he is given the numbers cut out in sandpaper in the same way that he has been given other objects, that is, according to the three different stages: "This is one." "This is two." "Give me one." "Give me two." "What is this number?" A child must trace the numbers with his fingers in the same way as he did the letters.

Exercise with numbers: association of the written symbol with quantity. I have had two cases made for the numbers. Each includes a horizontal tray divided into five compartments by small raised ribs, within which objects may be placed. A second tray is placed vertically at right angles to the first. This is also divided into five parts by vertical lines. Within each space there is a number. In the first tray the numbers are 0, 1, 2, 3, 4, and in the second 5, 6, 7, 8, 9.

The exercise is simple. It consists in placing within the area of the horizontal plane a number of objects corresponding to the number drawn on the vertical plane. To vary the exercise a child is given different small objects. I use small spindles which I had made for the purpose, Froebel's cubes, and discs used in playing draughts. A group of such objects is placed before a child and he has to put them in their place, that is, to put, for example, one disc near number one, two discs near number two, and so forth. When the child has completed his task and thinks he has succeeded, he calls the teacher to verify it.

Lessons on zero. We wait for a child to ask, pointing at the compartment for zero: "And what should I put there?" We then answer: "Nothing, a 0 is nothing."

But this is not enough. We must make a child feel that 0 is nothing. For this we use exercises that are highly amusing to the children. I place myself in their midst. As they are seated about me in their little chairs, I turn to one of them who has already performed a number exercise and say: "Come, dear, come to me zero times." The child will almost always run up and then return to his place. "But, my child, you have come to me once, and I told you to come zero times." "But what then should I have done?" "Nothing, for zero is nothing." "But how do I do nothing?" "Don't do anything. You must sit still. You must not move. You must not come even once. 'Zero times' means no times at all."

We repeat the exercise. "You, my dear, throw me zero kisses with your fingers." The child trembles, smiles, and stays quite. "Did you understand?" I repeat in an almost passionate tone. "Send me zero kisses, zero kisses." I stop. I lower my voice as if I were angry at their laughter and address one of them severely, even threateningly. "You, come here zero times! I tell you, come here zero times. Do you understand. I am speaking to you. Come here zero times!" He does not move. The laughter becomes even more boisterous, aroused as it is by my change of attitude, first of entreaty and then of threats. "But then," I sadly sigh, "Why do you not come? Why do you not come?" Then all shout in a loud voice, with their eyes gleaming and almost weeping from joy and laughter: "Zero is nothing! Zero is nothing!" "Ah, is that so?" I ask, smiling peacefully, "Then all of you come here to me at one time!" And they rush up to crowd about me.

When later it is a question of writing the figures, we will say at the zero: "Zero seems to be an *O*. Is it an *O*?" "No, it is not an *O*. Zero is nothing."

Exercises in remembering numbers. When the children recognize the written figures and know their meaning, I have them perform the following exercise.

I have various pieces of paper, on each of which are printed, or even written by hand, the numbers from zero to nine. For this purpose, I often use numbers cut from large calendars. I prefer these numbers to be red if possible, and I cut away any print that may be above or below the figures. I fold the pieces of paper, place them in a box, and let the children fish for them. A child draws out a slip, carries it to his place, looks at it stealthily, and folds it, keeping his secret to himself. Then one by one, or even in groups, the children possessing numbers, and these are, naturally, the eldest who can recognize them, come up to the large table of the teacher, where different objects are placed in piles. These may be cubes, or Froebel's bricks, or the tablets I have devised for exercising the baric sense. Each one takes the number of objects indicated by the slip he has drawn. The paper itself with the number on it, however, remains at the child's place mysertiously folded. A child must therefore remember his number not only while he moves among his companions as he approaches the large table, but also while he is picking up his pieces and counting them one by one. The teacher can at such a time make interesting observations on a child's memory.

When a child has gathered his pieces, he places them in a double file on his table, and, if the number is odd, he places the uneven piece at the bottom, centered below the two last pieces. The arrangement of the nine numbers will thus be as follows:

```
o   o   o   o   o   o   o   o   o
X  XX  XX  XX  XX  XX  XX  XX  XX
    X  XX  XX  XX  XX  XX  XX  XX
        X  XX  XX  XX  XX  XX  XX
                X  XX  XX  XX  XX
                        X  XX  XX
                                X
```

The crosses represent numbers. In the place marked by the small circle, a child must place the folded slip. When he has done this he waits for the teacher to verify his work. The teacher comes, opens up the slip, reads it, and expresses her satisfaction when she sees that he has not made a mistake.

At the beginning of the game it will often happen that a child will take more objects than are needed to match the number he has drawn. This happens, not because he does not remember the number, but because of his mania for possession. This is an instinctive bit of cheating which is characteristic of primitive and untaught individuals. The teacher tries to explain to the children that it is useless to have so many things on their tables, and that the real beauty of the game consists in taking the exact number of objects indicated.

They gradually grasp this idea, but not as easily as one might suppose. A child must make a real effort at self-denial to keep within the prescribed limits and to take, for example, only two of the objects which are heaped up before him when he sees his companions taking more.

I therefore look upon this game more as an exercise of the will than as a lesson in counting.

A child who has drawn a zero does not move from his place, even though he sees all his companions with slips rising up and going to take objects forbidden to him from the distant heaps. Very often the zero falls to a child who can count easily and who would be really pleased to get a fine group of objects and place them in order on his table so that he could then wait with pride and confidence for their confirmation.

It is most interesting to study the expressions on the faces of those who draw a zero. A child's reaction to such a lot reveals a great deal about his character. Some remain impassive, putting up a bold front, and thus conceal the pain of their disillusionment. Others, with a sudden gesture, express their disappointment. Others cannot conceal a smile at the novel position in which they find themselves and which will arouse the curiosity of the others. Some follow all the movements of their companions to the very end of the exercise with a bit of envy and an obvious desire to imitate them. Others, finally, show an instant resignation.

During the verification of the numbers, when they are asked what they have drawn, their expressions in admitting that they have a zero are also interesting: "And you, didn't you take anything?" "I have a zero." "It's zero." "I have zero," are the common replies that are given. But their expressive faces, the tones of their voices reveal widely different feelings. Rare are those who wholeheartedly admit that they have suffered something unusual. Most are troubled or resigned.

But some lessons on behavior must be given: "See, it is difficult to keep the secret about the zero. It can escape you. Act as if you didn't care. Don't let anyone know that you have nothing." In fact, after a while, pride and a sense of dignity prevail, and the children become accustomed to drawing a zero or a small number. They no longer become disturbed and deliberately conceal the slight irritations which first dominated them.

Addition and subtraction from one to twenty. Multiplication and division. The material we use for teaching the first operations in arithmetic is the same as that already used for counting, namely, the rods graduated according to length, already containing the first rudiments of the decimal system. The rods, as we have already noted, are called by the name of the numbers which they represent: 1, 2, 3, 4, and so forth. They are arranged in a numerical order according to length.

The first exercise consists in trying to regroup the shorter pieces in such a way as to make up tens. The simplest way of doing this is to take the shortest rods in succession, from one on up, and place them at the ends of the corresponding longer rods from nine on down. Orders to this effect may be given as follows: "Take one and add it to nine." "Take two and add it to eight." "Take three and add it to seven." "Take four and add it to six." In this way we make four rods all equaling ten. This leaves the five, but by turning it over lengthwise it reaches the other extremity of ten, and this shows us that two times five is ten.

These exercises are repeated again and again, and gradually a child is taught more technical language: "Nine plus one equals ten." "Eight plus two equals ten." "Seven plus three equals ten." "Six plus four equals ten," and, finally, "Two times five equals ten." At last, a child is taught the signs for "plus," "equal to," and "times," and he is invited to write them. The result is that we can see such exercises as the following written in the neat notebooks of our little ones:

$$9 + 1 = 10$$
$$8 + 2 = 10$$
$$7 + 3 = 10$$
$$6 + 4 = 10 \qquad\qquad 5 \times 2 = 10$$

When all this has been thoroughly learned and fixed on paper to the great delight of the children, their attention is drawn to the work which must be done when they come to replacing the pieces which have been grouped in tens. From the last ten, four is taken and there remains six. From the next, three is taken and there remains seven. From the next, two is taken and there remains eight. And from the last, one is taken, and there remains nine. We then say more accurately: "Ten minus four equals six." "Ten minus three equals seven." "Ten minus two equals eight." "Ten minus one equals nine."

As far as the remaining five is concerned, it is half of ten, and, if we were to cut the long piece into two equal parts, that would be to divide ten by two. Ten divided by two therefore equals five. When this is put in writing it reads as follows.

$$10 - 4 = 6$$
$$10 - 3 = 7$$
$$10 - 2 = 8$$
$$10 - 1 = 9 \qquad\qquad 10 \div 2 = 5$$

Once children have mastered these exercises, they can try new exercises on their own. Can we make a three from two pieces? Let us place the one over the two and then write down what we have done so that we can remember it: $2 + 1 = 3$. Can a four be made from two pieces? $3 + 1 = 4$, and $4 - 3 = 1$, and $4 - 1 = 3$.

The two piece bears the same relationship to the four piece as the five to the ten, that is, when turned end over end it goes from one extreme to the other. Therefore $4 \div 2 = 2$ and $2 \times 2 = 4$. We can therefore consider the following problem: With how many pieces can we play this game? The three with the six and the four with the eight, that is,

$$2 \times 2 = 4; 3 \times 2 = 6; 4 \times 2 = 8; 5 \times 2 = 10;$$
$$\text{and } 10 \div 2 = 5; 8 \div 2 = 4; 6 \div 2 = 3; 4 \div 2 = 2.$$

At this point we find that cubes used in playing the game for remembering numbers can be of help:

```
   2         4         6         8          10
X X X   XX X X XX   X X XX   X X XX X X   X X
        X X X XX   X X XX   X X XX X X   X X
                   X X XX   X X XX X X   X X
                            X X XX X X   X X
                                        X X X
```

From their arrangement it can be immediately seen which numbers can be divided by two: all those that do not have a cube at the bottom. These are even numbers, because they can be arranged in pairs, that is, two by two, and the division into two is very easy since all one has to do is to separate the two lines of cubes arranged under each other. By counting the cubes on each side of the line, the quotient is reached. To reconstruct the original numbers all that one has to do is to bring the two rows close together again, for example, $2 \times 3 = 6$.

Five-year-old children do not find any of this difficult.

Very soon, the repetition becomes monotonous. But what prevents us from changing the exercises? Let us take the series of ten lengths and, instead of placing the one over the nine, let us put it on the ten, and the two over the nine instead of the eight, and the three over the eight instead of over the seven. The two can also be placed over the ten, the three over the nine, and the four over the eight. In these instances the result is a length greater than ten, which must be learned and named: eleven, twelve, thirteen, and so on, to twenty. And why should games with the cubes be limited to the number nine, which is so small?

After the operations have been learned through ten, they are continued to twenty without any difficulty. The only difficulty lies in the decimals, which require several lessons.

Lessons in decimals. Arithmetical calculations beyond ten. The material necessary for these lessons consists in various square cards on which the figure ten is printed in large type about an inch-and-a-half or two inches high and other rectangular cards half the width of the squares, each bearing an individual number from one to nine. The simple numbers are placed in a row, 1, 2, 3, 4, 5, 6, 7, 8, 9. Then, since there are more numbers, we must begin again with the one. This one is like that section in the system of rods that extends beyond the nine in the ten piece. When we count along the steps of the staircase up to nine, there remains this one section which we again begin to mark with one since there are no more numbers; but it is a one that is placed higher and, in order to distinguish it from the other, we place near it a sign which has no value, namely, the zero. Thus we have ten. Then covering the zero with the separate rectangular numbers in the order of their succession, we have 11, 12, 13, 14, 15, 16, 17, 18, 19. These numbers are composed with the rods by adding one to ten and then, instead of the one, the two, the three, and so forth until we finally add rod nine to rod ten and thus obtain a very long rod which, when its alternating blue and red sections are counted, comes to nineteen.

The teacher may therefore direct the movements of the system of lengths, showing the cards of ten and a figure placed over the zero, for example, sixteen. A child then adds a piece of six to that of ten. The teacher takes the six from the ten card and places over the zero another rectangular card carrying another number, for example, the the number eight. This gives the number eighteen, and the child takes away the six rod and places in its stead the eight.

Each one of these exercises can be put down in writing, for example, $10 + 6 = 16$; $10 + 8 = 18$, and so forth. Subtraction would be carried out in a similar manner.

When the numbers begin to have a definite meaning for a child, the combinations are made with cards alone. The numbers are drawn on two long cards, as represented in the figures A and B, and the rectangles bearing the nine figures are placed over the two rows of numbers.

	A		B	
	10			
	10	11		10
	10	12		20
	10	13		30
	10	14		40
	10	15		50
	10	16		60
	10	17		70
	10	18		80
	10	19		90

The rectangular card bearing the 1 is placed over the 0 of the second 10 on card 1, and under this is placed the 2, and so on. Thus while the row on the left remains the same with the 1 of the 10, all the figures on the right are different going from 0 to 9.

In card B the applications are more complex. The cards with the separate numbers on them are laid down on the first row going from 1 to 9 in a numerical progression by tens. When the 9 has been reached, it is necessary to go on to the succeeding 10 and the process is continued until 100 is reached.

Almost all our children count up to 100, the number which was given to them as a reward for the curiosity which they showed towards it.

I do not believe that this teaching requires further illustration.

19. Further Developments in Arithmetic

It seemed important to us that the children should be able to count up to one hundred and to carry out the exercises connected with this operation, which unites a rational study of the primary numbers with simple reckoning, especially since a rational approach to arithmetic was given rather than a system based on rote memory.

For more than twenty years we limited our teaching to these exercises.

In general, like everybody else, I assumed that arithmetic was very difficult and that it would be foolish to expect more than what had been attained at so early an age.

Actually, experience showed us that children had only a slight interest in arithmetic in comparison with the enthusiasm which they had for, and the surprising results which they attained with, written language. This higher interest in the study of language apparently confirmed the common prejudice about the difficulty and dryness of arithmetic.

In the meantime I had prepared for older children in elementary schools, where we soon attempted to extend the system we had devised which had produced such wonderful results in younger children, material which represented numbers through geometrical forms and movable objects which enabled a child to make various combinations of numbers. We have called this splendid material "the material of the beads." Numbers are represented in it in their natural order from one to ten by sticks, or rods, made up of beads of colored glass. Each number has a distinctive color. There are so many of these objects that the numbers can be combined into groups. Thus when the ten is repeated ten times, it forms a square of ten rows containing a hundred beads. Finally, ten squares placed over each other and tied together formed a cube. The cube of ten is thus one thousand. This material had been described in a book that applies our method to the education of children in grammar schools. (*The Advanced Montessori Method.*)

Now it happened that some children about four years old were attracted by these brilliant objects, so easy to carry and handle; and, to our great surprise, they began to use them as they had seen the older children doing.

The result of this was such a great increase in enthusiasm for work with numbers, and especially with the decimal system, that arithmetic actually became one of their favorite exercises.

Four-year-old children composed numbers up to a thousand; and, later, children between five and six years of age made such remarkable progress that today six-year-old children can perform the four operations on numbers running into the thousands.

Mario M. Montessori has helped to develop this program so that children can extract the square root of two, three, and even four figures. Further, the children have been shown how to combine the numerical rods in such a way that they can solve simple algebraic problems.

The obvious pleasure which the children had in these exercises and their ability to handle the small geometrical solids prompted me to make objects resembling Froebel's famous "gifts" of cubes and prisms arranged into a square box. Instead of making all the cubes and bricks alike, however, I had a large wooden cube, about four inches on each edge cut into two unequal parts, then into three other unequal parts. When it had been cut in this way, the large cube became the source of other smaller cubes and rectangular prisms of various shapes. This material represented algebraic formulae, that is, the cube of a binomial and of a trinomial. Solids which had an equal decimal value were of the same color, and each group of like solids had different colors.

Thus, when a child opened the box, he saw a single object, a cube painted in many colors, with its individual components lined up and arranged separately into groups; for example, in the trinomial there were three cubes of different sizes and of three different colors; the same number of prisms with a square face of one color, for example, green; three other prisms also having a square face, but of different shapes, colored, for example, in yellow; three other prisms with a

square face, different from the other two sets, colored, for
example, in blue; and finally six prisms all alike and with
their rectangular sides painted black. The rectangular sides of
the three groups of prisms already mentioned were also
black. These small colored objects fascinate a child. He must
first of all group them according to their color, then arrange
them in various ways, making up a kind of little story, in
which the three cubes are three kings, each one having a
retinue identical to that of the other two, the guards being
dressed in black. Many effects can be obtained through the
use of this material. One of these if the following algebraic
formula:

$$a^3 + 3a^2b + 3a^2c + b^3 + 3b^2a + 3b^2c + c + 3c^2a + 3c^2b + 6abc$$

Finally, the cubes are placed back in the box in a definite
order, and there is thus reconstructed a large many-colored
cube $(a + b + c)^3$.

When playing with this material, a child forms a visual
image of the arrangement of the objects and can thus
remember their quantity and order.

The sense impressions received from these objects furnish
material for the mind. No object is so attractive for four-
year-old children. Later on, by calling the kinds *a*, *b*, *c*, and
writing the names of the separate pieces according to their
dependence upon their own king, five-year-old children, and
certainly six-year-olds, can store up in their minds the algebraic formula for the cube of a trinomial without looking at
the material, since they have fixed in their visual memory the
disposition of the various objects. This gives some idea of the
possibilities that can be attained in practice.

All this teaching of arithmetic and of the principles of
algebra by means of cards which assist the memory and by
other materials produces results which might seem to be
fantastic. They indicate that the teaching of arithmetic should
be completely transformed. It should start with sense perceptions and be based on a knowledge of concrete objects.

It should be obvious that these six-year-old children when
they enter into an ordinary school, where others are beginning to count one, two, three, find themselves out of place. If

they are to continue their wonderful strides in learning, the elementary schools must be radically reformed.

This system in which a child is constantly moving objects with his hands and actively exercising his senses, also takes into account a child's special aptitude for mathematics. When they leave the material, the children very easily reach the point where they wish to write out the operation. They thus carry out an abstract mental operation and acquire a kind of natural and spontaneous inclination for mental calculations.

An English child, for example, when he was descending from a streetcar in London with his mother, said: "If they had all spat, the fine would have come to thirty-four pounds." The child had noticed a sign which said that anyone who spat in the streetcar was subject to a fine of a certain number of shillings. He had then spent his time figuring out in his mind the sum total of fines, converting the shillings into pounds.

20. Drawing and Representative Art

The exercises which we have described as "drawing" actually were intended to train the hand so that it would be ready to write. These exercises were taken as a part of that complex preparation by means of which a child's small hand, still uncertain in its movements, could execute that minute kind of drawing that constitutes writing. These elements, or factors, are separated from each other, as we have already seen with respect to the movements required for writing, so that they may later be combined. In the case of writing, this synthesis is "explosive," and at times it may be found combined with other syntheses of a more general character. The particular kind of drawing which we have already described as a preparation for writing thus later becomes also a foundation for, and component of art and drawing in the proper sense of the word. By itself it is neither drawing nor writing, but rather an introduction to both the one and the other.

Much is said today about free drawing, and many people are surprised that I have set up rigid restrictions on children's drawing. They compose geometrical figures, which they then fill out holding the pencil in a special way, or they fill in with colored pencils figures that have already been outlined. To be better understood, I therefore feel obliged to stress the fact that the procedure which I am describing is only one of the factors in the analysis of writing.

The so-called "free drawing" has no place in my system. I avoid those useless, immature, weary efforts and those frightful drawings that are so popular in "advanced" schools today. And yet, despite this fact, our children draw figures and ornamental motifs that are much more clear and harmonious than those strange scrawlings known as "free drawings," which require an explanation on the part of the child who drew them as to what is meant by these incomprehensible essays. We do not give lessons in drawing or in modeling, and yet many of our children know how to draw flowers, birds, landscapes, and even imaginary scenes in an admirable way. Our children very frequently adorn the pages of their writing or arithmetic with drawings, sometimes adding to a page of calculations the figure of a child in the act of writing, or surrounding it with a fantastic decorative border. Even the geometric drawings frequently become frames for figures, or the outline of a geometrical figure is garnished with ornamental motifs. We must therefore conclude that the preparation of the hand and of the senses naturally assists both writing and expressive drawing.

We do not teach a child to draw by having him draw but by giving him the opportunity to prepare his means of expression. I consider this to be a great aid to free drawing since, being neither inefficacious nor incomprehensible, it encourages a child to continue.

Another type of help which we give to drawing is that which we give to every type of learning. This consists in an analysis of the difficulties of an object's various components. In drawing itself there are various elements, for example, outline and color. We help the child by having him trace the outlines of the insets and fill in the figures with lines. This prepares his hand by developing his muscular control. For colors, he has at his disposal paint brushes and water colors. With these he can paint even without first drawing an outline. We also give a child pastels and show him how to use them.

Finally, artistic figures may be made by cutting them out of colored paper, as has been done by the famous Viennese physicist Oswald.

These papers, scientifically prepared and graded according to color, are useful for making a child appreciate harmonies in various color combinations.

These two separate elements, line and color, are determined and perfected independently of each other. This is done by an individual who suceeds in expressing himself artistically by combining these two elements.

An individual's education is thus perfected through his own spontaneous efforts without the intervention of another. In fact, interfering in a work already completed is always an obstacle. It interrupts the inner drive for expression as can happen when direct means are used to teach drawing.

We call our system for teaching how to draw and write an "indirect method." When they are taught in this way, children become more and more capable of expressing themselves. They make hundreds and hundreds of drawings, producing at times ten in a single day with that same freedom from weariness that they manifest in writing.

This does not mean, however, that progress in drawing continues indefinitely as it does in writing, or that the drawings indicate that the children will all become artists. In almost every instance, there comes at a certain moment a lack of interest in drawing; and another interest, such as that of writing, takes precedence. This lessening of interest in drawing has been frequently observed, especially by psychologists interested in art.

Cizek noticed, for example, in his famous school of free art in Vienna that many children who seemed to have a real passion for artistic labors and were artistically endowed by nature, suddenly lost all interest in art and ceased to make further progress. Doctor Revesz, a psychologist who has specialized in the study of art, states, as a result of her own experience: "There are children who, as they develop their powers of expression and become more sophisticated, give up drawing completely, either because they have lost interest in it or lack artistic talent, or because they concentrate on matters of another character."

Thus, for example, it is frequently noted that children who are especially endowed with musical talent and strongly attracted to abstract subjects such as mathematics and logic do not at all succeed in drawing, or they abandon it.

This has been thoroughly studied from a psychological point of view in a child who was a real musical prodigy. His drawings give obvious proof of what we have just indicated. They are markedly inferior and immature in comparison with the pleasant musical pieces composed by the child during the same period.

This may be the reason why our children abandon drawing for some time when they become passionately interested in writing. It is only later, when they have mastered writing, that they begin again to decorate the margins of their pages. But if a child is endowed with an artistic spirit it takes complete possession of him and makes of him an artist, as in the case of Giotto.

The astonishing colored drawings of animals in motion painted on the walls of caves by primitive men show us that an artistic genius for drawing has existed from man's very beginning. But those beautiful drawings were not simply a manner of expression or a means of communicating pleasant ideas. They are rather, as it is generally thought, expressions of religious ideas.

Briefly, the instinct for self-expression looks for a means to manifest itself; and this may be in at least one of two different ways. One of these is through writing, which is used to express ideas; and the other is through representative art. But, in the majority of cases, this undeniable tendency of a child to draw is not connected with any innate artistic gift or radical inclination towards art. It is rather a kind of writing done with figures which a child employs when he cannot express the ideas and feelings that rise up within him as he comes in contact with his environment.

This means that a child's hand becomes a means of communication, and, as we see, just as a child is continuously speaking, so he draws. He expresses himself with his vocal chords and with his hand, showing latent tendencies of which he himself is still unconscious.

As a matter of fact, the history of writing shows us that writing originally consisted in drawing, that is, in pictography. Many of the earliest pictographs of different prehistoric people resemble the free drawing of a child, especially in the representation of the human figure. These strange drawings had a very clear purpose, that of communicating with other men through a means different from the human voice.

A period of transition followed that of the primitive pictographs. Through a process of gradual development, men discovered how to draw symbols of syllables. Many of these are unintelligible (like many children's drawings) and, as a consequence, the writing is poorly understood. Each of the evolving cultures invented its own system of writing, and this became distinctive of the race, as we see in the case of Egyptian and Hittite hieroglyphs.

Finally, with the discovery of the alphabet the drawings were simplified. They no longer represented ideas or syllables but the simple sounds that comprised the spoken language. An easy mode of writing was fixed that exactly reproduced the spoken language. It was as if the mind had inherited whole and entire the ability to express itself both with the hand and mouth.

We might note in conclusion that the best way to teach drawing is not to leave a child completely free, but to provide the means for its natural development by training the hand. True talent will spontaneously manifest itself and a child's drawing will thus not be hindered by lessons given to assist him, but which instead can stifle his natural interest in drawing. When a child gives up the effort to express himself with his hand, he hampers the free development of drawing. To avoid this loss, we should enrich his environment with means of expression and indirectly prepare his hand to carry out its functions in the best possible manner. The eyes observe things with greater accuracy and discover the beauties concealed in natural objects, and the hand becomes more skilled and flexible. A child will attain the goal towards which nature is urging him with greater happiness for having carried out the exercises required for attaining skill in drawing.

Dr. Revesz, speaking of our method and answering the general criticisms made against it in this matter of "free drawing," has said: "The Montessori school does not repress free drawing, rather it enables children to find the greatest pleasure in it as they develop their sense of color and form and continually exercise their hands and eyes."

The education of the hand is particularly important since the hand is an organ of the mind, the means which the human intelligence uses to express itself.

Dr. Katz, who has made a special psychological study of the functions of the hands, has observed: "The Montessori method, which is dedicated to the development of the use of the hand, shows very clearly the surprising versatility of this organ. My studies, extended over a period of a dozen years, have made me aware of the marvelous sensibility of this instrument of touch and movement. The hand is the means which makes it possible for the human intellect to express itself and for civilization to advance. Without the hand, intelligent beings, despite their natural superiority over other creatures, could not have survived on earth. The hand is an organ of expression, and in the area of artistic creation it has practically occupied the first place. In early infancy the hand assists the intelligence to develop, and in a mature man it is the instrument which controls his destiny on earth."

21. Introduction to Music

Our brief description of musical education in this book is not due to a lack of appreciation for the place of music in education, but to the fact that there can be no more than an introduction to it for children of tender age; only when they are somewhat older can they develop a real interest in it. Moreover, success here depends to a great extent upon having a child hear a good deal of music. His environment must be such that it can arouse in him a feeling for, and an understanding of, music. In a school which should be accessible for all, it is impossible to have ready at hand one who plays well or to provide the children with simple musical instruments such as those which Dolmetch has made for his wonderful children's orchestras. Nevertheless in the Model Montessori Schools musical education is cultivated in a serious way. As in all branches of his development, a child here is given a free choice and free means of expression.

Miss Maccheroni has already conducted some beautiful experiments in this regard. These have been partially published in my book, *The Advanced Montessori Method II*. Lawrence A. Benjamin, with the assistance of distinguished musicians of London and Vienna, has made some important contributions in this regard. The most significant of these has been a careful selection of pieces from the folk and classical music of many different countries. These were chosen after seveal years of experimentation in the Model Montessori School in Vienna.

We may proceed to a rapid review of the various factors connected with musical education.

Rhythm and metrical exercises. The preparation of the motor organs for rhythmical gymnastic exercises may be seen in the exercise called "walking on the line," through which children acquire a perfect sense of balance. At the same time they learn how to control the movements of their hands and feet.

It is during this slow and continuous motion that music may be introduced as a help to sustain their efforts. When balance has been attained, education in rhythm may then be taken up. Many lullabies make suitable accompaniments for these slow and uniform movements, which might be compared with the rocking of a cradle. This addition of music to the movements of these exercises is a real "accompaniment" to the already stabilized gait which it penetrates. In contrast to this slow rhythm there is another which corresponds to running; and it is these two contrasting types of musical rhythm that are particularly appealing to small children. Just as contrasting sensations provided the starting point for the education of the senses, so here contrasting rhythms are the basis of this type of education. Children like to run about or to go at a slow and deliberate pace that requires an effort to keep their balance. On the other hand, because of the proportions of their bodies, they do not have sufficient strength for a rhythmical leap, which moreover requires a perfect sense of balance. It is only at a later age, when a child is at least five, that he can begin to appreciate particular movements corresponding to different rhythms. These are analogous to the various gradations in the training of the senses.

Rhythmical marching on the line should be distinguished from the exercises carried out on it which are aimed at establishing a perfect balance and control of movements. These musical exercises are carried out by a child in different ways, by holding a flag, a glass of water, or a lit candle in his hand or by holding a small basket on his head. In order to carry out the exercise, a line is drawn on the floor to guide the steps in a particular manner. The direction of the line makes it rather difficult for a child to maintain his balance and therefore it enables him to practice and perfect this ability. These exercises are accompanied by soft and regular music which helps the children to sustain the efforts required to carry them out exactly.

But when children start to take up rhythmical exercises, their feet must be free and the line becomes simply a guide that helps them to walk, run, and jump in a row. It should be clear, then, that when they go on to dancing, the line has no further reason for existence, but it can serve as a means of giving the children a sense of order in their movements.

The technique for the education of music consists in picking out a single musical phrase that can be easily interpreted and playing it over and over again. This is analogous to the repetition of the other exercises. In addition to the two initial contrasting steps particularly suited for little children, rhythmical, musical phrases can be chosen and repeated to develop their sensibility to music. Otherwise they do not have an opportunity to receive musical impressions from their environment as they do in the case of colors and other visual objects. By repeating each phrase over and over again, some children between the ages of five and six can develop the capacity of interpreting rhythms which demand slightly different movements, for example, the slow step, the marching step, and so on (gradation).

A teacher can profitably give some instructions, showing how one step, for example, corresponds to a particular rhythm, just as she does in the "lessons" when she says: "This is large, this is small." But after she has given such an instruction, the child should be left to himself so that he can recognize and interpret the same rhythms that are found in different musical phrases.[1]

It is important to note, however, that it is a mistake to give too strong a beat to the rhythm. One should play the measures with all the expression that the melody demands, being confident that the rhythmical cadence will be brought out by the melody itself. To stress one note more than others simply because it has the rhythmical accent is to deprive the piece of its melodic value, and thus also of the power it has of arousing a motor response to the music. Music must be played exactly and with feeling, that is, it must be played and interpreted musically. This gives a "musical time" to a work which, as everyone knows, is not the mechanical rhythm of a metronome.

Children feel the rhythm of music played with feeling, and they often follow it not only with their feet, but also with their arms and bodies. Even very little children can at times show a sense of rhythm. Beppino, when he was about four years old, could keep time with his index finger. The music

[1] L. A. Benjamin, *An Introduction to Music for Little Children.*

which he heard, a song, had two alternating movements, one smooth and the other choppy. He would move his hand smoothly for the *legato*, and jerkily for the *staccato* parts.

Nannina, when she was four years old, could follow a gentle melody by spreading out her dress in a graceful manner and throwing her head back with a happy smile; but at the sound of a military march, she would straighten up, adopt a grave expression, and march along with a firm step.

Children are pleased when at an opportune moment they are shown a new step or how to move around more gracefully. Miss Maccheroni had among her pupils Erminia, Grazilla, Peppinella, Sofia, and Amelia. When she taught them some new movements of a rhythmical dance, they would embrace each other and their teacher. Othello, Vincenzino, and Teresa thanked their teacher for helping them to improve their walk and gestures.

Sometimes children also listen to music as they are seated about a room and watching their companions walking along a line, and they often keep correct time with their hands. Occasionally a child will impersonate a director. When Vincenzino was four-and-a-half years old, he would stand with his feet together in the center of the ellipse drawn on the floor on which the other children were walking and keep time with his extended arm, bending his body slightly at every beat. He raised and lowered his head at the exact interval between one beat and another and assumed an expression in perfect keeping with that of the melody.

The precise way in which a child comes to mark the tempo of a musical beat without having been taught the divisions into three-fourths and four-fourths time is a proof of the sense education derived from musical rhythms. At first children follow the time without regard for the rhythmical accent.

But the time comes when they suddenly sense the stress and follow it, that is, they make their movements correspond to the first beat of the bar.

Marie Louise who was only slightly over four, was walking to the sound of a march. Suddenly she called out to her teacher: "Look! Look what I am doing!" She was jumping up and down gracefully lifting her arms at the first beat of every bar.

Only when the children are older do they study the value

of the notes.[2] Their interest in this will be enhanced by the fact that they have already developed and analyzed within themselves a sense of rhythm.

Musical reproductions. Music that is heard and accompanied by rhythmical movements is only one aspect of a musical education, being simply concerned with a succession of sounds produced in a rhythmical pattern and with the stress given to each bar.

But such movements are followed by a study of harmony and melody. A child can exercise himself in these only if he has at his disposition simple instruments adapted to his size and potentialities, and if he is left free to use them, without being hindered by too many technicalities. When such instruments are available, a child is given a few brief lessons, or introductions, on how to use them, like those which he receives for the use of other materials. This puts him in the position of being able to play by himself; and, because of the simplicity of the instruments, he derives a continually increasing interest in them. The musical performances of the children are surprisingly good, and the fact that they can play together in a band is due to the individual practice of each child with his own particular instrument, which can give him a true feeling of music.

Excellent results have been obtained by Dolmetch in England. Wishing to bring back into use the exquisite musical instruments of the past which had fallen into disuse because of the predominance of the piano, he conceived the idea of making simple instruments for children. Dolmetch's faith in the power of music and in the soul of the child led him to formulate a method with fundamental principles like those of my own. He makes use of suitable material and a brief introduction, whose sole purpose is to make a child familiar with the material. He then leaves the child free to play his instrument.

In the magnificent English institute of Bedales, where there are model Montessori classes, one can meet children in the woods playing violins under the trees or small groups of them stringing together melodies on instruments that are a cross between a simplified harp and a lyre. Delicate harmonies may be heard coming from the windows. Many of these children

[2] For details on this method see L. A. Benjamin, *op. cit.*

have no knowledge whatever of notes or musical theory. They have never carried out rhythmical exercises. Their interest in music comes from their having heard the delightful performances given by their old and impassioned teacher wherever he happens to be—in one of the rooms, or in the woods, or in the meadows. The children follow him and stretch themselves out on the grass and listen to them ecstatically. Their interest in and their ability to play musical selections are enhanced by the opportunity they have of taking up an instrument whenever they feel like doing so and trying to reproduce some tune that has remained fixed in their hearts.

The writing and reading of music. But even in Children's Houses it is possible to start making musical notations.

This activity is based upon the sense exercises connected with the recognition of the musical sounds given off by bells, which are first paired and then arranged according to pitch.

It is a great help to be able to "handle" the notes, that is, the objects which produce the individual sounds. These objects are identical in every detail except for the sound they produce. Since they represent different sounds in a material way, they can be separated, mixed up, and then put back together again like the other objects used in the training of the senses. Since the children have already used this material, the only thing that is now left for them to do is to attach their respective names to the different notes, as they do in other exercises. The names *do, re, mi, fa, so, la, ti*, are cut on separate wooden discs shaped like notes, and the children place them at the foot of each bell according to its sound. In this way a child, by repeating the exercises, comes to know the relative names of the notes. The discs carrying the names of the notes are therefore not only signs to be arranged according to their place on the musical scale but they are in a special way symbols of sounds. When children begin to study the notes on the scale, they therefore do it as a written exercise on already known musical facts.

In order to help a child work alone, assisted by his natural instinct for touching and moving objects, we have prepared for him a wooden scale on which circular spaces have been hollowed out corresponding to the relative positions of the notes on the scale—*do, re, mi, fa, so, la, ti, do*. In these spaces can be set the discs bearing the different names of the notes on their upper face. To insure their insertion into the proper place, there is a corresponding number (1, 2, 3, 4, 5, 6, 7, 8) at the bottom of each space and on the lower side of each disc. Thus a child, by placing the objects according to their numbers, discovers that he has placed them on the scale according to the notes of the octave. For a later exercise, a child is given another scale on a board like the first, but without the hollow spaces and their corresponding numbers. Connected with this scale is a box of unnumbered discs having on their upper sides the name of a note. The same name is repeated on several discs. The exercise tests a child's memory for putting the notes in their proper places and is carried out in the following manner: The discs are picked up at random and placed on the staff, but with their names turned down and the black side of the disc facing up. Many discs can obviously be placed on the same line. Once the notes have been set out, they are turned over without being moved from their original position. The names on the discs can now be read, and this will show if the child has made any mistakes.

The third piece of material is a double scale on separate boards on which the notes are placed in a rhombus. By separating the two boards, the notes are arranged in treble and bass staffs.

When they have reached this stage, children can read little tunes and reproduce them on the bells. And, vice versa, they can write down little tunes after they have played them by ear on the bells or on an instrument and have found the proper notes for them.

In children of a slightly more advanced stage, that is, in the primary classes, musical notation has had a remarkable development. In the Montessori school in Barcelona the children have musical notebooks almost like those for writing.

It should be noticed that the three exercises which have been indicated: rhythmical movements, the reproduction of sounds on musical instruments and the writing of music can go on separately and independently. As a proof of this we may cite not only the existence of independent exercises but even of complete programs which take up only one of these aspects of a musical education. It should be sufficient to note the Delcroze method, which simply aims at perfecting rhythmical exercises, and that of Dolmetch, which trains the children in the art of producing harmonies on musical instruments. The old methods of teaching music begin with a knowledge of the notes on the musical scale apart from music itself. But our method is an example of what we call analyis, that is, the separating of the parts of a sufficiently difficult and complex whole into exercises which can by themselves provide an interesting task.

Rhythm, harmony, and the writing and reading of music are, however, ultimately united. They are thus three separate interests, three levels of graded work and pleasant experiences that explode into the fullness of a single conquest.

22. Religious Education

Religious education considered along the same general lines as those of our whole system includes the preparation of an environment wherein different divisions may be noted: those which pertain to practical life, and those which, on the other hand, corresponding to the development of the mind at school, are concerned with the promotion of a religious feeling, an education of the heart, and a religious knowledge that provides the necessary background for an appreciation of religion. There is thus a complete parallel between what has thus far been described with respect to a Children's House and the totality of religious education. This should be sufficient to indicate that it is impossible to treat the whole matter here. The observations that I shall make will simply aim at establishing the necessary connections between the two branches of education, one of which is concerned with a child's contacts with the realities of the external world and the other with his relations with the realities of the supernatural life.

The foundation for religious education according to my method were laid in the Model Montessori School in Barcelona. This was a public school, but one in which instruction in Catholicism was a basic subject.[1]

The first thing that was done was to prepare an environment—a Children's Church which resembled a place of worship reserved for the faithful but reduced in size for the benefit of the children. We furnished it with little chairs and kneelers and had holy water fonts set up that reached only to the knees of an adult. Small pictures were also hung closer to the floor than usual, and these were frequently changed

---

[1] See Maria Montessori, *The Child in the Church*, edited by Mortimer Standing (London, 1929; St. Paul, 1965).

according to the seasons of the year. There were small statues and groups of little figures representing the Nativity, the Flight into Egypt, and so forth. Fine curtains were hung at the windows so that the children themselves could draw them to shut out the light. They took turns taking care of the little church, putting the chairs in order, filling the vases with flowers, drawing the curtains and lighting the candles.

A priest gave the children instructions in religion and celebrated Mass in the chapel. Just as soon as it had been completed and opened up to the children, we witnessed something that had not been anticipated. We discovered that in many respects the church is a kind of goal towards which our method was oriented. Some of the exercises which did not seem to have any definite external goal in the school found their practical application within the church. The silence which had prepared a child to recollect himself now became that inner recollection to be observed in the house of God, in these half-dark surroundings, broken only by the flickering of candles. Walking silently, keeping still, moving chairs without creating a disturbance, standing up and sitting down and passing between benches and people without making a sound, carrying fragile objects without damaging them in the process, as for example, vases filled with flowers to be placed at the foot of the altar, and lighting candles without spilling wax on hands and clothes were little more than repetitions and practical applications of what a child had already learned to do within the walls of the classroom.

They must therefore appear to these tender minds as the goal of their patiently endured efforts. And they are a source of sentiments of gratitude, joy, and a new sense of dignity. The children carried out these exercises at first in response to an inner impulse, but without a definite external goal. They later performed them out of respect for God's service and experienced what was almost a revelation of the difference between the two different modes and places. It was like the difference between sowing and reaping. The very act of distinguishing between similar activities that have varied meanings and uses is in itself another important sources of intellectual growth. A child of four does not fail to notice the difference between the holy-water font in which he dips his slender little hand to bless himself and the basins in a neighboring room where he washes himself. Such intuitions as these in recognizing differences in things that are alike afford a real exercise for the intellect. A small child, who is thought to be almost incapable of rising to concepts that transcend the senses, begins to make such distinctions when he begins to realize that he is a son of God lovingly invited into the house of his Heavenly Father.

I have met many who had doubts about all this. "Do you know why," I was once asked, "my little grandson likes to come to school in time for Mass? Because you make him put out the candles in a basin of water. That is all. Would it not be better to use this pleasant exercise to teach him arithmetic? Could he not hold, for example, ten lighted candles and put them out as he counted one, two, three, and so forth?"

My critic who spoke to me in this manner certainly had little spiritual insight and scant knowledge of children. Her exercise in arithmetic with the candles would have lasted at the most a week, that is, the approximate time needed to learn how to count from one to ten. But children, as they grow in age and general knowledge, whether of a secular or religious character, will continue to light candles for years which will burn themselves out before the tabernacle. And they will understand that this is no childish game but a truly religious act because it is carried out in a sacred place preserved for the worship of the Lord.

A child who is interested in everything is all the more struck by that which is symbolical and seems to him to be clothed in majesty. From the very first the objects are set apart, and it is the acts themselves which attract a child's attention. He sees the missal, sacred vessels, priestly vestments, and the various acts of worship such as Signs of the Cross, genuflections, and kisses; and little by little their relevance and hidden meaning become clear to him.

When the priest began to explain the sacraments with the help of the objects used in the sacred rites and often went through them with the assistance of the children themselves, I thought that only the older children would be interested. But the youngest did not want to go away. They watched everything with the deepest attention. Even little children of three followed the proceedings enchanted. The priest would prepare, for example, the baptismal font and the ritual objects. He chose a godfather and a godmother from among the children themselves and had a number of infants only a few days old brought in and went again through each of the sacred rites used in the administration of the sacrament. On another occasion a larger child acted as a catechumen and asked for baptism. The children were greatly interested in discovering that baptism in the primitive Church was always given to adults when they were converted to Christianity. In this way the children gradually gained their first notions about the history of the liturgy.

When the children were able to read, another feature was added which helped them to teach themselves. This consisted in making on a miniature but accurate scale objects used in religious services, such as priestly vestments, an altar, and even some representations of historical events or scenes from the Gospels. Cards containing the names of the objects or simple sentences (like those used for giving commands in the first lessons in reading) were prepared so that they could be placed against the objects. This enabled the children to repeat the exercises as they had done before. We also decided to make groups of objects like those used in teaching spelling in the first reading lessons, were, as we may recall, words of the same difficulty are grouped together and placed against objects to which they belong. But here, instead, the group of objects had reference to what is necessary for the validity of the sacrament. The division of the material into separate visible groups and the separation and reuniting of the material in each separate group done many times over made it easy for the children to understand it and to memorize the details exactly, while the reading and placing of the cards against the objects guaranteed the learning of the proper terms. The exercise consisted in setting out the objects of one group, for example, those for the Sacrament of the Last Anointing, and taking the cards corresponding to these objects and placing each one of them on the object that it happened to designate. The Sisters of Notre Dame in Glasgow, Scotland, have made complete models of these objects. Among them is an altar in miniature only five inches wide, but with its details faithfully and exquisitely rendered. A child can look at it and place upon each particular object the card bearing its name.

Children, thus, it may be said, live in the Church from their earliest infancy and acquire almost imperceptibly a knowledge of religious things that is truly remarkable considering their tender age. Moreover, the habits which children have already acquired in our school, such as concentration on work, silence, calm in an environment where there are continual social contacts with other children, and where they must choose their own activities and adapt them to their own needs and those of others, predispose them for the attainment of another moral victory of the utmost importance.

Silence and controlled movements can lead to an inner sensitivity known as a "religious," or "spiritual sense."

In fact, only at the age of seven does a child feel a need of distinguishing between good and evil. A small child is not confronted with such problems. He accepts and believes everything. The only evil that he can imagine is "naughtiness," which draws down upon himself the severity of an adult.

A child is extremely "receptive," and an environment that touches his senses exercises a strong influence upon him. Therefore, it is important to realize that in the first period of a child's growth his environment and the impressions it produces are, one might say, engraved on his soul in an indelible way. A mother who takes her child with her to church provides him with an appreciation for religion which no teaching could arouse.

It is therefore a mistake to try to teach a child how to distinguish between good and evil at a precociously early age when he has yet no interest in the problem. He is as yet too immature to develop a moral conscience in this sense.

A feeling for what is good can be cultivated in a child at this early age by dealing sweetly and kindly with him. What a child really needs is a feeling of security that comes to him from the protection given by his elders.

His education should also follow along these natural lines. God, who loves and protects a child, and who sends His invisible angels to watch over him day and night should be the foundation of his religious aspirations.

Only later is the social sense awakened and responsibility felt for one's own actions. It is then that a child has need of a guide who will show him his way in the world and help him to form his individual conscience.

To speak of evil to a small child is to teach him something that he cannot understand or at least assimilate. Great prudence, therefore, is required in a teacher so that she does not hurt the soul of a child with arguments that are not suited to his years. On one occasion, for example, one of the Franciscan Missionary Sisters of Mary, when she was teaching Bible History remarked that Cain, when he was a boy, must certainly have been cruel to Abel. Some hours after the lesson, a little one, while he was working (meditation!) burst out into tears, saying: "Oh! I shall become like Cain!" And he confessed to the sister, who tried to console him, the small wrongs he had done to his companions.

Our method encourages children to be both devout and free in their intellectual operations. The result of this is that they are seen to be spiritually strong and robust. Growing up in this fashion, they are neither timid nor fearful but pleasantly self-possessed, courageous, and alert. Above all they have faith and confidence in God, the Author and Preserver of life. Children are so capable of distinguishing between what is natural and supernatural that they seem to pass through a period that is particularly sensitive to religion. Just as a child's bodily development is strictly dependent upon the natural laws which transform it, so he seems at this age to be very close with God. I remember a two-year-old girl who, when she was placed before a statue of the Infant Jesus, said: "This is not a doll."

Work in the fields as a part of religious education. We thought that it would be an excellent idea to have the children grow the wheat and the grapes to be used as the material for the Eucharist and thus incorporate the children's religious activities into their labors and joys in the fields. We therefore set aside portions of a large meadow where the children used to play in the afternoon for the growing of grain and vines. Two rectangular patches were picked out by the children themselves, one on the extreme right and the other on the extreme left of the field. A type of grain was then chosen that matures rapidly. Furrows for the grain were laid out in parallel lines, and each of the children sowed a portion of the grain in them. The actual sowing, the care required to see that no seeds fell outside the furrows, and the seriousness and solemnity with which the labors were carried out at once showed that the activity was suited to the goal intended. A little later the vines were planted. Those looked like shriveled roots and were so dry that they gave no promise of that marvel to come, the appearance one day of real bunches of grapes. The shoots were placed equal distances apart in furrows laid out in parallel rows. Then we decided that it would be well to plant flowers all around them as a kind of unending homage of fragrance and beauty to the plants which one day would furnish bread and wine for the Eucharist. The children continued to play in the other parts of the meadow. They made buildings of bricks, dug ditches, laid out little paved roads, ran about, and played ball, and their gaiety was increased by the flowers. Along with the pleasure of their games they experienced that deeper emotion of watching day by day the wonderful growth of plants.

Parellel rows of green blades actually began to appear in the field of grain. As they grew they created a lively interest among the children. Then the dry shoots of the vines also began to send forth pale green buds and leaves. The children would stand around in groups watching their growth. Some of the children were chosen to disinfect the vines to protect them from peronospora (fungi). When the clusters of grapes made their appearance, they covered them with little bags of white gauze to protect them from insects.

We decided to organize for the opening and closing of the school year two outdoor festivals, one corresponding to the grape harvest and the other to the reaping of the grain, and we enlivened these festivals with folk songs and rustic music made on primitive instruments. Some of these songs were very old and melodious and had been used from ancient times as sacred hymns in church.

Carefully and with obvious pleasure the children reaped the grain. They took noisy delight in binding the sheaves with colored ribbons and setting them in rows before bidding the grain good-by and waiting for the return of the flour.

These notes on our experiments in religious education represent only an atempt, but they show how religion can be brought practically into the life of a little child as a rich source of joy and inspiration.

The experiment in religious education was eventually abolished in our Children's Houses because it was aimd exclusively at instruction in Catholicism, which lends itself to exercises in moving about and preparing various objects, whereas there is no place for such activities in religions that are almost entirely abstract.

Nevertheless, much was prepared and even written on this

program. I can mention the following books: *I bambini viventi nella Chiesa (The Child in the Church), La S. Messa spiegata ai bambini (The Mass Explained to Children), La vita in Cristo (Elementary Illustrations of the Liturgical Year and of the Church Calendar), Il Libro aperto (Advanced Material for Reading the Missal),* and the *Manuale per la preparazione di un Messale per i bambini (Manual for the Preparation of a Children's Missal).*

23. Discipline in a Children's House

The experience that has accumulated since the printing of the first edition of this book up to the present day has repeatedly confirmed the fact that in our classes of small children, which number up to forty and even fifty pupils, there prevails a more perfect *discipline* than in ordinary schools. Anyone who visits a well-managed school is struck by the discipline of the children. Here are forty children from three to seven years of age, all intent on their own particular work. Some are doing the sense exercises, some arithmetic, some are touching letters, some are drawing, some are at the cloth frames, some are dusting, some are seated at a table, and some are bent over carpets spread out on the floor. A faint noise can be heard of objects being lightly moved about and of children walking on tip-toe. Every now and then a poorly repressed shout of joy is heard. There is an eager shout: "Teacher! Teacher!" or an exclamation: "Look at what I have done!"

But more frequently there is absolute concentration.

The teacher moves about slowly and silently. She goes up to one who has called her. Her supervision is such that anyone who needs her is immediately aware of her presence, whereas those who do not are completely oblivious of her.

Hours pass and all is silent.

As some visitors to the Children's Houses have noted, they seem to be "little men" or as others have described them, "senators in session."

The children are so engrossed in their work that they never quarrel over the objects. If anyone does something extraordinary, he finds someone who will admire and be delighted with his work. No heart bleeds at the good of others; the success of each is the joy and wonder of the rest. And this often creates eager imitators. All seem to be happy and satisfied with doing what they can. The activities of others do not arouse their envy or painful rivalry, nor are they themselves inflated with empty pride. A little child of three works peacefully alongside a boy of seven and is as contented with his own work as he is about the fact that he is shorter and does not have to envy the older boy's height. They all grow up in the most profound peace.

If the teacher wants something from the whole group, for example, that they should all give up their interesting work, it is enough that she say one word in a low voice or make a gesture for everything to be suspended. The children look at her closely, anxious to know how to carry out her wishes.

Many visitors have seen a teacher write some directions on the blackboard and have noted how joyfully the children obey.

But it is not only the teacher who is obeyed. Anyone who asks something of the children is struck at seeing how scrupulously they respond, and with what peace and serenity. Often visitors would like to hear a child who is painting sing. He will leave his painting to accommodate them, but as soon as he has carried out this act of courtesy, he returns to the work he has broken off. Often very small children will finish the work they have begun before obeying.

One of the most wonderful examples of discipline occurred during the examinations of the teachers who had followed my first course on methods. The tests were both theoretical and practical. Groups of children were put at the disposal of the one being examined. She had to put the children through different exercises drawn by lot. The children busied themselves in the meantime in our presence with occupations of their own choice. They labored continuously and, after the interruption caused by an examination, would return to their original undertakings. Every once in a while one would come up to give us a drawing he had finished during the periods of waiting.

We marveled at the patience, constancy, and eager readiness of the children.

All this might give the impression that these children are excessively repressed for the fact that they are utterly lacking in timidity. Their bright eyes, gay and disarming countenances, and their readiness in inviting others to observe their work or to listen to their explanations of it make us realize that we are in the presence of individuals who are masters of their own homes. The eagerness with which they embrace their teacher's knees or draw down her head to kiss her reveals their uninhibited emotions.

Anyone who has seen these children set a table must have become increasingly apprehensive and surprised. Little four-year-old waitresses set the table with knives, forks, and plates. They carry trays with as many as five glasses of water and pass from table to table bearing large tureens of hot soup. No one cuts himself, breaks a glass, or spills a drop of soup. During the meal the waitresses are silent and assiduously attentive. No one finishes his soup without being immediately asked if he wants a second helping; or, if he has finished, a waitress hastens to take away his empty plate. No child has to ask for a second helping or indicate that he has finished.

Anyone who sees children acting in this way must reflect on the ordinary behavior of four-year-olds who shout, break everything, and must be constantly waited upon. This is a moving spectacle which obviously flows from hidden sources of secret energy in the depths of the human soul. I have often seen the eyes of spectators at these little banquets fill with tears.

Such discipline could never be obtained by commands, exhortations, or by any of the ordinary means used for keeping order.

Actually, it is useless to depend upon scoldings and entreaties for the maintenance of discipline. These may at first give the illusion of being somewhat effective; but very soon, when real discipline makes its appearance, all this collapses as a wretched illusion in the face of reality: "The night gives way to day."

The first glimmerings of discipline have their origin in work. At a certain moment a child becomes intensely interested in some task. This is shown by the expression on his face, his intense concentration, and his constancy in carrying out the same exercise. Such a child shows that he is on the way to becoming disciplined. Whatever may be its particular occasion, an exercise of the senses, a fastening of some sort, or a washing of dishes, it is all the same.

We can help to stabilize such an experience by repeated lessons in silence. Perfect immobility, attention aroused to catch the sound of one's name pronounced from a distance in a whisper, and the carefully coordinated movements required for the avoidance of objects and for walking lightly all effectively prepare a child for setting his motor and mental operations and his personality in order.

When a child has succeeded in concentrating upon his work, we must supervise it with scrupulous exactitude, graduating the exercises as experience suggests. Our own success as teachers in establishing discipline will be dependent upon a strict application of the method.

One of the greatest difficulties is securing discipline lies in the fact that it cannot be obtained simply with words. No man disciplines himself by merely hearing another speak. Rather, he needs to go through a series of complex preparatory actions such as, for example, those that are required for the complete carrying out of an educational program.

Discipline is therefore attained indirectly, that is, by developing activity in spontaneous work. Everyone must learn how to control himself and how to engage in calm and silent activity, for no other purpose than that of keeping alive that inner flame on which life depends.

Work cannot be presented in an arbitrary manner, and this is what lies behind our method. It must be the kind of work that a man inwardly desires and for which he has a natural inclination, or which he can accomplish bit by bit. This is the kind of work that gives order to a person's life and opens up to it infinite possibilities of growth. We may take, for example, the lack of discipline in a little child. It is basically due to lack of muscular control. A child is constantly on the move but his actions are disordered. He throws himself on the ground, shouts, acts strangely, and so forth. Beneath all this, however, there is a latent tendency to coordinate and give fixed patterns to his movements. A child is a man who is as yet awkward in speech and movement but who must become their master. For the present he commits many painful mistakes as he struggles towards an instinctive but poorly perceived goal.

The movements which he must perfect are those which become a man. A child must acquire the customs prevailing in his environment. This is why he must have an opportunity to exercise himself in them. It is not enough that he see what others do. His movements are not those of a machine that only has to be regulated; they are rather those of a mechanism that has a definite task to fulfill. Motor activity, therefore, must have a goal and must be connected with mental activity. There is a close relationship between movement and the desire to learn. Children who are disorderly in their movements are not simply children who have not learned how to move about. They are rather children whose minds have not been properly nourished and are suffering from mental starvation.

To tell a child: "Stand still like me!" does not enlighten him. One cannot by a simple command put order into the complex psycho-muscular system of a still growing individual. When we attempt to do so, we confuse a child with someone else, that is, with a man who deliberately chooses to do wrong and who can (within certain individual limits) carry out the urgent bidding of another with respect to something he knows and can achieve. But if we wish to obtain obedience from a small child, we must teach him how to coordinate the natural evolution of his voluntary movements. We must teach him how to coordinate all of his movements so that he can carry them out in a harmonious fashion, analyzing them as far as we can and perfecting each one of them individually.

All the exercises that promote the coordination of movements are undertaken for a definite preconceived goal. By means of these exercises, children not only exercise their muscles but they also give order to, and enrich their minds. These activities strengthen the will, since they are based on various motives which arouse the activity itself. However, even though the movements have been coordinated, the individual who coordinates them occupies a central position. By means of these motor exercises he enlarges his own understanding, becoming ever more conscious of himself and his environment. A real coordination of movement perfects the whole person.

Those, then, who have learned how to move as they should are no longer children. They have enriched their personalities by freely choosing their own occupations and have thus disciplined themselves.

It is not surprising, but rather most natural, that a child at this age should become disciplined through these exercises as far as his muscles are concerned. As a matter of fact, when he moves, he is following nature's bidding; but, since his movements are directed towards a goal, they no longer have an appearance of disorder but of work. Here we have a discipline which represents a goal attained through a host of conquests. A child who has been disciplined in this way is not the same as he was before, when her knew how "to be good." Rather, he is an individual who has perfected himself, who has surpassed the ordinary limitations of his age, and made a leap forward. Through present conquests he has laid hold of the future. He has thus grown up. He will not always have to have before him one to tell him repeatedly: "Be still! Be good!" and who, in so doing, vainly confuses opposing ideas. The good which he has acquired can no longer make him be quiet in idleness; his goodness is now wholly expressed in his movements.

Actually, "the good" are those who "move towards the good" built up through their own efforts and through orderly and useful external works.

External works are at once the means of attaining internal growth and an indication of it. The two factors are woven together. Work perfects a child interiorly, but a child who is thus perfected also works better, and is fascinated by his progress. He therefore continues to perfect his inner self.

Discipline is not, therefore, a fact, but a way. It enables a child to acquire with an almost scientific exactness the concept of goodness.

But more than anything else he tastes the supreme pleasure of possessing an inward order that has been attained through conquests leading to a proper goal.

During the course of his long period of preparation, a child experiences joy, pleasure, and excitement. These make up the intimate treasures of his mind, and they afford a special strength and sweetness which will be a source of goodness. As a matter of fact, a child has now not only learned how to move about and to engage in useful activities, but he has acquired a special charm in his movements which make his gestures more correct and graceful and adds to the beauty of his hands, face, and eyes, which reveal through their brightness of the birth of an inner life.

A child's movements are gradually and spontaneously coordinated. Though his own inner efforts he establishes a harmony in his external activities. Muscles which nature has destined for movement find their rest in orderly movements, just as the normal rhythm of breathing in the open air represents rest for the lungs. To deprive muscles of all movements is to frustrate their natural tendency. This is not only a source of weariness but also of degeneration.

We should therefore be convinced that rest for anything which naturally moves is some definite form of motion corresponding to its own intrinsic end. Its rest consists in moving in a way that corresponds to the secret decrees of life. If we apply this principle to man we shall see that since man is an intelligent being his movements are restful in proportion to their intellectuality. A child that jumps about aimlessly and without restraint uses up his nervous energy, but intelligent movement which gives him an inner satisfaction and pride in having overcome himself increases his strength.

This "augmentation of his potentialities" may be physiologically explained as a development of his organs through rational use, through a better circulation of the blood, and through an active renewal of the substance of his tissues, all of which favor the growth of the body and promote physical fitness.

Something of the same could be said about a child's intellectual development. His mind is at first undisciplined, but it also has its own proper goal to achieve, but in the process it experiences many difficulties because it is frequently abandoned and even persecuted.

I once saw in the gardens of the Pincio in Rome a very beautiful child of about a year and a half. He had an empty bucket and a little spade and was busily collecting pebbles from the path to fill it.

Near the smiling child was a distinguished looking nurse, who was obviously well-disposed towards him and who must have been most affectionate and intelligent in her care. It was time to depart and the nurse patiently entreated the child to leave his work and let himself be placed in his buggy. In the face of the child's resistance, all her exhortations were of no avail. She finally filled up the pail with gravel herself and then put the gravel and the child in the carriage, certain that she had pleased him. The loud cries of the child indicated that this was not so. His shouts of protest at the violence and injustice which had been done to him struck me. What a weight of resentment filled his heart! The child had not really wanted to fill the pail with gravel; he had simply wanted to carry out the exercise needed to fill it and thus satisfy the needs of his growing body. The end sought by the child was his own inner formation, not the external act of filling a pail with little stones. His lively attachment to the exterior world was only an illusion; his vital need was a reality. Actually, if he had filled the pail, he would probably have emptied it so that he could fill it again many times over until he had completely satisfied himself. Before the intervention of his nurse, I had seen him pursuing this satisfaction with a rosy, smiling countenance. Inward happiness, exercise, and the sun were the three rays that had been illuminating that resplendent life.

This simple episode is an example of what happens to children all over the world, even to the best and most dearly beloved. They are not understood because adults judge them according to their own standards. They believe that a child is concerned with external ends, and they lovingly assist him to attain them. Instead, a child is dominated by an unconscious need to develop himself. He consequently contemns anything that has been attained and longs for that which is still to be achieved. For example, he would rather dress himself than be dressed, even magnificently. He prefers washing himself to the pleasant feeling of being clean. He would rather build a house than own one. And he is thus disposed because he must first form his own life before he can enjoy it. In this self-formation is his true and almost sole delight. In the first year of his life a child's formation is largely limited to assimilating food, but later it consists in stabilizing the psychophysiological functions of his organism.

The little child on the Pincio is a symbol of this. He wanted to coordinate his voluntary movements, to exercise his muscular energies in lifting objects, to exercise his eyes in judging distances, to use his intelligence for filling the bucket, to develop his will in deciding on the acts to be performed, and instead of this someone who loved him, thinking that he wanted to gain possession of little stones, made him unhappy.

We frequently commit a similar error by imagining that a young pupil is aiming at intellectual knowledge. We help him to gain it and in so doing place an obstacle in the way of his development and thus make him unhappy. It is generally believed in schools that a child gets his satisfaction from learning something.

But by leaving our children free we have been able to trace their spontaneous intellectual growth.

Knowledge attained is a point of depature for a child. When he has learned how to do something, he then begins to enjoy the repetition of the exercise, and he repeats what he has learned an indefinite number of times with obvious satisfaction. He takes pleasure in exercising himself since it is in this way that he develops his psychic activities.

Once we have realized this, we can be objective in our criticism of the teaching done in many schools. We can see an example of this in a teacher who asks a question of his class and then tells one of the students who volunteers to answer: "No, not you, since you know the answer." And then he asks one of the pupils who he thinks does not know it. In other words, the one who does not know the answer must speak out, and the one who knows must keep silent, though nothing lies beyond knowledge. And yet how many times does it happen to us in the ordinary course of events that we repeat what we know best, what we love dearly, and what corresponds to our own inner life?

We are especially fond of singing the tunes which we know well and which we have, as a consequence, relished and made a part of ourselves. We like to speak about what we know and love, even if we know perfectly well that we have nothing new to say and have said the same thing many times before. We always repeat with fresh interest the prayers we have learned.

But if we are to repeat in this fashion, it is necessary that what we repeat should have first existed. In this instance, it is knowledge that already exists, and this knowledge is the *sine qua non* for the repetition of the acts. Growth comes from the repetition of an exercise and not from the first apprehension of something new.

When a child has reached the stage when he repeats an exercise, he begins to grow interiorly as may be seen from his exterior discipline.

But this phenomenon does not always occur. The same exercises are not repeated at every age. In fact, repetition should correspond to a need. The essence of the experimental method of education consists in providing exercises that will satisfy the needs of a growing organism. And if a particular need has run its course, a child will no longer have the opportunity of attaining his full development because the time for it has passed. This is why children frequently are forever fatally deprived of what they should have had.

It is also interesting to note that children take different amounts of time to carry out specific acts. Small children, who are making their first solitary efforts, are very slow in carrying out their actions. Their life thus is ruled by special laws quite different from our own.

Little children take great pleasure in performing slowly and deliberately many complex actions, for example, dressing and undressing, cleaning up the room, washing themselves, setting the table, eating and so forth. In all these activities they are most patient, and they carry their laborious efforts to conclusion, surmounting all the difficulties that confront an organism still in its formative state. But we, when we see a child "toiling" and "wasting time" in doing something we could do in a moment and without the least difficulty, substitute ourselves for him and do it instead.

Always dominated by the same prejudice that the object to be attained is the completion of some exterior act, we clothe and wash a child and take from his hands objects which he ardently wants to handle. We pour soup into his bowl, feed him, and clear the table. And after we have served him in this way, we judge him harshly, as always happens when one patronizes another, as being awkward and helpless. We often look upon a child as being impatient simply because we do not have the patience ourselves to let him carry out the acts according to his own tempo, which is different from our own. Or we judge a child to be haughty simply because we ourselves are afflicted with the vice. Such hostile attitudes bear down heavily on the patient and gentle nature of a child.

Just as a brave man defends his right to live, so a child rebels against anyone who opposes the voice of nature within him which he must obey. And he shows his displeasure in violent actions, screams, and tears. He then appears as a rebel, a revolutionary, and a destroyer to one who does not understand him and who, though he believes that he is assisting him, actually is pushing him back on his way of life. An adult thus inflicts still another slander upon the one he loves, imagining that a child's defense of himself is a kind of innate wickedness that is characteristic of children of tender age.

What would happen to us if we were plunged into the midst of the Fregoli, who are very rapid in their movements, like those who amaze and amuse us in the theater with their rapid changes? And what would we do if, continuing to move in our usual way, we saw ourselves assailed by these Fregoli, who began to dress us and toss us about without any consideration, to feed us so rapidly that we had no time to swallow, to take our work from our hands so that they could complete it more rapidly, and to reduce us to a humiliating state of idleness and impotency? Not knowing what else to do, we would cry out and defend ourselves with our fists against such fanatics, and they, since they only wanted to help us, would say that we are wicked, rebellious, and good for nothing. But we, knowing our true fatherland, would say to them: "Come to our country and see the splendid civilization that we have erected; see our wonderful works." And these Fregoli, when they saw that our world, though slower than their own, was so fair, active, orderly, peaceful, and gentle would be carried away with admiration.

Something similar happens between us and children.

The education of the senses is attained through a repetition of the exercises. Their object is not that a child should come to know colors, shapes, and various qualities, but that he should sharpen his senses by paying attention, making comparisons, and forming judgments, that is, be engaged in real intellectual exercises. And these exercises, rationally carried out with various stimuli, further a child's intellectual development, just as physical exercises improve his health and regulate the growth of his body.

A child who exercises himself in perceiving isolated stimuli with his various senses learns how to focus his attention and gradually perfects his psychic reactions, just as he trains his muscles through various exercises. He is thus not limited to psycho-sensorial activities but lays the foundation for a spontaneous association of ideas, for reasoning processes based upon positive knowledge, and for mental stability. This secret training is the reason for those psychic explosions which bring so much joy to a child. It is then that he discovers the world about him. He admires the new things that are revealed to him and take delight in his growing consciousness.

And, finally, then is born within him, almost spontaneously, as a sign of his inner development, reading and writing.

The wife of a medical colleague of mine once brought me her two-year-old son. The child slipped from his mother's arms and practically hurled himself upon the objects on his father's desk—a rectangular pad of paper and a round cover for an inkstand. I was moved at seeing this intelligent child striving as best he could to do the exercises which our children ceaselessly repeat with the plane insets. His father and mother scolded him and drew him away. They explained to me that they tried in vain to keep the child from touching the papers and objects belonging to his father: "The child is restless and naughty." How often are children scolded for "touching everything" as if they were hostile to all correction!

And yet it is by guiding and developing this natural instinct for touching everything and for recognizing the harmony of geometrical figures that our four-and-a-half-year-old children have found the source of so many joys and emotions in the phenomenon of spontaneous writing.

A child wastes his nervous energies in hurling himself upon a pad of papers, inkstands, or similar objects, as he vainly strives to attain his goal. Despite his continued efforts he is constantly being overcome by persons stronger than himself and, as a consequence, he is in a constant state of agitation and weeping from frustration. Yet his parents still believe that he should rest. It is also wrong to look upon a child as wicked who is striving to lay the foundations of his intellectual edifice. Our children, on the other hand, when they are left free to remove and replace the geometrical plaques of the plane insets, are really happily at rest. They are given such objects to develop their powers, and they enjoy a perfect psychic peace, quite ignorant of the fact that their eyes and hands are being introduced into the mysteries of a new language.

The majority of our children grow calm in carrying out such exercises. Their nervous systems rest. Then we say that these little ones are good and tranquil. They have already far surpassed the external discipline so eagerly sought in ordinary schools.

But just as there is a difference between a calm and a disciplined man, so the obvious external calmness of the children is something partial, exterior and physical in comparison with the real discipline that is growing within them.

Often, and this is still another prejudice, we believe that all that we have to do to elicit a voluntary act on the part of a child is to order him to do something. We pretend that this is actually effective and we call this pretense "a child's obedience." We find that little children are particularly disobedient. When they are three or four years old their resistance is so strong that it can make us give up any hope of obtaining obedience. We persist in extolling the virtue of obedience to the children. It should be, according to us, characteristic of childhood, but actually, obedience is a child's virtue simply because it is so rare and so difficult to obtain.

It is a very common illusion to imagine that we can obtain something that is difficult or impossible by prayer, entreaty, command, or agitation. We ask, for example, for obedience from children, and the children ask for the moon.

Obedience can only be obtained through a complex formation of the psychic personality. In order to obey, one must not only wish, but also be able, to obey. When we give an order, we expect the person to whom it is given to do something or to stop doing something. Obedience therefore includes a training of both the intellect and the will. Any efforts made in this direction teach obedience to a child, even if only indirectly.

The method which we employ contains a voluntary exercise in each of its stages. When a child carries out movements that are directed towards an end, he reaches a predetermined goal; and by patiently repeating an exercise, he exercises his will.

Similarly, through a fairly complicated series of exercises he learns how to check and control his own activities. For example, during the lessons in silence a child must control his movements for a considerable length of time as he waits to be called, and even when he hears his name called, he must restrain his desire to cry out with joy and to run to the one who is calling him. Instead he must remain silent and move quietly, taking care to avoid obstacles so as not to make a noise. Another exercise that checks his impulses is that of arithmetic. A child who has drawn a number must take from a group of objects only that number corresponding to the one he has drawn. But, as experience shows, he would like to take as many as he could carry away. If he draws a zero, he must wait patiently with empty hands. Another exercise of this sort is the lesson on the zero. A child who has been called in many different ways to come zero number of times and to give zero number of kisses remains where he is, obviously conquering the instinct which would make him obey at once the call. A child who is carrying a large tureen of soup must drive away every distraction that would impede his task. He must resist the temptation to jump or to pay attention to a fly buzzing about his face and must be completely taken up with the great responsibility of not permitting the tureen to slip or spill.

A little four-and-a-half-year-old girl, every time that she rested the tureen on a table so that her little guests could be served, would make two or three little jumps. She would then take the tureen and carry it to another table, where she would jump again. But she never interrupted her round of work in serving twenty little tables with soup, nor did she ever forget the vigilance required for her task.

The will, like every other faculty, is developed and strengthened through methodical exercises. In our schools exercises for the will are to be found in all of a child's intellectual exercises and his exercises in practical living. A child seems to be learning how to carry out his movements with grace and accuracy, how to sharpen his sense perceptions, and how to read and count, but actually he is becoming the master of himself and laying the foundations for a strong and ready will.

It is often said that a child should be able to break his own will in the face of obedience and that the education of a child's will consists in submission and obedience. But such a claim is irrational since a child cannot relinquish something which he does not have. Rather, in expecting this, we hinder the development of his will and thus seriously injure him. A child is never given time nor even the means to test himself, to evaluate his own strength and limitations, since he is always interrupted by, and subjected to, us. Such an injustice causes him to lose heart. He hears himself bitterly scolded for not having something which is being continuously destroyed within him.

This is a source of timidity in a child, a kind of malady of a will that cannot develop and which, whether we are aware of it or not, we wrongly attribute to a child as a characteristic trait.

Our children are never timid. One of their most fascinating qualities is their fearlessness in dealing with others and sharing their efforts with them. Some children are timid and tearful in the presence of adults but they become little tyrants when left alone with other children. Their characters have been warped since they have not been able to exercise their wills except by stealth. But such aberrations disappear in our Children's Houses.

In addition to exercise of the will, obedience requires a knowledge of the act to be performed.

One of the most interesting observations made by my student Anna Maccheroni, first in the Children's House in Milan and later in the school on the Via Giusti at Rome, was particularly concerned with the role played by knowledge in a child's growth in obedience.

This virtue becomes manifest in a child just as soon as his personality begins to acquire a certain degree of order. A child, for example, makes an effort to carry out a certain exercise. Then at a certain point he suddenly does it perfectly. He is surprised, looks around and wants to do it again; but he does not succeed until he has made a number of other attempts. Later he will almost always succeed in doing the exercise. But if someone asks him to do it, instead of succeeding he will almost always fail. The external command is still incapable of effecting a voluntary act. But later, when a child almost always succeeds in doing what he wants to do by himself, an external invitation will arouse orderly acts sufficient to attain their intended goal. In other words, the child can now regularly carry out the command he has received.

That these facts, apart from particular exceptions, are dependent upon the laws of psychic development may be seen from our own experiences in school and even in life. We often hear a child say: "I have done it, but I can't do it anymore." Or a teacher, puzzled by a child's inability to carry out a command, will say: "He used to do it well, but he can't now." But then the stage is finally reached where a child not only can do something but he also retains the ability to do it.

There are thus three stages of development. The first consists in a subconscious stage during which a child's intellect, through a mysterious inner impulse, is passing from a state of disorder to order. This is revealed by a perfect external act, but since the act is still outside the range of consciousness, the child cannot reproduce it at will. The second consists in a conscious stage when the will assists in the production and fixation of the acts. In the third stage the will can elicit the acts themselves and respond to external commands.

Obedience develops in a parallel fashion. In the first period, of internal disorder, a child does not obey. He is phychically deaf and cannot understand the commands. In the second period he would like to obey and seems to understand the command and wishes to carry it out, but he cannot obey, or at least he does not always succeed in obeying. He is therefore not ready to obey and does not know the joys of obeying. In the third period he responds promptly and with enthusiasm, and as he perfects himself in the exercises, he finds happiness in being able to obey.

It is during this period that he responds with joy and leaves at the least command whatever he happens to be doing.

This order which replaces the former chaos of the mind provides the basis for a child's intellectual and moral growth. Light has been separated from darkness and his now orderly mind has experienced new sentiments and made new conquests. He already manifests the first flowerings of kindness, love, and longing for what is good. The soul of such a child is filled with a fragrance which gives a promise of the spiritual fruits mentioned by St. Paul: "Charity, joy, peace, long-suffering, gentleness, goodness, meekness, and modesty."

The children become virtuous because they practice patience in repeating the exercise, meekness by yielding to the desires and requests of others, and goodness by rejoicing in the good of another and not being jealous or hateful. They are happy and contented in doing good, and diligent to a marvelous degree.

These are the bare outlines of a program for securing discipline in a child. The means may be described as indirect since the rationally organized work and freedom of a child takes the place of a critical and demanding teacher. It presupposes a religious concept of life, a recognition of the authority of God and of those who visibly represent Him, but its immediate foundations are work and liberty, and these in turn are the bases for civil progress.

A child has thus acquired virtues through patient exercise.

These include civil virtues, which come from living freely with others, and religious virtues, which raise the intellectual and the moral virtues to a supernatural level and direct them immediately towards God.

24. Conclusions and Impressions

I believe that the portion of our method here described is clear enough for teachers to put into practice.

Anyone who grasps its general notion will understand how the part dealing with its material application is extremely simple and easy.

The figure of a teacher who makes great efforts to maintain discipline and to keep the children still and who wears out her lungs in loud and constant speaking has disappeared.

Verbal instruction has been replaced by "material for development." This material contains within itself its own control of error and thus affords children the opportunity of teaching themselves by their own efforts. The teacher thus becomes a director of the children's own spontaneous work. She is silent and passive.

Each of the children is occupied with a different work. As the teacher watches over them, she can make observations which, when they are later studied scientifically, can help determine a child's mental state and lay the foundation for further pedagogical experiments. I believe that with my method I have established the conditions of study necessary for the development of scientific education. Anyone who will adopt this method, will make of every school and every class where it is used a laboratory for experimentation.

From this we may expect real, positive solutions to all the problems of education currently discussed. Solutions for some have already been found. These include freedom for the pupils, self-education, and the intermingling of household, with formal class work for a more rounded education.

On the practical side, our method has, moreover, the advantage of being able to draw together children of very different backgrounds. In our first Children's Houses there were children of two-and-a-half, still too young for the simplest exercises of the senses, and children over five who, because of their attainments, could have passed after a few months into the third grade. In our schools each child advances and perfects himself according to his own individual ability. This method contains the further advantage in that it would make teaching in schools in the country and in small villages in the provinces, where the number of students and teachers is limited, quite easy. Our experiences have shown that a single teacher can supervise children ranging from the ages of three to seven. Since children in our schools learn easily how to write, if our method was more generally copied, illiteracy could be fought and reading promoted.

As far as the teacher is concerned, she can remain a whole day with children of such different stages of development without exhausting herself, just as a mother at home passes the entire day from morning to night with her children without growing tired.

Through working by themselves children acquire an active discipline, a practical independence, and a gradual increase in knowledge. When they are directed by an intelligent teacher employing our method for their physical, intellectual, and moral development, they can acquire both bodily health and largeness of mind.

There are some who still cling to the mistaken conviction that a child's natural education should be wholly physical; but the spirit also has its nature, and it is the life of the spirit that should dominate human existence at every stage.

Our method takes into account the spontaneous psychic development of a child and assists it with means drawn from observation and experience.

If physical care enables a child to enjoy the pleasures of a healthy body, intellectual and moral care introduces him to the higher pleasures of the spirit and urges him on to new insights and discoveries both in his external environment and in the intimacy of his own soul.

These are the joys which prepare a man for life and which are the only ones that are really suitable for the education of children.

Our children are notably different from those in ordinary schools. They have the calm look of happy individuals and the ease of those who are masters of their own actions. They run up to meet visitors and speak to them frankly. They gravely hold out their little hands to be shaken. They thank their visitors for coming more with their shining eyes than with their high-pitched voices. They give the impression of being remarkable little men and women. They show their accomplishments with the same simplicity and competence that they would if they were asking their mother's approval. They will sit down on the floor near the feet of two visitors speaking to each other and write in silence their names with a polite word of thanks as if they wanted to express their affectionate gratitude to those who had come to see them. When they give proof of their respect by their profound silence, they truly touch their visitors' hearts.

The Children's Houses seem to have a spiritual influence on everyone. I have seen business men, men of great influence, men preoccupied with painful work or with a sense of their own superiority become serene, shake off as it were the heavy burden of their authority, and become pleasantly forgetful of themselves. And this has been brought about by the sight of the human soul developing according to its true nature. This is what makes us call our little ones happy and wonderful children. They represent a childhood that is more advanced than was our own. I fully understand the great English poet Wordsworth who, having fallen in love with nature, began to hear the mysterious voice of its various movements and asked it for the secret of all life. At last it was revealed to him as in a vision: The secret of all nature is to be found in the soul of a child.

25. The Triumphal Chariot

The educational achievements of the Children's Houses show that there is a marked difference between them and the ordinary elementary schools. The Children's House is not a preparation for the elementary grades but a beginning of an education which continues without interruption. With our method we can no longer distinguish between preschool and school. In fact we do not have a program for instructing a child, but rather it is the child who, living in the midst of, and developing himself with the help of, physical and intellectual labors, achieves different levels of culture which, generally speaking, corresponds to his advance in age.

We have clearly shown that a child has a need to observe, to reflect, to learn, to concentrate, to isolate himself, and also from time to time to suspend his activities in silence. And we have done this so clearly that we can say with all confidence that the idea that a small child is in a state of rest when he is outside a place suited for his education is erroneous. Rather, it is our duty to direct a child's activities, sparing him useless efforts which would dissipate his energies, divert his instinctive search for knowledge, and be a frequent cause of nervous disorders and hindrance to his growth. The education of even a very small child, therefore, does not aim at preparing him for school but for life.

What interests us here is to determine the level of attainment that can be fixed as the point of separation between the two kinds of schools, that is, the Children's House and the elementary school.

Children in the Children's Houses have begun four branches of learning—drawing, writing, reading, and arithmetic, which they will continues to cultivate in the elementary grades.

These branches of learning are derived from the education of the senses in which are to be found their initial impulses.

Arithmetic comes from a sense of exercise in judging dimensions, that is, in determining the quantitative relationships between things. Drawing comes from training the eye in judging shapes and distinguishing colors and the simultaneous preparation of the hand to follow the outlines of determined objects. Writing comes from a more complicated group of tactile exercises which enable the hand to move lightly in specified directions. At the same time the eye is taught how to analyze shapes and abstract forms, and the ear to perceive the individual sounds of speech so that words may be fashioned from letters that correspond to these sounds. Reading flows from writing and enables an individual to share in the thoughts of others. Such conquests are powerful manifestations of an inner energy and they have a kind of explosive character. The onslaught of these higher activities stirs up joy and enthusiasm in a child. It is therefore not a kind of arid learning but rather a triumphant manifestation of a child's personality. The spirit of a child, erect and poised, is like an ancient Roman conquerer advancing in a splendid chariot. He is driving forward his four intellectual conquests. With these four horses of his triumphal chariot, he rushes on towards the ultimate goal of learning.

Nevertheless, the truly central point of this experience has been a discovery in the field of child psychology. Every further development has followed upon that first revelation given by the children of San Lorenzo. They showed that they were able to reproduce by means of a movable alphabet long words whose meaning they did not know. Their activities further broke out into a sudden explosion of writing, and on their own account they achieved an almost miraculous feeling for discipline for such small children. All this happened in an almost inexplicable way since they were not taught directly nor submitted to any compulsion. And yet such phenomena were not manifested at a single time and in a single environment but have been repeated in every part of the world where a system has been exactly followed.

These extraordinary phenomena have revealed an unknown aspect of a child's soul. And this is the real pivot of all our work. It is around these phenomena that it developed and from which it received its inspiration. This is why these experiments and the method which is based upon them cannot be understood unless it is recognized that they are connected with a particular mentality that is found only in the creative period of early childhood.

What emerges in particular from this great experiment is a proof of the fact that a child less than six years of age has a "mental form" different from that which develops after he has reached the age of six or seven and which is, consequently, different from that of an adult. The younger a child is, the greater is this difference of mentality. We call this the "absorbent mind" of a child, and we have discussed it for the first time in a work entitled *A New Education for a New World*. We are now preparing another volume which will soon be published, *The Absorbent Mind*, which deals with child psychology.

It is certain that mysterious facts which can be referred first to his unconscious and then to his subconscious mind show that a child has the capacity to absorb images from his environment. This is even true when these images are gathered into a kind of mental labyrinth, as may be seen in the truly miraculous fact that a child can absorb what is erroneously called his "mother tongue" with all its phonetic and grammatical peculiarities at a time when he does not as yet fully possess the faculties for learning—voluntary attention, memory, and power of reason. It is also true that things absorbed during this unconscious period by the very force of nature are those which persist in such a stable manner that they are identified with the person. This is so true that a native language becomes a true and proper characteristic of a race and a characteristic attribute of an individual.

On the other hand, adults who learn a foreign language after their minds have reached their maturity do it with difficulty, and they do not succeed in imitating the sounds of another language perfectly, nor do they ever lose their foreign accent, and they always make some errors in grammar.

During the first two years of his life a child prepares with his absorbent mind all his individual traits even though he is not himself aware of this. When a child reaches three, his motor activities come into play, and it is through these that he stabilizes his experience in his conscious mind. The motor organ used for this transformation is essentially the hand as it makes use of various objects. A child obviously wants to touch everything and is particularly fond of games which promote his intellectual development through the activities of his hands.

The importance of the hand as an instrument for the development of the conscious mind in childhood has not as yet been appreciated by educators.

The powers of the absorbent mind are gradually dulled as the conscious mind becomes organized. They persist, however, throughout childhood and enable a child, as our experiences with many different races throughout the world have shown, to absorb a far greater amount of learning than we would have ever imagined possible.

A child in his earliest years, when he is only two or a little more, is capable of tremendous achievements simply through his unconscious power of absorption, though he is himself still immobile. After the age of three he is able to acquire a great number of concepts through his own efforts in exploring his surroundings. In this period he lays hold of things through his own activity and assimilates them into his mind.

Nevertheless, he has not as yet reached that stage of maturity which will later enable him to learn from listening to an adult. This is why small children have been thought incapable of being properly taught in the ordinary schools.

But it is certain that the things acquired in the absorbent period are those which remain fixed, not in the memory, but in the living organism, becoming as they do the guide for the formation of the mind and character of the individual. Consequently, if a child is to be educated at this age, this must be done by the environment and not through oral instruction. The culture absorbed by a child kindles within him a blaze of enthusiasm. He is as it were suddenly on fire and moves on to further growth and other victories.

This is the age when a man works without becoming tired and when he draws food for his life from his knowledge. If a child's intellect does not have the opportunity of developing in accordance with nature's plan, he suffers and becomes abnormal.

Modern psychologists have began to recognize a kind of mental starvation in difficult children. They seem to have been arrested in their development and to have strayed from the straight route which they should have followed.

The surprising results obtained in our schools described in these pages are not, therefore, the result of a more perfect method of education. They rather reveal a special type of mind and psychological sensibilities that are only encountered in the creative period of growth.

Credit, therefore, should not be given to our scientific work, nor even to the new method we employed in instructing defective children and later adapted for use with normal children. The point of departure for a true understanding of our work is not to consider it as a method of education, but rather the contrary: Our method is the result of having observed the development of psychological phenomena which had hitherto been unknown and unobserved.

The problem, therefore, is not pedagogical but psychological. And education which leads to a better life is something which should be of concern to all men.

26. Grades and Sequence in the Presentation of the Material

In the practical application of our method, one should know the order of the exercises as they are given to a child.

In our exposition in this book we have indicated the progress of each exercise. Even though in the Children's Houses the most varied exercises are begun at the same time, there are different steps in the presentation of the material in its totality. These are as follows:

First Grade

Moving chairs silently, carrying objects, walking on tiptoe.

Various types of fastenings.

The solid insets (sense exercises).

The following gradation from easy to hard is found in the solid insets:

a) insets of the same height, but of diminishing diameter.

b) insets diminishing in all dimensions.

c) insets diminishing only in height.

Second Grade

Practical life: standing and sitting silently, dusting, pouring water from one container into another.

Walking on a line.

Sense exercises.

Material for dimensions, lengths, prisms, cubes.

The various sense exercises in the period of making pairs and contrasts.

Third Grade

Practical life: dressing, undressing, washing, and so forth.

Straightening up the room.

Eating properly with knife, fork, and spoon.

Exercises in movement.

Various exercises in the control of movements by walking on the line.

Sense exercises.

Drawing.

All the exercises according to their gradations.

Exercises in silence.

Fourth Grade

Exercises in practical life:

Setting the table, washing dishes, arranging the room, and so forth.

Exercises in movement; rhythmical marches.

Analyses of movements.

The alphabet.

Arithmetic: various exercises with the material.

Entrance of the children into church.

Fifth Grade

Practical life: all the exercises of practical life as indicated above with the addition of the following:

Delicate care of personal toilet such as cleaning teeth and nails.

Learning the external forms of society such as greetings and so forth.

Watercolors and drawings.

Writing and reading words: commands.

First operations in written arithmetic.

Reading scientific, geographical, historical, biological, geometrical, and other similar words.

Development of reading accompanied by games.

In the same class there should be found children of three ages: The youngest, who are spontaneously interested in the work of the older children and who learn from them and should be assisted by them. A child who shows a desire to work and to learn should be left free to do so even if the work is outside the regular program, which is here given simply for a teacher who is beginning a class.

Appendix

Inaugural Address Delivered on the Occasion of the Opening of the Second Children's House in 1907.

It may well be that the life of the poor is something which more than one of you here present have never considered in all its degradation. It may also be that you have only felt the misery and extreme human poverty through the pages of some profound book or the vibrant voice of a great actor.

Let us imagine that at a certain moment a voice should cry out to you: "Go and look at those houses of misery and darkest poverty. For there amidst terror and suffering have sprung up oases of happiness, of cleanliness, and of peace. The poor are to have houses of their own. In quarters where poverty and vice ruled, a work of moral redemption is going on. The people's consciences are being saved from the sluggishness of vice and the shadows of ignorance. Little children also have a "House" of their own. New generations will experience a new age when misery will no longer be lamented but destroyed, when the dark dens of vice and wretchedness will have become things of the past, and no trace of them will have remained."

With what new and changed emotions would we hasten to come here, like those Wise Men, who, guided by a dream and star, hastened to Bethlehem.

I have spoken thus so that you may understand the meaning and true beauty of this humble room. It seems almost to be a part of a home itself, destined, as it were, by a mother's hand for the happy use of the children of this area. It is the second Children's House opened in the ill-favored quarter of San Lorenzo.

This quarter is notorious. There is hardly a day when the newspapers of the city are not filled with reports of its misfortunes. And yet many are sitll ignorant of the origins of this part of the city.

It was never intended that tenements for the common people should be erected here. But San Lorenzo has become not a quarter for the common people but a quarter of the poor. It is an area in which poorly-paid and often unemployed workingmen live in a city without industries. Here men without jobs and the paroled prisoners live confusedly together.

The district of San Lorenzo has its origins between 1884 and 1888, when there was a building boom in Rome but no social or sanitary laws regulating the construction of new buildings. Builders covered acres and acres of land with walls. The more buildings they erected, the more profits there were for banks and stock companies. And the buildings themselves were erected with a complete disregard for the disasters that were bound to come. No attention was paid to the strength of the buildings since they never remained in the hands of the contractors who built them.

When the boom collapsed between 1888 and 1890, these poorly-constructed buildings remained unoccupied for a long time. Then when the need for housing began to be felt again, they were gradually filled with tenants. But since those who owned these vast apartments were neither willing nor able to invest more capital in them, the buildings, which had been erected without regard for hygiene and had been rendered still worse by temporary occupancy, were taken over by the poorest classes of the city. Five-, six-, and seven-room apartments were let out very cheaply in proportion to their size, but the rent was still too high for single families. This led to subletting and speculation, and eventually to overcrowding, promiscuity, and immorality.

When one enters into one of these tenements, he is struck by their darkness. He cannot distinguish even in full day the details of a room. When we speak of social problems we indulge in fantasies without bothering to discover the facts. We raise the question as to whether children should study and do their assignments at home or not, as if the poorest of them could write on the floor next to a straw mat. We would like to found circulating libraries so that the poor would read at home, and print pamphlets on education and hygiene for even the poorest to read. But all this only shows our profound ignorance of their real needs. Many of them do not even have a lamp by which they could read. The proletariat worry more about simply living than about educating themselves.

We must speak in a different way of the children who are born in such surroundings. They do not "come into the light" but into darkness, and they grow up in the midst of human degradation. They cannot help being dirty. The water that is available in a poor apartment is scarcely sufficient for three or four persons but must still be shared by twenty or thirty. There is hardly enough to drink!

We have a poetic concept of the word "home." It is a sacred place restricted to those who are dear to us. It is a place of beauty, peace, and pious sentiments. But the shocking reality is that very many have no such "home." They are housed within ghastly walls where there is no privacy, no courtesy, and often no light, air, or water. Consequently, we cannot speak of "the home" in the abstract as the foundation of the social order and a source of education for the masses.

Because of the terrible conditions of their dwellings the people find it more proper and healthy to take refuge in the street. And this becomes the ordinary domicile for their children. But frequently the streets are theaters of crimes and shameful sights that are difficult for us even to imagine.

Spectacles of extreme brutality may be seen here at the very gates of our city, the mother of civilization and the queen of the fine arts, because of the separation of the masses of the poor from the rest of the people.

During the Middle Ages, lepers were isolated and the Jews were shut up in ghettos, but poverty was never considered to be such a danger and disgrace that it had to be removed from the scene. The poor lived scattered among the rich. The contrast between the rich and the poor was a common literary theme even down to our own day. Men wrote of palaces that shut off the light from the neighboring hovels of the poor. As a lesson in morality a teacher could tell of the help sent by a princess to a poor cottage or how children of a wealthy home took care of a sick woman in a garret. All this would today be quite unreal. The poor can no longer expect help from their rich neighbors in times of dire need. Even the crumbs that were thrown to the poor have been taken from them. They are gathered together outside the walls of the city and abandoned to despair, brutality, and vice. We have thus created infected areas that are a threat to the city. In their desire to live in a city that is fair and beautiful, the people there have cleansed themselves from everything that is ugly and diseased.

When I first came to this quarter, where people enter as a rule only after death [the cemetery of Rome is located in San Lorenzo], I had the impression that I was entering into an area that had been struck by a great disaster.

It seemed to me that a recent sorrow weighed down upon the people who milled about the silent streets with a stupefied and almost fearful look. Their deep silence seemed to indicate that their lives had been broken and shattered. There were no carriages; there were not even the common, happy voices of street venders nor the sound of hand-organs being pushed around by their owners in search of tips. Not even these sounds, which are now prohibited in Rome as signs of poverty, broke the sad and heavy silence.

As I saw the deep holes in the streets and the rocks strewn over the ground, I could almost imagine that a great flood had overwhelmed the area. But looking at the bare houses with their broken walls, I thought that it might have been an earthquake that had struck it.

Then, when I saw that there was not even a store, shop, or inn except for some filthy taverns, I realized that the disaster that had fallen upon these people was poverty united with vice.

This sad and dangerous state of affairs has stirred many consciences, and individuals have come here to initiate generous charitable works. Every misfortune inspires some form of remedy, and all have been tried, from the introduction of hygienic principles into each house to the establishment of nurseries and dispensaries. But what has been the result? These acts of kindness seem to be little more than expressions of regret, of pity turned into action. Because of a lack of continuity of aims and means, the actual benefits have been few, and only a limited number have been helped. But the extent of the evil demands a more universal remedy which can bring relief to all.

The Roman Association of Good Buildings has adopted the policy of acquiring apartments, improving them, and administering them in a definite way. The first buildings it acquired were in this quarter of San Lorenzo. The apartments have been modernized and measures taken to improve the health and morals of their inhabitants.

One of the major improvements has been to divide up the large apartments into small ones so that there can be separate lodgings for individual families.

The aim of the project has been to furnish the tenants with neat, well-ventilated, and sunny homes.

But these benefits are not without cost to those who enjoy them. They must pay for them by their good will in keeping up their properties. The one who maintains his apartment in the best fashion receives an annual award. This means that all the inhabitants vie with each other in maintaining their homes. The buildings are kept in perfect condition. They are like the gleaming marble temples in the city that have come down to us from antiquity. The building in which we now find ourselves and in which the second Children's House is being inaugurated has for two years been under the sole care of the tenants, and the work of maintenance has been left entirely to them. Yet few of the homes of the upper classes can compare in cleanliness and freshness with these dwellings of the poor.

An experiment has been made and the results have been remarkable. The people have gained along with a love for their homes a love of cleanliness. They have also acquired a feeling for beauty and have adorned the courtyards with numerous plants and pots of flowers.

A new spirit of pride has risen in the quarter. There is general rivalry to have the best preserved apartment, to have attained a higher state of culture. The inhabitants have learned not only how to live but how to respect others.

This improvement in their homes has led to an improvement in the individuals themselves.

The Association has funished each one of the tenements with baths. Here all the tenants can go in turn to bathe in hot or cold water, just as they used to go to wash their clothes at the fountains.

But the Association met with a difficulty in attaining its ideal of a semigratuitous maintenance of its buildings. Working parents left their children who were too young to attend school in the tenements. Since they were unable to appreciate the sense of rivalry which prompted their parents to maintain their homes, they did a considerable amount of damage to the buildings.

Another reform was therefore begun. This was the establishment of a Children's House which is paid for by the savings in the cost of maintenance. But it has had wonderful moral effects as well.

Working mothers may safely leave their little children in the Children's House, which is exclusively reserved for those who are not yet old enough for school. This is a great boon to them since it frees their minds of a heavy burden. But even this help demands good will on their part in return. This is explicitly mentioned in the rules posted in the buildings: "Mothers must send their children clean to the Children's House and assist the directress in her work of education."

They are thus obliged to provide for the physical and moral welfare of their children. If a child will have shown by his words or behavior that the work of the school is being undermined at home, he will be sent back without recourse to the arms of his indolent parents. In other words, parents must appreciate the advantages of having a school for their young children in their own apartment building.

Mothers must go at least once a week to confer with the directress, give an account of their children, and receive the advice which the directress may have to give. This will be of great help to the children. Their health will be cared for by a physician who is assigned to the House.

The directress is always at the disposition of the children's mothers, and her own life as an educated and cultured person is a constant example to the inhabitants of the building; for she is strictly obliged to live in the tenement and thus be in close contact with the families of all her pupils. This is of great importance. In this area, where no one wanders about at night unarmed, there has come to live a cultured, gentle woman, who dedicates her life to the teaching of others. She is a kind of missionary among the people, and if she has sufficient tact and courage she will gain much fruit from her work.

This is really something new. Generous individuals in times past have gone to live among the poor so that they might educate them, but their work has been ineffective since it is quite impossible for people of a higher rank to live amidst the unsanitary conditions of the poor.

The organization of the Children's House is also something

new. It is not simply a shelter for children but a real school employing rational principles of scientific education. The physical growth of the children is watched and encouraged. The teaching is eminently objective and makes use of unusually rich supply of teaching materials. But it is impossible to discuss these in detail. I should mention, however, that there is connected with the school a room with hot and cold baths for the children and, wherever possible, a piece of land which the children can cultivate.

It is important here to say something about the progress in teaching which has been achieved by the Children's House. Those who are familiar with schools and their principal problems know that much attention is paid to the almost unattainable ideal of harmony between family and school in the education of children. But the family is always something far away and seems opposed to the aims of the school. The home is shut off not only from educational but also from social influences. In the Children's Houses we see for the first time the possibility of effectively establishing this ideal. The school is located in the same building as the children's homes and the teacher lives in their midst.

The parents know that the Children's House belongs to them and is supported by the rent they pay. They can go there at any hour of the day to watch, to admire, or to meditate. It is a constant stimulus to reflection and a source of evident blessing for themselves and their children. How many delicate attentions have the good mothers of these children paid to the teacher. They often place candy and flowers on the windowsill of the school as a silent, reverent tribute. After three years of such a novitiate, the mothers will send their children to the ordinary elementary schools. By this time they will be excellently prepared to cooperate in the work of educating their children and will have acquired the conviction that is rarely found even among the higher classes that they must merit through their own conduct and virtue the gift of having an educated son.

Another advance made by the Children's House pertains to scientific education. Hitherto this has been based upon anthropological studies of the child to be educated and has therefore treated only one aspect of the problem of transforming education. A man is not only a biological but also a social being, and the social environment of individuals who are being educated is the home. Scientific education will seek in vain to better the new generations if it does not succeed also in molding the environment in which the new generations have their origin and growth. All attempts to remedy the ills of education will be fruitless if the home remains closed to all progress. I therefore believe that by taking the home as an essential instrument of civil progress we shall solve the problem of directly modifying the children's environment and thus make it possible to provide them with a truly scientific education.

The Children's House represents still another advance. It is the first step towards the socialization of dwellings. The inhabitants enjoy the advantage of being able to leave their little ones in a place not only safe but also beneficial.

Up until now only wealthy women have been able to leave their children in the care of a nurse or governess while they tended to their own worldly occupations. Today the women who live in these remodeled apartments can say that they enjoy this same privilege. There is even a house physician who watches over their children and helps them to grow up strong and healthy.

We all know the advantages that have accrued to us through the socialization of our environment. We see examples of this in surface transportation, street lights, and means of communication. The working day has been lengthened by these means, and industrial progress has greatly increased the production of useful objects. Now everyone can have clean clothes, carpets, curtains, delicacies, china plates, silverware, and so forth. This improvement in the general welfare of the people has had a leveling effect upon society.

In the Children's House we have the first example of a socialization of personnel, that is, of persons engaged in such occupations as that of nurse or governess. This answers a need of the times. Because of the social and economic revolution of recent years a working woman is compelled to abandon those duties that are most dear to her. She must leave her children, even though it pains her to do so. Not only women of the laboring class but even those who are more educated can profit by such an institution. Otherwise, they must leave their children in the hands of maids and cooks when they go off to work. As a matter of fact, after the first news of the Children's House was spread abroad, many of the middle class sent urgent requests that such a healthy reform be extended also to their dwellings.

We are therefore socializing a mother's work within the home. This is a practical solution to what seemed to be an insoluble problem. What will become of the home, it is asked, if the woman leaves it? The home itself will be transformed and assume the ancient role of the woman.

I believe that in the future other forms of socialization will be adopted, for example, in infirmaries. A woman is the natural nurse for the dear ones of her own household, but how often today must she tear herself from the bedside of one she loves in order to rush off to work. Competition is keen and absence from work may lead to the loss of a job. It would be a great advantage for a woman in such a position to be able to leave her patient in an infirmary where she could go during the free moments in her day and watch without hindrance at night. This would also contribute greatly to the health of the family by isolating those affected with contagious disease. Who does not know, for example, the anguish of parents who have a child sick with an infectious disease? They cannot isolate their other children from the danger because they have no friends or relatives in the city to whom they might send their healthy offspring.

A similar program for preparing food would have great advantages. This has already enjoyed some success in America. A dinner ordered in the morning could be sent up by a dumb-waiter to individual rooms. Middle-class families could profit by such a reform since they would no longer have to entrust their health and happiness to an ignorant cook who burned the food.

The fact, therefore, that a woman is compelled by social and economic conditions to work for pay does not mean that the home and family will be destroyed. It simply means that tasks which were formerly performed by a housewife are now taken over by the manager of the apartment.

This gives a new freedom to a woman and she will be loved for herself and not for the blessings she confers. The goal of human love is not to secure one's own satisfaction but to promote freedom and perpetuate the species.

This ideal love has been embodied by Frederick Nietzsche in the woman of Zarathustra, who desires a son better than herself. "Why do you desire me?" she asks the man. "Perhaps because of a fear of solitude? ... To protect yourself from the trials of life? If that is the case, depart from me. I am looking for a man who has conquered himself and enlarged his soul. I am looking for one who has preserved his body clean and strong. I am looking for one who desires to unite with me body and soul so as to create a son! A son better, more perfect, more courageous than has as yet been born!"

Through marriage a man should wish to improve the race through his own pursuit of virtue. The home can become a place for the education and consolation of new generations as they begin their triumphant march in time towards eternity.

ABOUT THE AUTHOR

MARIA MONTESSORI was born at Chiara-velle, Italy, on August 31, 1870. In 1894 she was the first woman to graduate in Medicine from the University of Rome, and in 1899 she began a study of educational problems of handicapped children. Working on lines first laid down by the French physician E. Seguin, she achieved startling results and the children under her tutelage passed the state examination in reading and writing for normal children. Dr. Montessori concluded that similar methods might also be successfully applied to younger normal children and she began to work with toddlers in private and public schools in Rome. She encountered opposition from advocates of orthodox methods of education who regarded her system, which encouraged freedom of movement, as destructive of discipline, but she was warmly supported by enthusiastic reformers. From 1900 to 1907 Maria Montessori lectured on pedagogical anthropology at the University of Rome and in 1922 she was appointed government inspector of schools in Italy. She wrote more than six books on learning and the child, and the system of education which she developed bears her name. Her later years were spent supervising training courses in Spain, India, England, and the Netherlands. She died at Noordwijk, Netherlands, on May 6, 1952.

Learn to live with somebody... yourself.